70648067

Love Always,
Petra

Love Always, Petra

A STORY *of* COURAGE AND THE DISCOVERY OF LIFE'S HIDDEN GIFTS

PETRA NEMCOVA
AND JANE SCOVELL

WARNER BOOKS

NEW YORK   BOSTON

Photo insert page 4. *First row, left:* Photograph by Vanessa Von Zitzewitz, courtesy of Graff; *first row, center:* Summer 2004 Intimissimi by Marc Hom; *first row, right:* Photograph by Simon Atlee, courtesy of V. C. Pearce on behalf of Pearce Stoner Associates; *second row, left:* Photo by Kenneth Willard, courtesy of Grey Advertising *second row, center:* Photo by Spicer; *third row, left:* Photo © Giles Bensimon/*ELLE*; *fourth row, left:* Photo by Chris Militscher for winstonwest.com; *fourth row, center:* Christophe Jouany/*Sports Illustrated*; *fourth row, right:* Walter Ioos Jr./*Sports Illustrated.*

Photo insert page 5. *First row, left:* Walter Ioos Jr./*Sports Illustrated*; *first row, center:* Photographed by Pavel Havelicek/ © Hearst Communications, Inc.; *first row, right:* Photo by Michael Williams, www.michaelwilliamsphotography.com; *second row, center:* Photo by Spicer; *second row, right:* Photo by Christopher Micaud © 2002; *bottom, center:* Photo by Troy Word.

Photo insert page 6. *Bottom, left:* Photograph by Alan Davidson, courtesy of wireimage.com; *bottom, right:* Photograph by George Pimentel, courtesy of wireimage.com.

Copyright © 2005 by Petra Nemcova
All rights reserved.

Warner Books

Time Warner Book Group
1271 Avenue of the Americas, New York, NY 10020
Visit our Web site at www.twbookmark.com.

Printed in the United States of America

First Edition: December 2005

10 9 8 7 6 5 4 3 2

Library of Congress Cataloging-in-Publication Data

ISBN: 0-446-57913-0
ISBN 13:978-0-446-57913-1
LCCN: 2005934580

Book design by Charles Sutherland

For Simon

Acknowledgments

From the bottom of my heart, I would like to give thanks to all who helped me to make this book happen.

Besides all the family, friends, and colleagues mentioned in the book, I want to thank all the doctors, nurses in Thailand, the Czech Republic, and New York, all my agents and everyone working at the agencies in New York, London, and Paris, and especially Jurgen Wagner, Lorenzo Pedrini, Mimi Obadia, Barbara Fisher, Maury DiMauro, Joel Wilkenfeld, Rob Shuter, Keesha Johnson, and Caroline Bubnis. I would love to give a special thanks for changing my life and the lives of so many to my spiritual family, S.H.Y. and Master Dang. Many thanks also, to Emily Griffin, Diane Luger, Chris Dao, Tareth Mitch, and all of the wonderful people at Warner Books. My gratitude to Caryn Karmatz Rudy, a thoughtful and caring editor, and to the thoroughly modern Jane Scovell.

—*Petra*

I would add to the above, my personal thanks to Lewis Black, Leigh Crystal, Jamison Ernest, Faith Kates, Olga Nemcova, Diane Smith, and especially Jeff Levy, for sharing their thoughts and observations with me. I thank Todd Shuster, agent and friend, and Sydney Sheldon Welton for her invaluable guidance. Thank you to my children Amy, Lucy, and Billy Appleton. A good editor never can be thanked enough, so here's to you, Caryn, and your assistant, Emily. Finally, I thank you, dear Petra—"the hand that hath made you fair hath made you good."

—*Jane Scovell*

Contents

Prologue

DECEMBER 26, 2004
KHAO LAK, THAILAND
10:30 a.m.

Pain.

It brought me back to consciousness, a sharp, agonizing, throbbing pain racking my body, my legs.

My legs.

I opened my eyes and looked down. Black filthy water covered the lower half of my body. I couldn't even see my legs. My arms, bare, scratched, bleeding and aching, were wrapped around a palm tree. I was holding on, leaning against the trunk. Black, oil-slicked, muddied water choked with debris was everywhere. I looked up. The sky was blue, clear, untroubled, the sun was shining. Where was I? Where was Simon? What had happened?

I remembered.

Simon and I were in the bungalow when a rush of water rose up so suddenly there was not even a second to think, a rush of water that came from all directions, hurtling us out into the furious current. For one split second, before the water separated us, I saw Simon's face.

"Petra!" he screamed. "Petra! What's happening?"

I couldn't answer. I didn't know. Then I lost sight of him. Seconds later, I saw him again, whirling in the tumbling waters. He was a few yards ahead of me. Behind him a rooftop was sticking out of the water.

"Catch the roof! Catch the roof!" I shouted. Then he was gone. I don't know whether he heard me or not. I prayed that he would catch hold. I was sure he would. He was a strong swimmer; he had to be okay.

It was impossible to tell in which direction the waters were streaming. I needed to grab onto something or be swept away. I saw another rooftop. I reached out my arms, and sending out every bit of energy I had, I grabbed the edges and held on. Instantly, my legs were sucked underneath, and everything accumulated by the raging water, the wood and metal objects, all the trash, began slamming against my hips and legs. I hung on, screaming with pain and fear. I would be crushed into nothing. For the first time, I thought of dying.

Miraculously, the pressure of the water began to lessen. I pulled myself up onto the roof. My clothes had been torn from my body. I was naked. Then, as quickly as the first, another tremendous wave rose up and poured over the rooftop. I lost my grip and was drawn down beneath the water. Frantically, I flailed my arms, trying to get out from under the thick layer of filth between me and the surface. Desperately, I fought to get some air until I had no breath left. I stopped fighting, stopped struggling, and began swallowing the inky water. A great feeling of peacefulness came over me. I surrendered to the calmness. Whatever was meant to be, whatever God will decide, it's okay.

At that moment, without any effort on my part, I was thrust through the barrier of debris to the surface. I threw my head back and gasped for air. Above me was the blue, blue sky. I was never so happy in my life to see the sky.

9:58 a.m. (twelve minutes before the tsunami strikes)

I don't remember ever being happier. I was in Thailand, a country I loved, with my love, Simon Atlee. Simon was a photographer, and we'd been a couple for eighteen months. We were going to spend our second Christmas and New Year's together in a very special way. Usually, Simon booked our holidays, but this time I did everything. That is, I made all the arrangements through a travel agent in Los Angeles. She was Thai and took particular interest in helping me create the perfect vacation. This was my fifth visit to Thailand and Simon's first; I wanted him to experience with me the lush green of the land, the smells, the sunshine, the ocean, the food exploding with taste in your mouth, the culture, and most important, the people. The Thais are the kindest people I ever met, and it comes from inside—it's not learned, it's natural. They put their hands together and bow their heads to greet you, taking the moment to show respect in such a gentle way. The gracefulness and peacefulness are addictive, and this land is in my heart. It had been nearly three years since my last visit, but the minute we arrived, I knew I was "home."

At Bangkok International Airport, we changed planes and flew on to the first of our three stops, Chiang Mai. This was my first visit to this city, so Simon and I were seeing things through the same eyes. We went on different tours, including guided visits to nearby Buddhist temples. One tour guide explained that, in the past, there had been a war between the Burmese and the Thais. Bad things happened, but the good thing was, the Burmese brought Buddhism to Thailand. I am inspired by the gentle teachings of the Buddha, so this was especially interesting to me.

We went to see a giant, seated Buddha on a nearby mountaintop. It wasn't a very touristy place; in fact, Simon and I were the only visitors. As is customary in many sacred places, we took off our shoes and went inside on our knees to pay our respects. We lit a candle and incense and placed flowers before the golden statue. Off to the side, two young monks wearing saffron robes were seated at a table with a checkerboard on top. The monks were playing checkers with flower petals and broken matches for the game pieces. Simon wanted to take a picture, but the minute he took out his camera, the monks put everything away and ran off. Obviously, they didn't want to get caught playing games.

We went to see the Long Neck Ladies, tall, thin, and elegant women who wear golden rings around their necks. These rings are a sign of beauty. They are put on starting when the women are little girls, and in time their necks stretch up many inches. I think they are a tribe from Burma.

Simon took lots of pictures, especially of one adorable little girl. She kept smiling and repeated every word Simon said.

"Hello."

"Hello."

"Can I take a picture?"

"Can I take a picture?"

"Thank you."

"Thank you."

Simon giggled like a schoolboy.

We went to the umbrella factories and the silk factories and bought presents. We went to see the amazing elephant shows. The elephants play football with their feet, play harmonicas with their trunks, and most incredible of all, they paint pictures on large pieces of paper. The keepers put brushes in their trunks, and the elephants paint with such a concentration— not all over the place, but very precise. The keepers change the colors, and the elephants make flowers and trees. It is unbelievable, and even more unbelievable, the paper is made from elephant dung. Simon bought two of these specially prepared paintings for his niece and nephew. We fed bananas to the elephants and played with the cute little babies with the spiky hairs on their heads. Of course, we took an elephant ride through the jungle.

Before we left Chiang Mai, Simon and I went to a special temple where monks give out cloth bracelets. The threaded cloth comes in one very long piece; the monks tie an end around your wrist, make a knot, and cut it as they chant a prayer. The bracelet is for protection and once on, must remain until it falls off. Women get the bracelet on the left arm and men on the right, but for some reason, both of ours were put on our right arms. When we got back to our hotel room, Simon said his bracelet was in the way and he was going to switch it to his watch hand. I told him to let it be.

"You're not supposed to undo it. You're not supposed to let it get away from your skin."

"Don't worry, Petra, I'll keep it in close contact with my flesh. It'll be okay."

He kept his arms pressed against each other as he undid the bracelet, slipped it around his left wrist, and quickly knotted it again.

"See?" He smiled, holding up his arm to show me. "Everything's okay."

From Chiang Mai we flew south to Phuket, and from there we drove an hour and a half to the Khao Lak Orchid Resort. Khao Lak is noted for its scuba diving school, and Simon was eager to scuba dive. Recently, I'd had some inner ear problems and couldn't dive, but I wanted Simon to enjoy it. We checked into a front-row bungalow on a beautiful stretch of white-sand beach with palm trees everywhere. The bungalow was a big room with a large bed on one side and a sitting area with a table and chairs on the other. At the entrance was a door to the bathroom. The bathroom had a shuttered window that opened onto the main room. You could open the shutters and look out from the bathroom through the living room window to the ocean. We stayed that night in the bungalow happy to be in paradise together. We spent the next day playing on the beach, where Thai ladies, carrying cooler boxes, walked up and down, crying, "Pineapple, papaya, watermelon, massage." You could get fruits or a massage or both. There is nothing like a Thai massage—so relaxing. I learned how to give them on my first visit, and though I was good at it, I wanted Simon to experience the real thing.

Early that evening we checked out of the hotel and went to the scuba center. From there we took an open van to the harbor, where many boats were lined up side by side. After scrambling over a number of boats, we reached ours. I have to admit I was nervous about climbing from deck to deck in the dark, but holding Simon's hand made me feel safe. Once we got on our boat, we had to remove our shoes, and they stayed off for the three days we were on board—I loved it. If I could, I would stay barefoot all the time. Simon and I were shown to our living quarters, a little cabin with bunk beds—we slept on the bottom spooning happily together. The divers were a mixed group—English, Swedish, American, and Australian—of about twenty-four people, plus the Thai crew.

Every morning there was an on-deck briefing, to go over the dive site, the currents, the rocks, the depth, the fish, etc. Then you'd suit up, get your oxygen tank, and go over the side. There were four dives a day. I was with Simon every time he prepared for a dive, and I was waiting for him when he came back. He was so happy; he loved the scuba diving. And he was making everyone else happy, too, with his good spirit and his silly humor. While Simon was in the water, I read, took some sun, or chatted with the crew. Simon and I never said that we were a photographer and a model—we were happy to leave our public lives behind.

We became friendly with a Swedish couple, who at one point came over to us carrying a Swedish magazine.

"Isn't this you?" they asked, opening to a full-page photo. I had to admit that it was. You can't keep a secret even in a boat in a harbor in Thailand. Although the others learned that we were a model and photographer, nobody bothered us; it was a very casual time. In between dives we went snorkeling or swimming in the bay. Diving or snorkeling, everyone gets excited about what they've seen. Simon was bubbling over with details about his undersea adventures.

The second night, Simon and I sneakily went up on deck, climbed into a hammock, and slept out under the stars. It was a beautiful experience. Really all we did on that boat was eat, sleep, scuba dive, sunbathe, and make love. It's the best holiday you can imagine.

On the last morning, December 24, one of the instructors came out on deck wearing a white beard, a red suit and hat, and full scuba gear. Santa Claus had joined the dive! I took a picture of him and planned to send it to friends as a Christmas card. After lunch we sailed back to Khao Lak and disembarked. We returned to the diving center, where we dropped off the equipment and exchanged addresses and telephone numbers with the others. Simon and I went back to the Orchid Hotel. We were given a different bungalow, same layout and still on the beach, but this little house was in the second row. Instead of overlooking the ocean, our room overlooked the pool.

Before dinner that night Simon and I went to an Internet café. The connections were so bad I couldn't send individual messages, so I e-mailed a group message, something that I'd never done before. I couldn't put the picture of the scuba Santa on the e-mail, so I just wrote "Merry Christmas." We left the café and returned to the hotel for dinner. It was a hilarious evening. People wore silly hats, and there were balloons to blow up and funny competitions for the children, as well as a magician doing his tricks. This was Christmas Eve Thai-style, easy and delightful.

The next morning, Christmas, we woke up late, and went to the beach, where we spent the day. We swam, we read, and we played. We found a coconut and tossed it around like a football. We took a stick and played tic-tac-toe and hangman in the sand. Everything was laid-back; we were like kids. We sat on the beach in the late afternoon talking about the future. I asked Simon what his wishes were now, what he wanted to accomplish next. He thought a moment and then answered.

"Everything I dreamed of doing, I've done. I think I've achieved all my goals."

Just before dinner we called our family and friends. Simon spoke to his mother and his sister, Jodi. He told them how much he loved Thailand and how much he loved them.

"I'm so happy," he said, "and I'm so in love." He looked at me with his beautiful blue eyes and handed me the phone.

"You should see Siddy," I said. Siddy was Simon's nickname. "His eyes are shining."

That night we had dinner on the beach on plastic tables underneath a roof of palm leaves. There was a barbecue pit made from half a tin drum. We had fresh fish grilled with delicious Thai spices, chicken *satay* on skewers with delectable peanut sauce, and many varieties of vegetables and fruits. I've dined in five-star restaurants around the world, but none were better than this feast.

After the meal we sat at the plastic table and talked by

candlelight. We looked out at the ocean and at the stars shining in the dark sky. I brought up the subject of children, and for the first time, we spoke about how many we would have together. We decided that we'd have two and adopt at least one. We had been talking about marriage for a while, and Simon had asked me for a signal to let him know he could propose. We established that when I started talking about children, it would be an indication that I was ready for marriage. Children became our "c"-word. It wasn't a question of "commitment"; it was a matter of timing. I wanted to continue my modeling for a while. Whenever I talked about children, and the subject came up often because I adore them, Simon would smile and say, "Be careful, Petra, that's the forbidden word." That evening he didn't say anything. It was a confirmation that both of us were ready.

We went back to our little bungalow, where we curled up together on the bed and watched movies. Because I grew up under a communist regime and was unfamiliar with Hollywood films, Simon was giving me a crash course in great old movies. One of my presents was a DVD of *White Christmas.* We put it on and cuddled. We saw about a quarter of the movie before we turned out the lights and fell asleep in each other's arms.

At 7:30 the next morning Simon woke me with soft kisses.

"Do you want to finish the movie or go for a walk on the beach?" he asked.

"Let's watch for half an hour, then we can go to the beach."

We turned on the TV and watched, cuddling and spooning. We didn't watch it all because we wanted to go for an early morning stroll, something that we hadn't yet done. We got dressed, left the bungalow, and headed toward the water. How beautiful and still the morning was! The warm sunshine kept us company as we walked along the beach. The tide was quite low. I knew there was a full moon around that time and that the moon moves the waters around the world, so I didn't pay much attention. Every so often, we would start to sing "Sisters, Sisters" from the movie. Lucky for us, no one else was on the beach, because we were the worst singers. We took a brisk walk and then went back to the bungalow. We were leaving in two hours for Koh Lanta, our final Thai destination. Simon went into the bathroom, and I started to pack. I was wearing a bathing suit and standing with my right side toward the window.

What did I hear first?

I think it was the screams. Hideous shrieks filled the air. Out of the corner of my eye I saw people running. I put my head up and looked out. Men, women, and children were dashing helter-skelter, some jumping into the pool—there was no concept of running in one direction. Next came steady ear-splitting, crack-cracking thunderclaps of hideous noise as bungalows, buildings, everything crumbled before the onslaught of flooding waters. One minute I was packing a suitcase, the next second I was fighting for my life.

That's how fast it was.

Released from under the thick layer of accumulated trash, I was back in the rushing current. I had to find something permanent to hold on to. Ahead of me, I saw a palm tree sticking out of the water.

Okay, I have to catch it. I have to catch it, I said to myself, or maybe aloud.

No use. I swept by the tree so quickly I couldn't even touch it. No time for despair, another tree was in my path.

Again, try again. Get your arms out!

As the debris-choked water rushed me past the tree, I grabbed at a branch, curled my fingers around it, and held on with every bit of strength I had. It was enough. The waters rushed on. I stayed and began to pull myself closer to the tree. The water was below my chest, and I could feel another branch beneath my feet. I tried to stand on it. It was too painful. I couldn't do it. I hung on to the upper branch trying not to get pulled away by the current and at the same time, trying different positions to relieve my agony. By the intensity of the pain, I knew bones were broken. I maneuvered my back toward the tree trunk in order to brace myself against it and let my legs float out in front. I managed to hold this position, and it did ease the pain. The water, which had caused all this horror, was now helping by cushioning my body.

It didn't last. A couple of hours later the floodwaters started to recede; my legs were no longer being supported. As they lowered down, the pain became more intense. I had to keep moving my body to find the most comfortable position, and at the same time, I had to make sure my legs didn't get trapped by the debris. I lay down on the branch with my legs stretched out. Every movement brought excruciating pain. The air was full of horrible sounds, crashing, smashing, violent sounds. I was terrified that they meant another wave was coming. I heard the tree cracking, and for a moment I thought that the weight of the trash surrounding me would cause the tree to collapse and take me under the water again.

Dear God, I prayed, please, dear God, don't let another wave come.

I looked around. I couldn't see anything—a jumble of floating objects blocked my vision—but I could hear people crying out. Two women were on a tree behind me. I knew there were two because one was speaking English, the other was speaking Thai. They were screaming for help. In the distance I heard a child crying; after a half hour or so, the crying stopped. I was thinking of all the people, of Simon, and I was sending energy to them, praying for them, and hoping for the best. It helped me to stay focused.

Time passed. The sky stayed blue, and the sun beat down. Cuts and scratches covered my arms and legs, none of them very deep. Even so, the water was bloody around me. I thought I must have been having internal bleeding, but I put it out of my mind. For many hours the water steadily lowered. I eased myself down with the water, staying on top of it to help soften the pain. I kept splashing water in my face so I wouldn't faint. I know I must have drifted off quite a few times. Once, I was brought back into consciousness by a tickling, pinching sensation on my left leg. I looked down and saw a little crab crawling around my ankle. I couldn't reach it because I couldn't move, so I broke off a branch from the tree and tried to get the crab onto it. I wanted to set him down somewhere where he could crawl. Every creature has a right to live, even a little crab.

As the water receded, I saw that a patch of mud had formed below me and I tried to get on it. I hung on to the tree branch and began lowering myself. The stabs of pain stopped me. I couldn't do it. I passed out. The sun woke me. It was so very strong. My whole body was hot, and the scratches were stinging. I splashed water on myself, that filthy black water. I put my head down and passed out again. When I awoke, I saw that the water had gone down so far I couldn't reach it anymore—nothing to ease the stings of my flesh. It was now getting toward evening. Soon the sun would go down. The day had been filled with the sounds of people crying and screaming for help. I didn't call out. I knew that screaming wouldn't help, and I had to save my energy. Did anyone know we were there? Even the helicopters that eventually flew over went off quickly. I remember thinking there must be many people worse off, so the helicopters should go where they were most needed.

It was around 6:00 p.m. when I heard different kinds of calls. "Hello. Hello. Hello. Hello."

These weren't cries for help; they were cries of help.

The others around me began screaming, "Here! I'm here!"

"Here, I'm here!" I was screaming, too.

In the distance I saw two Thai men pushing their way through the chest-high water toward me.

"I'm here! I'm here!"

They reached me, and I was so happy I burst into tears. "Kop Khun Kha, Kop Khun Kha. Thank you. Thank you for coming," I cried.

The men bowed and smiled. They didn't speak English. One man opened a can of juice for me. It had been nearly eight hours since I'd had anything to drink. I was lying flat out and couldn't sit, so he helped me swallow by holding my head up. The other man was wearing swimming trunks with swimming shorts over them. He took off the outer pair and tried to slip them over my legs. I had forgotten my nakedness.

"I can't. Thank you, I can't put them on," I told him. "I can't move my legs."

The poor man was trying so hard to cover me. And I was so not caring about it. He stopped his attempt to clothe me and laid the shorts over my lap. I pointed to my pelvis. "Broken, broken."

Both men nodded their heads, their faces full of compassion. How brave these men were to put others' safety ahead of their own and to come back into the ever-threatening danger. I soon learned that many people were doing the same thing. Again the men tried to help me up. I screamed.

"I can't sit up."

One of them motioned with his hands, asking if he could give me a piggyback ride.

"No, no," I cried. "Not possible. Too painful, too painful."

They looked at each other and then at me. I understood that they could do no more; they would have to go and bring back more help—at least I hoped they would. I motioned to the man who had covered me with his shorts, asking if I could have his T-shirt. Immediately, he took it off and tried to put it on me. I shook my head. "No, no." I didn't want to wear it, I wanted to use it. The water had gone so low, I couldn't reach it with my arm anymore.

I took the shirt, let it fall into the dirty water, and then drew the dripping cloth up to my face. It felt so good, so refreshing, that filthy water. The men bowed and went off. I dropped the shirt again, pulled it up, and rubbed the dripping cloth over my neck, my breasts, and my arms. On my right wrist, muddied and shredded, was the bracelet from the Chiang Mai temple. I lay back, put the wet shirt over my face and chest, and closed my eyes. I read once that when people are dying, their whole life is flashing before them. I wasn't so sure I was dying, but while I waited, and prayed for help to return—for both myself and all the others—I began to think about Simon first and then my mother, my father, my sister, my grandfather, my grandmothers, my friends . . . my work.

I believe that there is a pattern to life, and lying there, cradled in the palm tree, I could see how what had gone before in my life was making it possible for me to survive.

Part I

1

Karvina

My name, Petra, means "rock." Kvetrinka, my nickname, means "little flower." Quite a contrast, but contrast is okay: If it's always hot, you don't know what cold is; if it's always good, you don't know what bad is. My names reflect the two sides of me: the rock and the flower, the hard and the soft. That's my personal duality, and I celebrate duality in all things. The world would be so dull and gray if everything were the same. I know this because that's what communism was like, and communism was all I knew for the first eleven years of my life.

I was born on June 24, 1979, in Karvina, Czechoslovakia. My country has had many names over the centuries; it's now the Czech Republic. Karvina is a small town in the industrial Ostrava-Karvina coal-mining region of Moravia, four or five hours from Prague and close to the Polish and Slovak borders. The Czech Republic is divided into two big parts: Bohemia, where Prague is, and Moravia, where I am from. There are many differences between the two regions. For example, Bohemians speak short; Moravians speak long. In Prague they say "hello"; in Karvina it's "hel-looooo." They call us simple country folk and make fun of the way we talk, but, of course, we make fun of them, too.

There were four of us in my immediate family: my father, Oldrich Nemec, my mother, Bozena Nemcova, myself, and my younger sister, Olga. In Czech all women have "ova" after their last name, so you cannot make a mistake about whether it's a man or a woman. My last name is pronounced *Nyahmsova*, but in English it's easier to say *Nemcova*. My mother has the same name as one of the most famous of all Czech writers. When we studied about that Bozena Nemcova in school, the kids teased me to death.

"Let's hear one of your stories, Petra. Can you write like your mother?"

It got on my nerves, even though I loved Nemcova's works. She wrote down many of the fairy tales and legends that we Czechs, especially Moravians, adore. When I was growing up, I read them over and over; my favorite was "Salt Is Better Than Gold." In the story a king asks his three daughters how much they love him. One loves him more than precious jewels; the second, more than precious metals; but when the youngest says she loves him more than salt, the king banishes her, saying, "Salt is common and not precious at all. You don't love me." In the end the king discovers that one can live without jewels and gold but salt, like love, is essential.

For someone like me, who came from a poor family, the idea that love is basic and has nothing to do with riches was very important. My mom had no jewelry, just a small amber heart and a few cut stones of little value. She kept them in a small wooden "treasure" box, and when I was alone at home, I would sneakily go to the place where she put the box. I would lift the lid and gaze in at those treasures. Honestly, I got more pleasure out of looking at those inexpensive stones than I do modeling jewelry worth thousands and thousands of dollars.

As far as how we are looking, my family is a mixed group. My dad has blond hair and dark olive skin, while my mother has white skin and dark hair. My sister and I are a combination. She has ginger hair and white skin, and I have caramel skin and brown hair (right now, anyway; I love to change the color, and by the time you read this, I might be a redhead!). My sister has brown eyes like my father; my mother has green eyes; mine are hazelnut, a combination of both. All four of us are tall.

I was baptized in the Catholic Church, but I didn't grow up with religion. This isn't surprising, since the communists didn't encourage religion any more than they did humor. After the regime fell in 1989, religion started to come back. We could go to mass, but I never went . . . oh, maybe once with my grandmother, to please her. My grandmother Anezka Sikorova still goes all the time (she says she prays for me), but religion wasn't a part of my family's life. We didn't go to church or anything like that. I'm not a traditional type of religious person, but I do believe that there is a greater power, and that we often lose track of this. Sometimes we think we are more powerful than anything, which is foolish. We should respect the greater power or energy, or God, whatever we choose to call it. In my childhood the only "power," communism, was not so good.

The communists took over my country in 1948. By the time I was born, most people didn't remember—or never knew—anything better. Now I know. From history books I learned that the Soviets crushed any attempts by the Czech people to make a democratic society; I was too young at the time to understand the full picture, how people were imprisoned, sometimes executed, for believing in freedom. The regime killed personal ambition; nobody had big goals. Every day was a struggle for people like my parents. Even so, they wanted the best for Olga and me. For them the best meant that we get an education and enjoy our learning before we had to devote our lives to the Communist Party.

Everything was limited, even travel. We could only take trips in our own country or to countries that were part of the regime. If you journeyed outside, you had to answer millions of questions: Why are you going there? How long will you stay? Do you have family there? Sometimes they would make parents keep their children in the country as a kind of security, or they'd take away passports. They didn't want anyone escaping. In all my childhood I remember my parents taking only one trip, and it was just my mom going to Bulgaria, which, of course, was part of the system.

I never traveled. I never saw the ocean, just lakes and mountains, and castles. Lots of the castles were haunted, and I loved the ghost stories connected to them. One of the most famous is the legend of Perchta, the White Lady who appears in castles in the towns of Jindrichuv Hradec, Trebon, Cesky Krumlov, Rozmberok, and Telc. (I guess you would call her a portable spirit.) According to tradition, when the apparition of Perchta appears, you can predict the future by the color of her gloves. If they are red, there will be fire. If they are black, she is warning of disaster or death. White gloves are an omen of good things, like a wedding or a birth. I was enchanted by stories like this because through them I could travel into a world of fantasy. I yearned to see the big wonderful real world beyond our borders, but this was an impossible dream for a little girl living under communist rule.

Young as I was, during the first decade of my life, I did have a sense of the heaviness all around. It's difficult for people in the free world to imagine what it was like. I can tell about some of the repressions and deprivations, but what's harder to tell you about is the "grayness," the sadness, which was in the very air we breathed. The regime had an iron fist, and we were weighed down by rules and regulations. You had to be part of the system to get an apartment or a job, and they were always checking up on you. We were required to go to meetings where the local officials gave lectures on how wonderful everything was—propaganda, to be sure, but you had to go. Books were handed out, and at each meeting you were given a stamp to paste in the book. At the end of the year, if you didn't have enough stamps, you were in big trouble.

Everything was serious, very, very serious. Mostly, the communists worked day and night to keep out the Western influence. We never saw Western magazines or newspapers, or heard news reports. Movies were considered to be one of the biggest threats, especially the ones from Hollywood;

they simply weren't shown. Control was the key, and it was everywhere, from the big motion picture screens in the run-down cinemas to the little black-and-white TV screens at home. And when it came to education, you really could see how the party ruled.

In primary school our studies were dominated by the Soviets. For instance, only one foreign language was offered: guess which? Actually, discipline was the most important subject, and it was rigidly enforced. When you were in school, you had to sit holding your hands behind your back so you wouldn't play with them. We had no type of recess; we couldn't run, we couldn't even walk around on our own. During breaks we marched around in a circle in pairs. Every time we passed a teacher, we had to cry out, *"Cest praci,"* which means "Viva work." We were always saluting work. The regime was all about work. People were afraid. So many things were prohibited—even play activities for the children.

Personal appearance also had to reflect the party's no-frills formula. If you dared to wear makeup or nail polish, and the teacher caught you, there was hell to pay. If it was makeup, she would order you to go the bathroom and scrub your face clean. And if it was nail polish, she would take scissors from her desk and fiercely scrape the polish off your nails.

The one thing the party encouraged was sports. Ice skating was extremely important in the Eastern bloc, and the biggest dream anyone could imagine was to be a great skater who could win medals and prizes. When I started school, I took ice skating lessons twice a day, before and after my classes. My training was intense—honestly, the sessions were on a professional level. I think I had potential, but I was getting really bad marks in school. One day my mom said no it's not happening and took me out of the skating. I don't remember if I was relieved or sad about it. I didn't get on the ice again until I was fourteen. I went skating with two friends who had to stand on either side of me and push me along. If they let go, the only way I could stop myself was to bump into something. Today I can't skate at all!

The communist ban against Western culture included food from outside the Soviet bloc. We had a grocery store and a butcher shop, but they never had much, if anything, to sell. Still, there were always long lines in front of them. Meat was usually served with potatoes and lentils. Most of the time, though, you didn't get the meat, so you'd stick to lentils. I didn't mind, and to this very day, I love lentils. To get fruit, you also had to stand in lines. You could wait for over an hour, and there was still no guarantee that there would be anything left, if indeed it had been there in the first place. In those days, when a person saw a line, he would immediately get in it, not knowing what it was for, but hoping he could get whatever it was. I assure you, crazy as it may seem, all those stories about the endless lines to get nonavailable items are absolutely true.

In the Czech Republic there was only one fancy store, Tuzex. It was the only place in Karvina where you could get chocolates and jeans and other exotic stuff. Tuzex was for the rich, and they paid with *bony*, a privately issued paper money, not crowns. I never went to Tuzex in my whole life. My friends, who were richer, shopped there and bought incredible things like Swiss chocolate bars with air bubbles in them. My delights were a lot cheaper. I saved my pennies, picking many of them off the ground, to buy a certain kind of lollipop. They were transparent and different-flavored, like orange and lemon; they were covered in a plastic wrap that had a picture from a fairy tale, like Little Red Riding Hood, on it. I would save for weeks for one of these pops, or maybe I'd buy chewing gum.

There was one very special treat. Once a year on Christmas, we got clementines. They were our candy, and oh, the scent of them, and oh, the taste of them! Even now, when I smell clementines, it brings me back to the past, straight to Christmas.

Growing up under communism was severe, but I had one powerful weapon against the harshness of the regime: my family. Outside the family it was endless oppression; inside, while it could be strict, two special ingredients made life bearable: love and laughter. When I was born, we lived with my grandmother Anezka, her husband, and my mom's two younger sisters, Renata and Jarka. My mom, dad, and I were in one very small room. Later my parents were fortunate enough to get an apartment with a kitchen, two bedrooms, and a living room.

Karvina itself was rich because of the coal industry. Even under the communist rule, there were several levels of society, and we were more on the bottom; not bottom bottom, but the middle of the bottom. The very bottom was made up of families with only one parent, or parents who didn't work and were getting money from the state. My parents worked, but they were paid very little, which is why we were in the middle of the bottom. My mother and father gave us whatever they could, yet even with both of them working we never had enough.

Miners made a good living, but my father did not work in the mines. He was first a truck driver, then a bricklayer, and always took on extra jobs to make more money.

My mother was a teacher. She was born in Slovakia, and while she was in primary school, my grandmother moved them to the Czech Republic. My mom went into the Czech school system, and though the Czech and Slovak languages are similar, she had to learn a whole new system of grammar. She finished primary school, but because they didn't have enough money, she couldn't go to secondary school. She took a job in a store and did her studying behind the counter. She was determined to get her diploma so that she could earn more for the family. When I was two years old and she was pregnant with my sister, my mother still worked at the store. Somehow she managed to go to university and get her degree while keeping up all of her work and family responsibilities. She did it so that we could have a better life—and because she wanted to prove that she *could* do it. I admire as well as love both my father and my mother.

My sister and I were brought up with loving care and were taught to respect people and things. Respect is very important in the Czech culture. My parents were very loving in the Czech way, which is to say we didn't go around telling each other how much we cared; it was just there. Czechs are not comfortable talking about their feelings; we don't express emotions, but after much time in other cultures, I've adopted the view that it is important to talk about feelings. I am always concerned about the welfare of my parents; they would never complain, but I've learned how to worm things out of them. If I want to know how they are doing, I ask directly. I'll sit them down and say, "Okay, Mom, Dad, how do you *really* feel?" It seems weird to be like a psychologist with my own mother and father.

At home there was a lot of love, but not a lot of contact. We'd hug, sure, but not every second, and we didn't go around saying, "I love you," to each other. In Czech I say to my mother, "Mam te rada, maminko," much more often than I say, "Miluji te, maminko," which means, "I really love you a lot, Mother." *Mam te rada* means more than "I like you" and a little less than "I really love you a lot." It's a subtle difference, which, again, I think, is part of the culture. If I didn't hear "I love you" all the time, I felt it in everything my parents did, from my mother painstakingly ironing my clothes to my father cooking my favorite foods. They couldn't give us presents, so they gave us love from the first to the last, a far greater gift. Even today, when I call my parents and I say, "I miss you," and they answer, "We miss you, too," "miss" really means "love."

My father and mother each came from a family with three children. My maternal grandmother came from a family of eleven. Many aunts, uncles, and cousins live around Karvina. We often visited each other but not all at once. There are too many for all of us to get together at the same time. My aunts Renata and Jarka took care of Olga and me when we were little. They still tell stories about how naughty we were, particularly my sister. (Wait till my sister reads this.) I was more or less a good girl. I had one pigtail on each side of my head and a big smile on my face. Olga had a short bowl haircut, and she didn't smile so much. She was more a tomboy and very good at sports—which I wasn't. Olga didn't clean up after herself, either. When she came home, she took off her clothes and dropped them in a corner of our room and you had to force her to do the dishes. I always hung my clothes up and helped with the dishes. If my sister didn't like something, she would come right out and say it, and me? Never! I had a hard time admitting to myself what I liked or didn't like. What she wanted, Olga would go and get. (Oh my God, wait till she reads *this*! Be patient, Olinka, I have lots of good things to say about you later.) We used to fight all the time, but now we're really close—my sister's one of my most trusted friends. Olga has great instincts and a great ability to see the big picture. I can get lost in details. She's always had a confidence in herself that I, her big sister, often lacked.

Growing up, I thought that everyone else was special and wonderful, not me. I didn't speak up for myself and never expressed my own opinion. In secondary school I sat in the back of the class; when I had to go up front to read, I would stand there and my voice would get thinner and thinner, almost like I was crying. I was so nervous and so shy, and so tall—at least a head taller than all the others, including the boys. My nicknames were Giraffe and Eiffel Tower. Olga was tall, too, but it was different for her. She had more friends partly because she was so active in sports. I had friends, but I was more a loner and such a scared rabbit. To compensate, I tried to be perfect, to do things perfectly. Not so easy.

One particular incident has never left my mind. It wasn't anything major, but for some reason it has stayed with me. I was about eight years old, and I was supposed to bring a special book to school. I was nearly there when I realized I had left the book at home. I could have gone on to school and simply said, "I forgot it." That's what my sister would have done, but I, on the other hand, felt I *had* to have that book. I had been told to bring it, how could I disobey? I turned around and went back to get it. Now I had the book, but I would be late for school. All the way there, I kept thinking, Oh my God, I'm late, oh my God. I was so nervous I could hardly walk. My feet were dragging, and I was panting for breath. I was near collapse when I finally reached the school yard. The teacher didn't even ask for the book—she just punished me for being late. So much for seeking perfection.

At home I loved to clean and organize things for my mom because I knew this was a way to ease her workload. We didn't have money for gifts (except maybe birthdays), so I used my ability to neaten up the home as a present for her. In some Czech families the woman did everything; our house was very balanced, work was divided between my parents. Both of them had outside jobs, and both of them took care of the house and us, too. I can remember seeing my dad vacuuming as much as I remember seeing my mom do it. They both cooked, which my father loved to do, and still does—matter of fact, all the men in the family were excellent cooks.

Mealtimes were especially important in the Czech Republic. Despite the scarcity of certain foods, we were eating continuously. In the morning, for breakfast, we'd have a slice or two of bread with butter or marmalade or honey; sometimes we'd have scrambled eggs, or toast made with marjoram, like French toast, only salty. This was my favorite, so delicious! When we were little, my parents made breakfast for us, and when we got older, we made it ourselves. In school we'd have another piece of bread with butter or ham for a snack. Then came lunch—soup, a main course of meat with cabbage, lentils, or potatoes, and dessert. In the afternoon we'd have more bread, and then around seven o'clock came dinner, usually lentils with eggs. Wait, it's not over: At ten o'clock we had another dinner. Can you imagine? Six meals a day—and not a green vegetable or a citrus fruit in sight. It wasn't a healthful diet, even though we were eating practically every minute. For me, coming from that background, the hardest part of being a model was having to eat like a bird.

Stark as life could be, the Ostrava-Karvina region had its own particular charm, especially out in the countryside where my father's parents lived among beautiful hills and forests. Most weekends we went to Tyra, the village in the mountains near my grandparents Karel Nemec and Marie Nemcova. How I loved those weekends! And how I adore my grandfather. He has always been a driving force in our family. He's in his eighties now and still full of life and energy and practical positive thinking.

I have many great memories from those weekends in the mountains. Early on Saturday we'd board a train for the thirty-minute ride to the town of Trinec. (My parents didn't have a car until three years ago, so we always used public transportation.) I'm sure the train was dirty; I never noticed because I was too busy looking out the window at the passing countryside. From Trinec we took a bus to get closer to Tyra; next came the hard part. First, a long hike on a dirt path and then straight up a really steep hill. It was so difficult to climb that we had to take at least one break to catch our breath.

At that time my grandparents' house had no plumbing, no shower, and no toilet. On the most freezing days we had to trudge in the snow to the little wooden shack where the outhouse was, a one-holer. To wash up, we boiled water on the stove and poured it into a bowl. Then we'd scrub ourselves with soap and wash it off with the water. In summer we'd fill a big metal tub with water and leave it in the sun to get warm. Then we'd take a bath. To this day I don't need hot water to bathe in; what's more, I don't even need a bed to sleep on. Why? My father had a back problem and needed to lie on a firm surface. He'd often spend the night on the floor, and many times I'd lay out a thin blanket next to him and lie down. I got so used to it I can still sleep on a hard floor.

My grandfather had been a tailor but couldn't make a living at it, so he went into the mines. From his tailoring days he had this old sewing machine, which you pedaled with your foot, and a pair of huge heavy scissors that took all your strength to pick up. I never saw him use either the sewing machine or the scissors. I think he may have kept them as a reminder of the days when he worked above the ground. He's a cheeky man, my grandfather, and full of fun. He teased Olga and me all the time. There were wild boars in the mountains, and when my sister and I walked around the house, my grandfather would hide in the tall grass making wild-pig sounds to scare us. We'd run off screaming more with laughter than fear.

There was a great sense of community in the mountains. One neighbor had a farm with horses and cows, and we would get fresh dairy products from him. We got fresh milk with thick cream on top and the most delicious butter you can ever imagine. The butter was put into a bird-shaped mold, and it would come out, not white, but a shiny sparkly yellow in the shape of a bird. Oh, the taste of it! In exchange my grandfather would help the neighbor cut the grass, gather it, and place it in the sun to dry.

Food was something my grandfather was very serious about—he was almost obsessed with it, perhaps because his generation had lived through the world war. He wanted to make absolutely sure we got proper nourishment, so when we came to his house, we had to store up like camels. At mealtime there was no such thing as leaving a morsel on the plate. My grandmother poured the soup first, and the bowls were so full it was simply impossible to eat neatly. Then we'd have a second course, a mountain of potato, red meat, and cabbage. You had to sit there till you finished. Even if I was stuffed, I couldn't stop as long as something was on the plate. Sometimes Olga and I would beg our grandmother to help us out, and when my grandfather wasn't looking, she would take the food and hide it. Thank goodness for my darling grandma; otherwise, I would have been the size of an elephant.

We played lots of cards and games at my grandparents', especially one game called Man, Don't Be Angry. It was a very easy game, which also taught a big lesson. You could be on the verge of winning and suddenly, as in life, you could lose it all. It was very frustrating, but if you had patience and did not get angry, you could get back into the game and again have the chance to win. Both my sister and I learned a lot from playing that game. We don't really get angry, we keep on trying. When I'm frustrated because I can't influence what's going on, I realize maybe it's meant to be that way, so I don't go there. I try to remind myself that if something's not happening, don't push against the wall; follow another path. It's a simple philosophy which has helped me so much in my work and my life.

Another lesson I learned in the mountains was respect and love for nature. Whenever we entered the woods behind my grandparents' house, there were rules to be followed. We watched carefully where we walked, and we spoke softly. Respect has many rewards. If we watched our steps, the beautiful flowers were there to admire; if we trampled them, they were gone. If we were quiet and still, we could see the deer; if we made noise, we scared them away.

Speaking of animals, I haven't mentioned the cats yet. About twenty of them roamed around the property and in the woods. It all started when a neighbor went away and left his cat on its own. The cat jumped out the window and came to my grandparents' house. My grandfather began feeding it and called it Philip. Philip turned out to be Philippa, and from her started this gang. They weren't allowed in the house, so Olga and I would play with them outside, chasing after them and carrying them around.

My grandfather had a tent on his property. It had a wooden floor covered with dry grass and a blanket laid out over the grass. After lunch Olga and I would go inside the tent, curl up on the blanket, and take a twenty-minute nap to relax our tummies. We begged to be allowed to sleep there overnight, and sometimes we got our wish. One evening Olga and I were on our way to the tent when my dad told us we couldn't go in. Olga and I were very disappointed.

"Why can't we sleep there?"

"Come," said my father, "you'll see."

He led us over to the tent, picked up the flap, and we looked in. What a wonderful sight! A cat had just birthed three little kitties, and the four of them were nestled on the blanket. Olga and I were enchanted and quite willing to give up our places.

I used to take a lot of nature's gifts back home, things like abandoned wasps' and birds' nests and clumps of green moss. The simple truth is, everything to do with nature fascinated me, and I wanted to know all about it. There was no better place to observe nature than in the beautiful forest behind my grandparents' house, watching it change with the seasons, going from the bright green of summer to the snow-covered landscape of winter. Each season brought something different, and I loved all of them.

In summer we hiked in the woods and picked berries and herbs. I had a little book that gave the names of herbs and described their uses—whether for healing or for beauty. Some herbs were good for the hair, some for the skin, and still others had medicinal properties, like healing wounds or stopping bleeding. I knew a special place where the herbs grew, and I would go and pick them. I'd lay them out to dry in the sun, and later I'd make balms and teas with them. In times of stress I imagine myself back in that place where the herbs grew, and I find it so relaxing. I think of myself sitting on the little hill by the forest, looking over at another hill, with a beautiful silence surrounding me. Often I would lie down on the grass, smell the fresh earth, and feel at one with nature. Well, it wasn't always so serene. Sometimes Olga and I would lie on our sides and roll down the hills. We'd get up, pick the grass off our clothes, and sneak into the neighbor's garden. We'd steal peas and hide behind the trees, where we'd open the pods and one by one pop the peas into our mouths.

Mushroom hunting was a favorite activity. My dad, my grandfather, my sister, and I would head into the woods; my mom came with us sometimes, but usually she stayed back with my grandmother. We had a contest: Whoever found the most mushrooms was the winner. Each of us had a favorite place to find them. (Olga and I tended to cheat a little bit. We'd find a space where they grew, and then we'd come in and water it so that more would grow.) That way, we could gather the most mushrooms. The ritual was the same: We'd gather the mushrooms, cut them, put them to dry on newspapers, and save them for the winter. The funny thing is, while I loved hunting for mushrooms, I didn't like them and I wouldn't eat them. Today I adore them.

We also picked blueberries, blackberries, and red currants. We would carry pails filled with berries back to the house and hand them over to my grandfather. He used the berries to bake a special pastry—a sweet crust with the berries on top. They were the best cakes, sweet and tart all at once. Delicious! Olga and I wanted to eat them right away, hot from the oven.

"You have to wait or you'll get stomachaches," my grandfather warned.

Then he'd go out of the room, leaving us surrounded by the two temptations of sight and smell. Olga and I would stand over the cakes and begin whistling. If my grandfather heard the whistling, he knew we weren't eating the cakes. When the whistling stopped, he knew that we were sneaking bites.

In the evenings we'd build a fire outside to cook supper. We'd break off a branch from a tree, clean it, and sharpen it with a special knife. We'd put the stick through a sausage and hold it over the flames until the meat's juices bubbled. Meanwhile we'd put a hunk of bread on another stick and hold it over the fire until it browned. Then we'd pull the sausage off the stick with quick little tugs so not to burn our fingers, and put it on the bread. Finally, we'd smear on mustard and eat it down to the last bite. Our bellies full, we'd lie down on benches and look up at the stars. My father knew a lot about astronomy and he would tell us which stars were which, pointing out the different constellations, the Hunter, the Big Dipper, the Dog—so many of them and each with a story. Many times falling stars would shoot across the sky, and we would cry out, "There it goes!" Tracing the stars' paths in the clear, velvet sky remains a treasured memory of my childhood.

Autumn was a festival of colors, a beautiful symphony of flowers and changing leaves. We'd pick apples and walnuts from the trees on my grandfather's land and use them to make strudel—I make a wonderful strudel, if you'll allow me to compliment myself! We also saved the walnuts for winter to make Christmas cookies. We'd gather the root vegetables from the garden, eat some, and store the rest for the cold months. Autumn was the time for cutting the firewood, and I loved using a saw and ax. In fact, I love all tools and mechanical things. Many times I worked alongside my father helping him with tasks like laying tile. Although I'm no longer chopping wood or laying tile, I still enjoy working with my hands. I find it incredibly calming.

Winter meant snow—so beautiful, so cold, and so much fun to play in. We didn't have store-bought toys or equipment; everything was handmade. My father cut out blocks of frozen snow and built igloos for Olga and me to play in. My grandfather would take a very thick plastic bag, stuff it with dry grass, and close the top with a twist tie. Olga and I would sit on the bag and slide down the hill on our "sled." It took no time to get to the bottom of the very hill we struggled for ages to walk up. I don't know how fast we were going; I only know it felt like we went faster than the wind.

In spring the beautiful little white and yellow flowers

poked up through the snow, announcing new life, and the whole cycle of seasons would begin again. All four seasons were incredible—each had something special to offer—and I never tired of watching this cycle repeat itself throughout the years.

In the mountains we could laugh; in the narrow streets at home, things were more serious. The communist regime frowned on humor. Almost more than anything, I love to laugh. It's one reason why I look at things the way I do, trying to find the good in all situations, even sad ones. Laughter is a big part of my life, and that's why I adored Simon—he was so funny. In the mountains, away from the city, away from the iron rule of the government, and surrounded by nature's beauty, we found the flavor of life, which made it a bit difficult to go back to Karvina. The only time I really looked forward to returning home was right before Christmas.

Of all the holidays and seasons, I loved Christmas the most. Two weeks before the holiday my family would start baking cookies, and we'd make ten or fifteen different kinds from flour and nuts. We'd glue them together with marmalade and put them on the table to cool. The cookies were put on the balcony overnight to keep them cold, and—surprise, surprise—my sister and I would creep onto the balcony and do our usual nibbling.

A few days before Christmas we would go to the store and buy a couple of live carp. We'd take them home, fill the bathtub with water, and put them in; Olga and I played with them for hours. Early on the morning of December 24 my dad would close himself and the fish in the kitchen, and only one creature would emerge alive. People used to say,

"You play with the fish and then you eat them?" I'm afraid that's exactly what we did.

On Christmas Eve the four of us (sometimes my grandma Anezka came over, but my other grandparents stayed in the mountains) sat down at the kitchen table to a dinner of soup, fish, potato salad, and cookies served on special gold-striped plates, which were used only for the holiday. Christmas is a time to think about others, and my mother always put an extra plate out, to welcome any stranger who might come by. According to tradition, once we sat down to dinner, we had to remain seated, so everything had to be set up next to the table.

Although we had little of material value, my country is rich with traditions that have been going on for centuries (even the communists couldn't stop those old ways). I remember many of them. For instance, you'd cut an apple in half, and if the center core formed a beautiful star, then you'd be healthy for the next year. Or you'd take a walnut, break it in half, take out the nutmeat, put a little candle in the shell, float your "boat" in a pot of water, and light the candle. In another custom, older girls stood with their backs to the door and threw a shoe over their heads. If the shoe pointed to the door, it meant they'd be married in the next year. While there are many, many customs of the season, these stand out for me.

After dinner my mother rang a bell, the signal that we could go to the tree where we gathered around to open our presents. Before the evening ended, we had one last ritual. My mother put honey on special cookies that looked like giant communion wafers and gave one to each of us. At the same time, she took some of the honey and put it on our faces. This was supposed to make us more beautiful in the year to come. Then we all smeared each other with honey, sort of like a honey war. I think if there has to be war, it should only be a honey one. These are some of the reasons why Christmas in the Czech Republic is so meaningful to me. Even today it's my favorite time to visit my country.

Right before we left for Thailand, Simon came home with me for a Christmas visit to the Czech Republic. He joined in on all the preholiday festivities, trimming the tree and baking the cookies. My grandmother made strudel just for him, and he couldn't get over how delicious it was—he didn't want to share it. We all had a wonderful time together, and I am thankful that he was able to enjoy the season with me and my family.

2

A Model Beginning

Things did not change overnight in 1989. The communist rule was finished, but the atmosphere was leaden for many years after. There were some transformations. Censorship, especially in movies and TV, was lifted. Under the communists, only certain movies had been available—mostly Russian or approved ones from places like France, but never from America. At home my parents were kind of strict about our viewing. For example, if a movie had a kissing scene, a star was put next to the listing in the paper, meaning that the movie was not for children. One time Olga and I were sitting in front of our little black-and-white TV watching *Angelika*, a historical French film from the sixties. Such a beautiful movie and with a few kissing scenes. Kissing! Even though my parents let Olga and me watch, whenever the hero and heroine puckered up, we had to put a blanket over our heads.

With communism gone, people smiled more, they stopped wearing the drab colors, they walked with a quicker step, and more fruits and vegetables returned to the diet. It can take a long time to realize freedom, and, in some ways, my country is still recovering from the communist coma. Recently, I was talking to my friend Karolinka Bosakova, who also grew up in Czechoslovakia. We call ourselves "children of the change." We remember what it was like to be under the regime and are very aware how lucky we are to be doing things we never dreamed possible— traveling, exploring, learning, and earning. In a funny way, though, growing up under communism turned out to be a gift, because it made me appreciate more what I have now. All too often we only begin to appreciate things, or loved ones, after we have lost them.

Okay, if I'm telling my life story, I suppose I have to make some true confessions—like I have to tell some *bad* things about me. I guess this would be the place for it. The communists were out, but my parents still weren't making much money, which meant that lots of material things I really, really wanted were out of reach. In the early 1990s, leggings, or tights, were very popular for girls; they came in all kinds of styles, with flowers or stripes, and in different colors. I couldn't afford them, so two of my friends and I would go to a market and steal them. Usually, I'd hold the bag and they'd stuff the leggings into it. I was more an accomplice, although I have to admit that sometimes I took them myself. I wasn't caught in the market, but I was caught stealing in a drugstore. I went to buy some tampons, and I was kind of embarrassed to ask for them from the male clerk. I stupidly slipped a pack into my coat. I was walking out when the cashier came from behind the counter and stood in front of the door.

"What have you got in your pocket?" he demanded.

I couldn't say anything; I burst into tears, took out the package, and handed it over. I had been too shy to ask for the tampons, and for that, I had the bigger embarrassment of being a thief. The cashier was very nice and let me off. He warned that if it ever happened again, he would call the police. (Probably if the communists had been in power, I would have been put in jail.) From that day on, I *never ever* stole anything again. I'm not proud of what I did, but I think that every child does something bad and maybe it's good to know that anybody can do a stupid thing. To this day I don't know how I managed to keep my mother from finding out; she seemed to know everything I was doing. My sister and I couldn't lie to her or do naughty things because she could see right through us. I think this was because she was teaching teenagers and knew all the tricks. Somehow my thievery escaped her detection. When this book is translated into Czech, my mom's gonna get a really bad surprise about her good little girl.

It's not anything like stealing, but I was crazy for dancing. I started going with boys when I was thirteen, and dancing was the best thing to do with them. We young people went to a dance hall, and I'd dance and dance for hours and hours. At first I had to be home pretty early, but as I got older, I'd find excuses to stay out really late. A bakery was in the same building as the dance hall, and after the dancing we would go to get fresh hot bread right from the oven. Oh was it delicious, the perfect end to a wonderful evening. I still love dancing, and I can dance for hours on end. I still love bread, too, the dark, thick-crusted kind. Dancing wasn't such a terribly bad thing, even when I stayed out way too late; what wasn't so good was my last sin: smoking. A friend of mine taught me how when I was thirteen. She took some cigarettes from her apartment, and we went out behind the building. I didn't know how to inhale, so she explained it.

"It's like you have to get scared," she said. "Like, say, your mom is coming and you get frightened that she'll catch you, so you pull in your breath."

I did what she said and, of course, choked and choked. But I recovered enough to start enjoying it. I have to say my friend was a great teacher. I smoked for many years— first on Saturdays and Sundays, then half a pack a day, and finally a pack a day. I stopped because one of my boyfriends told me it was not good. Later, when I went to Italy to model, people looked at me like I was crazy. "You are a model and you don't smoke? Unbelievable!" I guess I wanted to be like the others, so I started smoking again. Somehow, though, I knew that I would stop before I was twenty-one. Sure enough, at nineteen I went on a trip to the Seychelles and brought along a carton of cigarettes. I said to myself, When you finish the last cigarette from this carton, you are going to stop. Someone told me that if you make longer the time between one cigarette and the second, you will smoke less. This is what I did. Instead of one pack a day, I cut down to between three and six cigarettes, and when I finished the last cigarette from the last pack, I stopped cold. It took me a week. The next week I was on a casting; one of the girls was smoking and I was thinking, Ooogh, that's disgusting.

Giving up cigarettes was easier than I thought, and I'm very happy I did it, not because I can smell and taste things much better, but because I know it is more healthful. I like challenging myself, and giving up smoking was a challenge I met and conquered. I believe that anything you put your mind into doing, you can do. (Try it yourself, if you don't believe me. Just focus on your goal, visualize it, and go for it! You'll be amazed at how much you can accomplish.) So now you've learned about my bad childhood—stealing, dancing, and smoking—and all before I graduated secondary school.

SPSCH-AK Heyrovskeho, my secondary school, was in Ostrava, about an hour's ride from Karvina. I had to get up at quarter to five, eat breakfast, and catch the bus. It was worth it. I was so happy to get into that school because I could concentrate on design and creativity. SPSCH-AK Heyrovskeho was a boys' chemistry school and named for a famous chemist. (Maybe in English you would call it a technical school.) The boys were studying to be chemical engineers or lab workers. Classes in fashion and design were also offered, but only for girls. There were thirty-three of us girls, and those were some happy boys when we arrived; finally, they got girls to look at.

At school I had four close friends: Jana, Lucka, Silva, and Kamilka. For four years we did everything together. We sat together in classes, we studied together, we ate together, we went out together. I was especially close to Kamilka Po-

A Model Beginning

Iakova. Kamilka looked after me like a big sister. She was the one I could confide in completely. She worried a lot about me, especially when it came to boys. She thought I was too trusting and would be breaking my heart over them. She is so kind, so gentle and caring, and is always thinking of others. Plus, she is smart—right now she's in Spain getting a Ph.D. in marketing.

My friends and I were crazy about the movies, and with the regime over, we got to see the ones from Hollywood. I loved the old ones on the TV, especially those with Audrey Hepburn. She was my favorite, and I adored *Breakfast at Tiffany's*. I also loved *Dirty Dancing* and *Pretty Woman*. Television programs that had been dull, dull, dull, were replaced with shows that had no big moral content but maybe just entertained you. Especially wonderful to me was the sudden appearance of Fashion TV—with models like Claudia Schiffer, Cindy Crawford, Naomi Campbell, and Christy Turlington. I'd never seen anything like it before!

I had always been interested in fashion. I played with paper dolls, and making paper clothes for them was one of my favorite activities. (My parents encouraged both Olga and me to explore many different pursuits, from handicrafts to cooking to painting to sports to reading.) How my mom found time in her busy schedule to teach me how to sew is still a mystery. Olga was too impatient with it, but I loved it. Soon I was designing and making my own clothes. Mostly, I made them because we didn't have the money to buy them, but I really liked doing it. (Too bad I couldn't sew leather—I had the same pair of winter shoes for five years.)

Fashion kind of exploded. Not only did we have the movies and Fashion TV, we at last could get magazines and mail-order catalogs from other countries. My favorite clothing catalog, Otto, came from Germany. I couldn't buy the clothes in Otto, but I would copy some of the designs and make them on my own. I loved working with my hands, sewing, drawing, modeling with clay. All of that took a lot of patience, which I still have. The TV shows, the movies, and the magazines inspired me; I wanted to make fashion my career, but at that point I wasn't thinking about modeling. So how did it happen? How did this "giraffe" from Karvina get to be a supermodel? I'll tell you.

One afternoon Kamilka, Jana, and I were fooling around at my parents' apartment. We put on different outfits that we'd designed and started posing: parading around the room or lying down on the couch and looking up with these dreamy expressions on our faces like we saw in the magazines. We were changing clothes and photographing each other and trying to be like professionals. This was my first "photo shoot," and after that, I started to get a little interested in modeling, in a kidding-around, experimental way. I needed to have photographs of myself, so I went to a passport photographer's shop. He did some regular passport shots and a few full body shots of me. This really was my first "professional" photographic experience, and one of those pictures is currently posted on my Web site, www. petranemcova.org. For the shoot I wore a lime-green dress, which I made myself even before I started studying design. The dress was a bit provocative, with holes on the sides. I don't know where I got the idea for it; it surely didn't look like anything out of *Otto*. I made a portfolio of the photographs, but I didn't do anything with it.

Then one day Kamilka came into school very excited. She heard about a talent search in Ostrava, sponsored by a local model agency, to find spokespersons and models for radio and TV. She said that we should go and try out. I wasn't so sure. I didn't want to do it because I was too shy. Kamilka got after me. "Come on, Petra. You *have* to do it. We have to go together." She wouldn't take no for an answer, and because she was going with me, I got the confidence. She *pushed* me into it. Believe me, if it hadn't been for Kamilka Polakova, I'd still be picking berries in the hills of Moravia.

We went to the model agency along with a whole bunch of others. The agency people looked me over and asked lots of questions. I gave answers, they thanked me for coming, and I left. Both Kamilka and I were pretty sure nothing would come of it. What a surprise when they sent a letter to my parents saying they wanted to represent me. I was shocked. My parents weren't a hundred percent thrilled with the idea of my modeling: I was only fourteen. Then my mom decided that it would be an opportunity for me to get some independence and make a little money; she thought I would grow with the modeling and go somewhere with it. She encouraged me. Later I found out that she was a lot more concerned than she let on. When things started escalating and I left home, she really got shook up.

I signed on with the agency, and now I was a model as well as a schoolgirl. Here's how it worked: The agency would call my mom and tell her where I should go for a "casting." Wait, maybe I should explain what a casting is. When a client needs a model, they call an agency, and the agency sends over a model. The client looks at the model and her portfolio and, if she's right for the job, casts her. A model may be very lovely but not suitable for that particular assignment—like, if they want a very tall girl or a very young-looking girl and you're not tall or very young-looking, you're not going to be hired. Sometimes you can go for a lot of castings and not get any jobs. You have to learn to accept this and not let it break down your confidence.

On one of my first castings, I was sent to Prague, where I had never been. I was excited about seeing the capital city of my country. I rode the train, along with some other girls, for around four and a half hours. The minute the train pulled into the station we tumbled out of the car and rushed over to the toilets to do our makeup and change into fancier clothes. From there we went right to the casting. The client looked us over, and that was that. We went back to the station and caught the train home. My first visit to Prague and about all I saw was the toilets in the railroad station.

Not long after this, I entered my first beauty contest, a regional competition to become Miss Moravskoslezsky Kraj (can you imagine this on a sash?). In the Czech Republic "Miss" contests, there's a bathing suit promenade, a question-and-answer, and finally, you have the freestyle expression of whatever you want to do—dance, drama, singing, etc. As far as my shyness keeping me from performing, I had not really a choice; I had to do something. In the first set I danced around a chair to a Janet Jackson song. For the final round, and believe me, I pulled the guts to do this, I performed card tricks while wearing a witch's costume. My thinking was, since I wasn't really that good at anything, I should do something with a little twist. I practiced and practiced to get the card trick right and then got the idea to dress up as a witch. It makes me laugh now to think that I would appear as an ugly hag in a beauty contest. I like to be original and I was—and I won the title of Miss Moravskoslezsky Kraj.

For a while I did magazine work, but mainly, I was doing tests, lots of tests. Trying out different things helps a model become accustomed to working in front of a camera. You get to understand how your body works, the different positions and poses that are good for you, and how your face works—what looks funny and what doesn't. I was learning the business from the grounds up.

Not long after I started working with the agency, I was sent to a very special casting; not a modeling job, but an important modeling competition, the Elite Look of the Year. This was a very big international event, sponsored by the Elite Modeling Agency, and was held every year all over the world. Each country had regional competitions, and the regional winners competed in a national contest. The national winner went to the international finals to compete with the girls representing their countries. Where do you think the Czech Republic regionals were held? You will never guess, so I will tell you—McDonald's. I went to the McDonald's in Ostrava and found many other girls there, very pretty ones, too. I gave my photos to the judges, local talent agents. They looked them over and then told me to walk. I walked up and down in front of the food counter. I walked like an elephant; I still walk a little like one, I think. (When I'd clump around in the apartment at night, my parents were always calling out, "Stop banging around. Stop being so noisy.") After the walk the judges took my measurements. That was it. The contest was over—I didn't even get a McNugget. What I did get, later that week, was a letter telling me I had passed the first level. I was so excited I couldn't breathe. Of all the hundreds of girls trying out, I was one of the lucky ones.

The Czech Look of the Year, the second stage of the nationals, took place in Prague. I hoped that on this trip I might see a little more of Prague than the railroad station toilets. I did see a little more, but not much. The contest was held in the Prague Public Transport Museum. Again we girls had to do our stuff—this time we had to do the special walk models use in fashion shows, the "catwalk." How to describe the catwalk walk? Well, normally when you walk, your feet stay parallel to each other as you move forward; on the catwalk it's different. You walk an imaginary straight line—so one foot goes directly in front of the other. In the meantime your head is up, your chin is up, and you're keeping your back very straight. You tilt a little backward, swing your hips, and let your hands hang loose. In motion you kind of go with the flow. It takes a while to learn how to do it right, so that it looks natural, which is funny because it's *unnatural*. At first you can't do it, then it comes to you—you learn how to do spins, and things like that. It's elegant and glamorous, and soon you begin to do the catwalk all the time, even out in the streets. When I

A Model Beginning

was recuperating in the hospital in the Czech Republic after the tsunami, I had to learn to walk again. They put me on a walker, and for a few days I was just standing. Then they told me to take some steps. I slowly began to move. The physical therapist took one look and cried out, "Oh my God, that's not normal; people don't walk like that!" The catwalk had stayed with me, and that's what I was doing. But now I had to learn to walk like a normal person all over again.

That night in the Prague tram station, we had three disciplines. First was sporty: We wore T-shirts and skirts from Replay. Then it was a bathing suit parade. Last, we came out in evening dresses. You wouldn't believe how nervous I was. My knees were knocking, and my legs felt like they were made of jelly. After the last discipline the judges conferred and then began the announcements. The chief judge took the microphone and called out the third-place winner's name. Actually, names—two girls tied. They came up and hugged each other. Next he announced the second-place winner. Again two girls were chosen, and those two went up and hugged each other. I stood there thinking, This is nuts; they can't pick one person. Mentally, I was preparing for the train ride back to Ostrava. The girl next to me leaned over and whispered in my ear, "You're going to win." The minute she said it, I began to tremble. The next thing I knew, the judge looked at a piece of paper in his hand and said, "Ladies and gentlemen, the first choice to represent the Czech Republic in the Elite Look of the Year, 1996, is . . . Petra Nemcova."

What do you think I did? I burst into tears, a waterfall

55

of tears. I was in such a daze. Everyone was coming over to me to say congratulations. There were flowers and gifts. (I can only remember one present, a painting of a cat.) My eyes were so full of tears I couldn't see anything, and my mascara was all over my face. Every time someone came over to me, I would kiss them on the cheeks and they would walk away with black marks smeared on their faces. The next day my photograph was in the paper. My face was completely smudged with mascara. But who cared? I was the Czech representative for the Elite Look of the Year, and the next stop was Nice, in the south of France.

One thing stood in the way: my boyfriend.

There are many stories about boyfriends who don't want their girlfriends modeling; they are afraid they will lose them, I think. My boyfriend at the time was like this. He really didn't want me in the Elite finals, and he started giving all sorts of reasons why it would be bad for me. I desperately wanted to go, but I loved him, and in the end, I gave in. Looking back, I find it hard to believe that I was so serious about this puppy love, but at the time, I was convinced that he was the one.

I told my parents I wasn't going to Nice. Now, my father is a very calm person. Like my mom, he respected my choices and usually let me do the things I wanted, within reason. When I told my parents my decision, however, my father said, very quietly and very firmly, "You *are* going." There have been a few moments in my life when my dad stepped in and took the lead, and always it had a good effect. This was one of those times. If he hadn't put his foot down, I would have missed one of the best experiences of my life. On another occasion an agency tried to switch contracts on me, and I didn't know what to do. My father did; he got a lawyer. I am so lucky to have my family looking out for me.

I was excited to go to France, especially to be in Nice where there was ocean—my first ocean, the beautiful blue Mediterranean. And what a thrill to meet girls from all over the world, as well as some very famous people (Quincy Jones was one of the judges). There were seventy of us contestants, and we shared rooms. My roommate came from China. She spoke Chinese and I spoke Czech. We couldn't talk to each other, but we didn't need words to communicate, we got along beautifully. There were many activities, luncheons, dinners on the beach, receptions, and, of course, rehearsals for the big event. This was the year of the macarena craze. We practiced dancing it onstage again and again. I could do it in my sleep. It was a whirlwind wonderful week.

The finals took place in the grand ballroom of a big hotel. Okay, I'm gonna get this over with quickly. I didn't win. People from the Czech agency were in the lobby when I walked out. They gathered around me. "You were great, Petra. Don't be sad. You did fine." Obviously, I *was* sad— maybe hurt because I didn't even make the last ten. You put so much energy into it; you try so hard, that you can't help thinking, I'm not good enough. I felt that way for a little bit, and then I pulled myself together. I didn't get it, but I wouldn't give up; I'd try again, another route.

Believe it or not, I was able to look at this and see it as a positive thing. Girls who win big the first time out often don't push themselves hard enough afterward. They are sometimes getting an attitude. "Oh, I won this contest and I got this contract, so I've already achieved the goals." They're like those shooting stars I used to see in the sky— beautiful, quick . . . gone. I believe that if you slowly and steadily build a career, you have a better chance of reaching the top and staying there.

Despite my disappointment, Nice was an amazing experience for me. I met beautiful people, I learned about different cultures, and I made a career decision. I discovered that I wasn't interested in beauty contests or going the conventional "Miss" route. I didn't want to try for Miss Czech Republic or Miss Universe. From the very beginning, from those first shows I saw on the television with the supermodels, I wanted fashion and modeling. Now I decided to go after it full-time.

3

Milan

I didn't return to Karvina as Elite Look of the Year, but I was the first in my family to visit Western Europe, and I spent long hours telling stories about the beautiful south of France. For a while I was walking on air; then I had to come down to earth. Much as I wanted to concentrate on fashion and modeling, it would have to wait. I was still a student. For the next two and a half years I went to classes full-time during the day and to castings at night. It was rough. Many castings were in Prague, and they had to be fit into my daily schedule. After school I would take a train, arrive in Prague in the evening, go to one or two appointments, and catch the last train back. I would sleep on the train, and sometimes when I got home in the early morning, I could sleep a bit more. Then it was up and out, and back to school. It was a lot of pressure, but I was excited about the work. My mom was concerned but also happy to see me so happy. She did everything to help, like ironing my clothes late into the night so that I would be dressed nice and proper. And she always made sure someone was going with me, like another model or someone from the agency. While my mom encouraged me, she was very strong on one point.

"The modeling is good for you, Petra," she told me. "I think you'll do well and it will take you far, but"—and her voice got real serious—"*you have to finish school.*"

She didn't need to tell me that. I'd thought a lot about it myself. I loved modeling and what it offered; it could make me self-sufficient, and I really wanted to take care of myself, and my family, too. But at this stage I couldn't be sure that I would have a successful modeling career. It was too indefinite. Having an education, having a diploma, that was definite.

My routine was simple, school by day and, two or three times a week, castings by night. Simple but complicated. Not all castings resulted in jobs, especially in the beginning. Of course, I was disappointed when I didn't get the jobs, and even when I began to get them, they didn't pay much money. Even so, I tried to save. Before I started the modeling, I had saved money by skipping school here and there and taking the bus fare to buy things for myself. Okay, sometimes I bought candy. I continued to get jobs, mostly for magazines and catalogs, and I tried to further my knowledge about fashion. I had a book on how to make your own cosmetics. I remember one beauty hint that said to put honey on the lips before going to sleep so they would be healthier and fuller. Every night I put the honey on. I don't know if it made my lips any healthier or fuller, but I do know it made the pillowcases sticky.

I spent two years in this hectic life. It was hard, but I loved it; I was totally focused. Anything I do, I give one hundred percent of myself—maybe more. There were obstacles. If a modeling job was scheduled for a school day, the agency would write a letter to the school telling them I had to be excused. Since I had to be in classes a certain number of days or be expelled, I had to be careful not to skip too many. Believe me, I missed the most I could. My marks began falling, and by the end of my senior year, with final exams coming up, I realized I couldn't juggle my two lives anymore. On my own, without a word to my parents, who were getting more and more concerned, I went to the agency and told them no more castings until I finished school. I stopped modeling and concentrated on my studies. I know it was the right thing to do.

My finals were tough. I was studying all the time. As a student I was never really that bright; I was good—not bad, but not great, sort of in the middle. I was focused and patient—I had to be, because things never went straight into my head. In order for information to sink in, I had to go over and over it. I got so involved in studying I didn't pay attention to anything else, especially food. I forgot to eat. At this point my friend Marian Mrozek stepped in. We'd known each other for years, and he was very encouraging about my modeling, and about my schoolwork, too. He'd call and ask how things were going and give me little pep talks. Most often, he called to see if I was eating properly.

"Have you eaten anything?"

"No," I'd answer, "I don't have time to eat. I have to study."

I'd go back to the books, and then Marian would show up with huge pizzas. He made me take a break to eat, and he did this quite a few times.

The night before the final exam, I still had studies to finish. I had to sew up a coat and do lots of paperwork. I was at it the whole night and into the next morning. I was getting ready to take the bus when Marian appeared at the door.

"Okay, Petra," he said. "It's a big day for you, and to make it easier, I'm going to drive you to school."

I was very happy. Not to hassle with public transportation was a big help. We went down to his car, got in, and took off for Ostrava. The next thing, a siren was wailing and a policeman drove up and made us pull over to the side of the road. Marian was speeding. While the officer filled out the ticket, I was getting more and more nervous. All I could think was, I should have taken the bus. I didn't say anything to Marian; I didn't want him to feel bad. Despite the delay, I got to school in time, took my exams, and you know what? I did very well. Much better than I thought I'd do. I was very happy about it. If I had tried to keep up modeling along with my studies, I never would have graduated.

I have many people to thank for sticking with me during this tough time: my parents, Marian, and my boyfriend, Janis—wait a minute, maybe here I better say a little about boyfriends. I have had a few of them in my life—well, a little more than a few, but always one at a time. Also, with one exception, I was with each one for a long time, from one and a half years to four years. I am not flighty; I am sincere in my affections. If I love, I love a hundred percent like everything else I do. It's hard for a model to keep a relationship going, especially a successful model. Success in my business means travel, a lot of travel, which makes it difficult to maintain a connection.

Back to Janis. He was half-Greek, half-Czech, and a wonderful person, the one who got me to stop smoking. Janis had a plan for us after my graduation. Like many Czechs, he wanted to go outside the country to work, to get money to send back. Janis had relatives in Namibia, and we were going to go there together. I had no idea what I would do in Africa; I just wanted to be with him. Janis went first, and I was supposed to follow him a month later. He called once, sent two letters, and that was it. I didn't hear any more; I was heartbroken. I waited for two months, and boy, was I sad. I really loved him. (Years later Janis and I reconnected, and I learned that a series of unfortunate family circumstances had prevented him from contacting me. All was forgiven and we are good friends now.) With Janis gone, I had to change my plans. I went back to the modeling agency and back on the casting circuit. Soon I had a breakthrough.

The fashion centers of the world are New York City, Paris, Milan, and London. New York is definitely the main fashion city—I know Paris is going to fight that, but it's true. (Milan used to be, but now it's mainly for high-end fashion shows; the regular modeling jobs aren't that well paid and not as glamorous as New York.) An agency in

Milan wanted to take me on and contacted my Czech agency. Models can be represented by different agencies in major cities. It was an amazing opportunity, but I was scared to leave home and go so far away. Always at these moments my fears try to take me over. Once again my family and my friends gave me the strength. They convinced me that if I wanted to be on the world stage, I couldn't get there by staying in the Czech Republic. I got up my courage and prepared to leave. The last night, I was packing and crying. Tears were all over the clothes in my suitcase. Partly I was scared of leaving home, and partly I was still crying over Janis. My mother was crying, too. She and my father were afraid of what might happen to their little girl in the big world. The wonderful thing is, despite their fears, they had the strength to let me go. "Our parents give us roots and wings" is a beautiful saying, and that's exactly what my mother and father did. They had the trust to let me fly away. I think I have honored their trust.

I took a plane from Prague to Milan and was met at the airport by representatives from the agency. Unfortunately, there was a problem at passport control. It was such a mix-up. An agent took me out of the line and into an office. He called the Czech Embassy and began screaming, "No, no, no," into the phone. That much English or Italian I understood. I was put into a holding room filled with every kind of person from everywhere in the world. I stayed there for hours. The agent came back and told me I had to go home. They put me on a plane, and I flew back to the Czech Republic. That was my first visit to Italy—not the best start, but I wasn't discouraged. I looked for another route to get there. A few days later I boarded a bus. This time it took several days to get to Milan, but I got there.

Going to Nice had been a small step; going to Italy was a giant one. Try to imagine moving to a major world metropolis and not speaking one word of the language or anything much of an international language that might help you. I had studied a little English at school. After the communists were gone, most people didn't want to continue studying Russian. The primary schools now offered other languages, German and English. I chose English, but learning how to say, "Good morning, teacher, how do you feel?" does not do it when you are a model trying to get to a casting. A few other Czech girls were in Milan, and one agency employed a woman who spoke Czech. I dealt with her and I could talk to the Czech girls, but I was more or less on my own. I did manage to keep up ties to home. I bought phone cards and called my parents frequently. I sent them postcards and bombarded my friends with letters, especially Kamilka. They were all very worried about me.

Looking for work was the same in Italy as it had been at home. They gave you a piece of paper with a list of all the castings and appointments, and then you had to get there. And always the agency would caution, "Don't be late. You have to be punctual." I tried my best, but it's hard to move fast when everything is in a strange language. All I could say in English was, "Hello, my name is Petra" and "How are you?" I couldn't say, "I'm hungry" or "I need a toilet" or anything else of use. I had a little Czech/Italian phrase book, which I carried everywhere. The phrase book got me through restaurants and lavatories but wasn't much help in my struggle to master the subway system. Many times I got on the wrong train and did not find out until I reached the end of the line. If there were multiple castings that overlapped, I was a cooked goose.

Milan is a tough city. In fact, I believe Milan is the hardest place for the young models, and most of them start there. The life is fast, and you have to be on your toes all the time. You work through agencies and public relations firms, and while most of them are good people, there are others who want you to do this or that to get the jobs and you don't want to do either this or that, you just want to model. You have to be supercautious because so many people will try to abuse your naïveté. I may have been an inexperienced girl from Eastern Europe, but I had some things working in my favor. I paid attention to what people told me, I listened carefully, and I knew how to distinguish good advice from bad advice. That was the plus side.

On the other side, I was eighteen years old, and for the first time in my life, I didn't have my parents on my back. Guess what I did? I partied. Two or three times a week I went to clubs with my new Italian friends from the fashion industry and danced my feet off. They warned me to be careful in the clubs, especially with drinking. Their advice was always the same: Buy your own drink, and if you put it down, don't touch it again. What I discovered was, people put drugs in your drinks and terrible things could happen. You could wake up somewhere with someone you didn't know and not have a clue what you did. I actually knew girls who got in big trouble this way, and it wasn't their fault. I don't drink—I like to be in control of things, and that's probably why I don't, especially in situations where there's the possibility of real trouble. I took my own bottle of water with me to clubs or parties, and even though it was only water, if I put it down, I left it there.

Believe me, there's a lot of dirt in the business and sometimes from people you trust. Some girls were not aware of the big picture; they thought they *had* to do things, that this was the way things were done, and they were easily manipulated. Often girls are taken advantage of by so-called boyfriends. A model makes some money and gives it to her boyfriend because he says he'll invest it for her. Well, he'll invest it, in himself. I learned that you must always be on guard and if you get burned, *c'est la vie.* I believe that each experience fits a piece of the puzzle into your life and shapes who you are. Only time will make such things clear.

Within a month I could speak basic Italian and began to find my way around Milan. I went on castings and began to get jobs. I didn't take off like a rocket; my career was steady and slow, a gradual ascent. I was proceeding like a snail. Looking back, I see this was not such a bad thing. Some girls soar, and overnight are on the moon. Everybody wants them for campaigns and magazines; then after half a year they're "yesterday," totally overexposed. The girls can be amazingly gorgeous, but the attitude is, "Oh, we've seen it. We want something different, something new, something fresh." Always they want "fresh." That's why a girl has to strategize. In most cases a career must be planned; it doesn't just happen, and a smart model will discuss her career with her agency and her agent. One true thing they say about supermodels: They're not only models, they're business-women.

There are two major modeling categories: editorial and commercial. Editorial girls work for magazines and do fashion shows, but they don't make much money. You can be on the cover of *Vogue* or *Elle* or any big magazine and still not get paid a lot. Editorial girls are more edgy and interesting-looking. Commercial girls are more traditionally beautiful and make very good money because they are in advertising campaigns or doing TV commercials. Sometimes they want to do the editorial because it's more creative, but they can't.

Me—again I'm lucky. I could do shows, editorials, commercials for TV, and the catalogs. Later in my career I could also do talk shows. I had the spice, all the flavors needed, to bridge the two worlds of modeling. In my career, from the very beginning, if it made sense, if it was worth it, I did every job, big or small, and I never complained. Some girls don't go to certain castings. They say, "Oh, I don't want this, I'll wait for something else." For me it's always been, "I'm there!" And when I'm there, I'm totally focused and do everything—in all kinds of conditions. Very often you are shooting a bathing suit scene when it's really cold out. It can get so cold that you are turning completely blue. This happened to me one winter in Cape Town, South Africa. We were on the beach where there was such a strong wind that people in the crew were wearing jackets and sweaters. I was in a bikini. My teeth were chattering, and I was turning blue. On other occasions I've had to get into freezing water that went straight into my bones. My body was numb; I couldn't feel anything, but I smiled for the camera. It sounds like torture, and it is in a way, but I never complained. I accepted it and went on. No matter how hard it is, I really love my work.

Doing the modeling is a great school of life. I learned so much about people and cultures and countries. And I learned languages. Besides Italian, I've also picked up French and a little Spanish. As for English, I now consider it my first language. I think in English. My sentence structure and my spelling may be more Czech, but every day I'm getting better with English. Modeling also made me stronger, able to stand on my own two feet and to use my own judgment. I learned to think fast and handle myself in strange and difficult situations—none ever so terrible as the tsunami. But even in the face of that horrific event, I was able to call upon the life lessons I've learned and make it through.

Much as I love modeling, right here I am going to say some things about it that are not so wonderful. I have already mentioned that young girls starting out can be taken advantage of, and just as awful—or more awful—is the need for models to be skinny, skinny, skinny. Even though I think that is not a good or healthy way to go, I follow the line. In that sense I am a victim of my profession. Models in Europe are required to be even thinner than in the States. (In the United States they like a healthier look.) Right away when I moved to Milan, they told me that I had to lose weight, and I was pretty thin already.

I had the bad luck to start my career when a horrible "look" became the rage. It was called "heroin chic," the most unhealthy kind of appearance you can imagine. Models were skin and bones and had dark circles under the eyes; if the circles weren't there, they were painted on. It was grotesque and terrible, yet for a while heroin chic was the standard. I was told the designers more or less started it. Back in the eighties and nineties gorgeous supermodels like Cindy Crawford and Claudia Schiffer had beautiful feminine bodies. Some people say that because the supermodels were becoming more powerful and getting bigger and bigger paychecks, the designers wanted to get the power back. They wanted change, and they wanted to shock people—fashion is always about changing the *look*. So it went to this heroin chic—no curves, just sticks—and they were hiring young girls whom they didn't have to pay much and who would do anything to be in the campaigns.

I was never in the heroin-chic class, but I did work to make myself ultrathin. That meant dieting big-time. Believe me, I have been through many, many diets. In Milan I kept a little packet of crackers to munch on during the day, and ate nothing but a plate of rice with sea salt in the evening. Normal salt is supposed to keep water in the body, which means the cheekbones can't be seen, whereas if you use sea salt, the cheekbones stay prominent. I stopped the rice thing when I realized that normal or sea salt, I had water retention. My cheekbones hadn't "fallen," but I had bloat.

Next I started eating only protein and vegetables, which sounds like a smart thing except that I was eating lots of canned foods—too much sodium, so, again, bloat. I stayed out of the cans and concentrated on eating protein, still a very unbalanced diet. In fact, this is the point where I messed up my metabolism for years to come.

Later, when I moved to Paris, I went on a fruit diet. I ate two kilos of apples a day. I thought it was healthy, but there was too much sugar in the fruit. Then I bought a book that introduced a protein and carb diet. This made sense to me, and I started eating that way. It worked well, especially when I combined the teachings with another book, which was all about fiber. The second book talked about the level of sugar in our blood and how we have to eat foods that don't bring the level up too high, because it turns to fat. I made a regimen for myself by uniting the knowledge from both books. I started to eat in a very healthy way, and have continued to do so. I eat sensibly—not a lot, but my diet is good.

I refuse to traumatize and abuse my body simply because of what I do professionally. I think that I have learned from all the crazy diets. I'm taking care of my body now, but it suffered from what happened before. One thing I could never do anymore is eat six Czech meals a day. It's not just because my stomach has shrunk, either. It's that my body is much more sensitive and reacts completely differently. My metabolism got messed up, which means I cannot eat certain foods. What I do is eat small amounts of everything, including brown bread, brown rice, and yogurt (but only goat's yogurt because I cannot digest the cow's). I can eat only a little bit of carbs.

One of the first times I was in the United States, I was eating the right things, chicken and vegetables, sort of a protein diet, and I was exercising every day. Still, after a month, I realized I was growing! My hips, my whole body, were gaining inches, and I thought, What is happening? I did some research and discovered that it was because of the hormones injected in the chicken. I was shocked. People are not aware that hormones are being put into their food, and not just in chickens.

Since that experience, I've been very careful. I eat only organic foods. I am not vegetarian, but I will have only *organic* chicken and fish and, occasionally, an *organic* steak. I used to hate salads when I was a kid; I never would eat them, I thought it was rabbit food. Now I love salads. The same with spinach, yogurt, dried fruits—all the things I disliked as a child, I now adore.

The hardest time for me is when I have to prepare for the fashion shows, which means I have to be even more skinny than during the rest of the year. During the shows I go strictly on protein. It's not what I like to do at all. Unfortunately, it is part of the business, and if I want to work, I have to conform. Still, I do think something should be done about setting standards that call for extreme skinniness. I am sad that normal teenagers who are looking at magazines want to be like the skinny, skinny girls in the photographs. It can mess up their whole lives, not just their body images. Some become anorexic and, worse, bulimic. I was never like that, although I know of models who went that route. Fortunately, I think that the trend of healthy-looking women is coming back, and I am glad, because health is more important than anything. The sooner we look after our bodies, the better our health will be and the less pain we will have when we are older. You have only one body, and if you don't take care of it, no one else will.

Maybe this has been a little preachy, but believe me, I want so much that young people be realistic about their bodies and not try to conform to what they see in the magazines. Here I must make a confession. I know personally how bad this wanting-to-be-skinny thing can be. I was never anorexic or bulimic, but for a very long time I did something dangerous. It became an addiction and could have permanently ruined my health. If it hadn't been for Simon Atlee, my story might have been a lot different. I will tell you all about it later on.

4

The Apprentice

I love to challenge myself. I like to put goals in front of me and try to reach them. I like looking back to see how little by little I came closer to those goals and at the same time how I grew in so many other directions. When I was in the Czech Republic, my goal was to be a model—that's all I could hope for. When I got to Italy, I wanted to be not just a model but a top model, and I worked hard at it. I lived in a residence with other girls, and my days were pretty much the same. I'd wake up around 7:30, have breakfast, and then go for the castings. Sometimes there could be a dozen in a day, and they could be all over the city. I got a Vespa motorbike and scooted from casting to casting. I was on the go every minute. I didn't have time to sit down. By the time I got home, around seven in the evening, I almost couldn't feel my legs. I'd make my dinner of rice with sea salt, and depending on what my schedule was, I'd either go to bed or go out with my housemates or Italian friends to a corner café for *panini* and cappuccino. One thing I have to say, though, I was never bored. My career was moving steadily. For a while I was torn between the commercial and the editorial, the money or the creative. I thought I'd have to concentrate on one or the other, but I never had to make a choice. I was lucky enough to be used in both disciplines. I was modeling for some top designers, and I began appearing in Fashion Week, which is about the biggest event in my business, the grand slam of modeling.

Fashion Week is held twice a year starting in New York, then London, then Milan, and finally Paris, always in that order. When you start out, it's easier to begin in London, more difficult to get shows in Milan and Paris, and even harder in New York. During Fashion Week there will be ten or more shows a day. You arrive a week to ten days before the shows and start going for castings, sometimes as many as seventeen different in one day; that's seventeen different designers. The pace is killing. You have all these appointments, as do hundreds and hundreds of other girls. You go there to be hired, and if you're lucky, you are—but you could as easily get nothing. If the designers like you, they call you back—and if they still like you, they may do fittings, and yet they don't have to use you. Sometimes you spend ten days and you only get three or four shows. Some girls don't get any shows because they don't have the "look." They can be skinny and perfect, but it's not the look. Maybe they want tomboyish girls, or girls with big breasts, or girls with strong noses, or girls with little noses.

Each season is different, and you either fit the look or you don't.

If you are optioned to appear, you get excited, but it's only an option and it could be dropped. Sometimes you get a confirmed option, have a fitting or two, and are scheduled for three or four shows. Then the day before, they change their minds and cancel everything. It has nothing to do with you; it's about whatever fits for that season. It's true that the top models are requested to appear, but only the very top models, and even they have to go and see the designers to make sure that they have the right sizes and everything fits. The thing is, when you're young and you're turned down, you automatically think, Oh, there's something wrong with me. It plays with your psychology so much, this roller coaster of highs and lows, but you have to learn not to take it personally.

For me, loneliness was more difficult to deal with than rejection. That's when I started thinking about all my friends at home and reaching out to them through letters and phone calls. They always answered the call, but they were far away. I've had low times, and it gets even more depressing when you see the other girls feeling the same way. Some don't eat anything and are tired all the time. Being tired is understandable when you consider that you get little if any sleep. You start at four and five in the morning with hair and makeup, and you're on the go practically around the clock. Oddly, all the parties you read about that sound so exciting are often a required part of a model's schedule. They start late at night and end early in the morning, and you have to be there. Then it's time to start all over again. There are so many parties, so many fittings, so much commotion, the designers often put out cots, and models flop down on them to grab any rest they can. Behind the glamour, Fashion Week is physically, emotionally, and psychologically draining.

At my first shows I was very stiff. Then with practice I got more confident. Whenever I got sad, depressed, or frustrated that I'd lost a job, I'd say, Okay, I'm going to change the thoughts and think positive. Maybe they didn't choose me for this job, but I'll get another, even better one. Each time, I tried to think what I could take from the situation in a positive way. You have to expect the unexpected, too. For example, I have a problem, if you want to call it that. For a 5'10" model, I have a small foot, a size 38 (U.S. size 7). Whenever I tell people my shoe size, they look at me like I'm crazy. "So small a foot? How can you keep your balance?" Most of the girls, they are size 40 or 41, and those are the sizes that are brought to the shows. I'm always wearing high heels two sizes too big. At a Fashion Week in London I was going down the runway and one of my shoes came untied. I leaned over, took off the other one, threw them both over my shoulder, and continued walking. If that had happened earlier in my career, I would have stopped dead in my tracks. You have to have the confidence to take disadvantages and turn them into advantages, and that comes with experience.

One evening after an Armani show, I went to a party. I was standing near the dance floor, and a nice-looking man started talking to me. He was a model, too. We had a pleasant conversation, which was unusual at such parties. Then

I had to leave. A few months later I was at a club, and someone came over and asked me to dance.

"Is your name Petra?" he asked.

"Yes."

"I'm Donaes. We met at the Armani party."

I remembered him.

Donaes Valentine Platteel is the full name of this amazing gentleman from Holland. He's charming, intelligent, and talented. He speaks seven languages: Dutch, German, Italian, French, Spanish, English, and Latin. He's a musician—a pianist and drummer. He's kind, always helping others, and very spiritual as well as knowledgeable. He also has a great dry Dutch humor. All the women who meet him find him fascinating, and they should, he's the perfect man. I don't feel the least bit strange saying all these wonderful things about someone other than Simon, either. Donaes Platteel played an important role in my life. He lived in Paris and came regularly to Milan for castings. We hung around together for a few days, as friends. I liked him very much; he was easy to talk to, wonderful to listen to, and possessed an amazing inner calm.

I discovered the source of this serenity when I went to meet him at his hotel. I walked into the room and found him sitting cross-legged on the floor, his hands on his knees and his eyes closed. Obviously, he was doing something special and private. I waited. In a while he opened his eyes.

"What were you doing?" I asked.

"Meditating, and working with energy."

"What is this energy?"

"We are made of energy, and energy is all around us."

"So what does this energy do?"

"It helps you get stronger. It helps your body get stronger. It can help you to get healthier, and it can help you to heal others."

Wow, I was thinking, this sounds good. I asked more and more questions, and soon Donaes was introducing me to meditation and energy work. This was my initiation into the beautiful world of spirituality, which I have been exploring ever since.

In my studies I have drawn strength from the connection between body, mind, and spirit. It has changed my entire life, making me stronger physically, emotionally, and mentally. Physically, I didn't get sick for six years, whereas before, I had many colds and frequent bouts of the flu. Emotionally, I grew more and more confident in myself—now the "giraffe" could stand tall in front of any group. Mentally, it sharpened my senses. I think much more clearly and am a much calmer person.

An introduction to the spiritual was only one of the amazing gifts I received from Donaes. He helped me professionally. Really, he didn't just *help*—he actually molded and created my professional self. In Milan we talked about my career. He had some suggestions. The first was that I move to Paris. Being in the business, he knew where to find the best opportunities; he felt that Paris was the place for me.

Donaes's words got me thinking. I felt I'd gone about as far as I could go in Milan. I wasn't so thrilled living there, either. At that time, more than any of the other fashion capitals, Milan was full of "sharks," people who wanted a piece of you, on the personal side, and on the business and the agency side as well. If you were even slightly naive, you could get so easily in over your head. I believe that the situation has changed, but in those days I found it a strain to deal with certain people that I didn't quite trust. After Donaes left, I carefully considered what he had to say, and on my next photo assignment tour, I scheduled a stopover in Paris.

When I got there, I met with some agencies. (I also renewed my acquaintance with Donaes.) I returned to Milan and began strategizing. Of course, I was scared to make such a big move, and I'm sure if Donaes hadn't been living there, it would have been a lot harder to make the decision. I was doing well in Milan, and yet I was not really confident about myself or my successes. There were hundreds of girls like me. I did better than some, and many did better than me. I still wasn't totally comfortable in my own skin; I didn't have the self-assurance I needed to have in order to be what I wanted to be. Again I was at a crossroads. I made my decision and moved to Paris and into Donaes's apartment.

Being in Paris was exciting but difficult. I didn't speak any French and had to learn my way around a strange city again. I wanted to bring my Vespa over, but Donaes discouraged me.

"In Paris," he said, "they don't look when they drive. You wouldn't last two minutes on the Vespa."

Sadly, I had to get rid of my little motorbike. Once again I was relying on public transportation. My first day, I went for three appointments and got two jobs! Two out of three! Miraculous! One was for Lancaster cosmetics, the other was for a photographic test in Majorca. Two weeks later I got a contract from Wolford for a bathing suit campaign. I quickly discovered there were indeed many more opportunities for me in Paris. My career, nurtured by Donaes, began to blossom. And I, also nurtured by Donaes, blossomed. Donaes is about ten years older than me, and very worldly-wise. He helped me grow professionally by nurturing me in a spiritual, not an emotional, way, which in turn helped me build my confidence. He did this in many ways, first by making me stand on my own two feet.

"Petra," he said to me one day, "you know I want you to be here with me, but I think it's important for you to be self-sufficient. I think you should get your own place. That way you'll have the freedom to do whatever it takes to make you realize your potential."

I think he was wonderful to do this. Selfishly, he could have made it easy for both of us by letting me stay, but selfish is not in his vocabulary; he gave me the wings to fly. I got my own apartment, and for the first time in my life I was completely on my own. Six months later my career was flourishing and so was I. After proving that I could be self-sufficient, I moved back in with Donaes, and we were together for four years. We were in love, but we did not put any chains on each other. Our relationship was based on trust, honesty, respect, and freedom. Freedom is very important to me; maybe it has to do with my communist-controlled childhood. A good relationship means not saying you *can't* do this or you *can't* do that; it's saying you *can* do anything as long as you respect the relationship. For

Donaes and me, freedom included seeing or dating others if we wished. From the beginning we established that if one of us met someone else, we would tell the other. Even with the freedom to do what we wanted, never in those four years did either of us see anyone else.

Love Always, Petra

5

The Top

I had two solid years in Paris—many jobs and much learning. I traveled all over doing shoots and fashion shows. I was like a Gypsy, always on the run, but I loved the experiences. At home I attended classes in meditation—they were in French, so Donaes had to translate everything for me. Soon I picked up enough of the language to study on my own. My studies in Spiritual Human Yoga gave me a completely different perspective and were filled with knowledge they never teach in school. This knowledge brought me inner confidence and strength—the strength to help others as well as myself, and the energy allowed me to reconnect with nature. One of my most important discoveries was the realization that happiness is mine and no one can take it away from me. This understanding, combined with meditations, filled me with joy. I felt grounded, I felt happy. It was a major turning point in my life.

During my first year in France, I was working for the Next agency in Paris and was sent to a fashion show in London. Agents from all over were there, and one of them, Leigh Crystal of the Next agency in New York, came back to talk to me. We liked each other right away. I went back to Paris and soon began getting calls from Leigh. She and Faith Kates, a director of Next, had a great job for me with photographer Gilles Bensimon for American *Elle*, a huge deal, so I flew over to New York to do it. I was a bit nervous. I find that when I do something the first time, I get a little jittery. Once I get going, I relax and begin to enjoy myself. Really, it's like a performance: You get the butterflies in the stomach.

After the American *Elle* job, I got another assignment, this time for Clarins in St. Bart's. It was a great job, and when it was over, we all swapped modeling stories. Here's a silly one. I was told that another girl had been there before me for a bathing suit shoot. The bathing suit was too big in the top, but they didn't have any silicone fillers, which is usually what's put in to make the bosom look all nice and curvy. So they improvised by taking fresh chicken breasts and inserting them under the bra. The model looked "nice and curvy," all right, but by the end of the day, the chicken was cooked from the heat of the sun. That's only one of the many secrets of modeling. Here's another—sometimes, if the bathing suit top is too loose, you stick a toilet paper holder in the back strap and twist it around to make it tighter. There you are doing all these sexy poses with a toilet paper roller on your back.

A few months later I was doing fashion shows in Milan

when I received a call from Next in New York. They wanted me to do a bathing suit shoot for some American magazine in Lake Como, Italy. The magazine was *Sports Illustrated*; I had never heard of it. I had no clue that the SI annual bathing suit issue was about the most prestigious assignment imaginable. All I know is, I did the shoot, and had the pleasure of meeting Diane Smith, who is the editor for the bathing suit issue. I adore her; she's like a (young) mom to all the models. I spent two days in Lake Como, and though it was work, it was a pleasure, too, because of the great people I worked with. This shoot was a happy experience, and at the same time it was probably the decisive moment of my career. Who would believe that a magazine I never heard of, an American magazine dedicated to sports, would be my catapult to modeling "stardom."

Every February, *Sports Illustrated* hosts a big party in New York City to launch the bathing suit issue, and all the girls who have posed for it are sent airplane tickets. I got an idea that this might be a big thing when I saw that my ticket was for business-class (I was strictly an economy flier then). They put the models up in a hotel and told us to get nice dresses and be ready for the party. Leigh was going with me. A *limousine* and a *bodyguard* came to pick me up, and all of a sudden I was like, Oh my God, this is really big!

Leigh began prepping me. "There's going to be a lot of photographers. First we'll do a picture of you by yourself and then with the other girls. After that, you'll do interviews with fourteen or fifteen different television stations from around the world."

I was shaking. I barely spoke English, and I was going to be appearing on television? I stood in front of the TV cameras braying like a donkey. All I said was, "Ah, ah, ah, ah." I guess it didn't matter what I said, because the "donkey" was asked to do the bathing suit issue the next year, too.

This time we went to Bahia in Brazil for another fantastic shoot with Walter Iooss, a photographer I've worked with many times and who I adore. When February came around, I was much better prepared for the party; for one thing, my English was much improved. Usually when you work, it's the job of the moment, and that's it. *Sports Illustrated* is different. If they like you, they keep using you. It's one big family. In September 2002 I was asked to pose for the 2003 issue. We shot in Vietnam, and then, early in January, we finished in Barbados.

After the *SI* shoot I worked nonstop to the end of the month, traveling from Morocco to Barbados, to Hawaii, and finally to Cape Town. There I had a meltdown. I was so overworked I was getting migraines, and I had no time to meditate—I had lost control. I remember putting blackout curtains in my hotel room so I could lie there and rest. At the end of this assignment I was scheduled to fly out of South Africa to New York for the *Sports Illustrated* party. I called Leigh Crystal and told her that I couldn't make it; I was completely washed-out and had to take a break. I expected her to be sympathetic and tell me it was okay, but I got a surprise.

"Petra, I don't know how you're going to do it, but you've got to do it. You'll get the energy when you get here."

Leigh never pushed me. Usually, she would say, "You should think about doing this; it's good for you," something like that, and leave the decision to me. I had no idea why she wouldn't let me off the hook this time, but I knew her well enough not to question her reasons. Leigh always has my best interest at heart. You would think I would have suspected something was going on when I saw that my ticket was first-class, but I could never imagine the reason.

Traffic caught me on the way to the airport. I missed the flight to Johannesburg and the connecting flight to New York. I had to make a big change in itinerary and fly from Cape Town to Atlanta, Georgia, and then to New York. I flew into Atlanta and was informed that New York had a major snowstorm; all flights were canceled. I called Leigh, then checked into a hotel for the night. I was in the room preparing for bed when the phone rang.

"Diane Smith from *Sports Illustrated* calling Petra Nemcova," the operator said.

"This is Petra," I answered. Why was Diane Smith calling me?

"Petra," said Diane, "I'm so sorry to have to tell you like this, but you really have to get to New York for the party. You're on the cover. And you're scheduled for a television interview tomorrow."

"Oh my God," I cried. I couldn't believe it. I was in shock. How would I get to New York? I called Leigh again. She told me to get out to the airport early the next day and grab any available flight. I went to bed, and excited as I was, I was even more exhausted and quickly fell asleep. I got up at 4:00 a.m. and went to the airport. The storm was over and I caught the first flight out. I was met at the airport in New York and hurried into a limousine, where I was dressed and made up on the way to the hotel. We reached the hotel, went through the lobby, and then I walked into a room where there was a huge poster of the 2003 issue—with me on it!

Unlike any magazine I've worked for, the cover of the SI swimsuit issue isn't photographed specifically as a cover; every girl in the issue has an equal chance to get it. As I understand it, the magazine chooses its favorites, takes those photographs to a shopping mall somewhere in the middle of the United States, and puts them on a big board. Then they ask guys in the mall to vote for their favorite; the one with the most votes gets the cover. Diane Smith told me that that year, the top three photographs voted by the mall men were all of me! The number one photo, the cover, was the last one I posed for in Barbados. I loved the shot, but never expected it would get so much attention. I'm so glad it did.

The next days were madness. I did all the events, all the shows, the parties, the interviews. I remember I was very skinny at that time; I was so overworked I'd gone down to nothing. (I would never let that happen again.) In Cape Town I had no life in me at all, and then, just like Leigh said, I got a burst of energy that carried me along.

Once the New York event was over, I had to fly to Los Angeles and appear on the Jay Leno show and on *The Late Late Show with Craig Kilborn*. I threw everything together fast, but I needed something special to wear. Faith Kates sent out an SOS, and Donna Karan was so kind to lend me clothing. Los Angeles was nonstop interviewing—even in the car between TV appearances, I was doing radio spots. The Leno show was good fun, but being with Craig Kilborn was especially meaningful. I'd been on Craig's show twice before, and Craig had been talking about me for a long time. He had kept saying that I should be on the cover of *Sports Illustrated.* When I actually got it, he was as proud as could be, like I was his protégée. He's a very special person.

I was in Los Angeles for two days, and I don't think I ever slept. But I had this incredible energy. I took the red-eye to New York and went right on to *Good Morning America.* The madness continued until April. When it ended, I flew to Jamaica to meet Donaes and collapse—I mean relax—no, I mean collapse.

The *Sports Illustrated* cover was the big break that pushed me onto another level. It was amazing and exciting and I was blown away. Of course, there are always pluses and minuses. The pluses are obvious, but I entered a new period that was even more work-oriented than before. New York became my headquarters, and I focused more intensely than ever on work. I became a complete workaholic. They say it's harder to stay on top than to get there, and I think it's true. You have to work doubly hard to maintain what you've achieved and to create new ways of keeping work fresh and capitalizing on every new opportunity. I loved it; I loved the challenge.

What I didn't realize was that I was flying too high and too fast. Donaes tried to keep me grounded, but he was mainly in Paris, and I was going around the world. There's a saying: Life is not about how many breaths we take but

Love Always, Petra

how many moments that take our breath away. At that period of my life, I lived incredible moments which most people, including me, only dream of. Yet, although I was living
my dream, I was feeling no real joy, just work and stress.
And then I met Simon Atlee.

Part II

6

Simon

On January 21, 2003, I took the Eurostar from Paris to London to do a four-day shoot for Freemans, an English clothing catalog. That evening I checked into a small hotel, had dinner in my room, and went to bed. The next morning I arose early, washed up, got into a pair of pants and a shirt, and was out the door and on my way. When I'm working, I'm always on time. (When I'm not working, sometimes it's a different story.) The Freemans assignment was scheduled for four locations. The first was two days in an old-fashioned English manor house that had been turned into a retirement home. I walked up to the front door and rang the bell. Someone buzzed me in. I entered and saw a few old people sitting in a large room off the front hall. They seemed to be sleeping in their chairs. A woman stood in front of me.

"May I help you?" she asked.

"I'm here for the Freemans shoot."

"Oh, of course; you want to go to the second floor, first room on the right."

I walked up the stairs, reached the landing, turned right, and walked into the room. At the far end a few people were setting up equipment. One man, with short dark hair and dressed in jeans and a T-shirt, was giving directions, motioning to the others where to put the lights. Obviously, he was the man in charge. Someone noticed me standing in the doorway.

"Simon, she's here," said the assistant.

The man in the T-shirt looked up and came over immediately with his arm outstretched and a lovely smile on his face.

"Hello," he said as we shook hands. "My name is Simon Atlee, the photographer."

"Hello," I answered. "My name is Petra Nemcova, the model."

We both laughed.

That's how it began. I went for a job and met him. Simon Atlee was pleasant and cheerful, and we had a very good humor together, nothing more. There was no bolt of lightning. I was still very much in love with Donaes, and when I'm in love, I don't look at other men. Two things, however, made this shoot special: Simon's humor and his thoughtfulness. He made me laugh, and not just me: He got the whole crew laughing. He did silly things like pretending to drop his equipment, but what he was really doing was putting people at ease. At the same time, he was considerate, which is not always what happens. A photography shoot is hard work, and people can be very serious about it—to the point where it has a negative effect. Sometimes you get people screaming at you. They look at you as more or less a "hanger" to put the clothes on. There's no respect whatsoever. You feel left out and strange, something not human. The photographer has a big responsibility. He has to be on top of everything, and if anything goes wrong, it falls on his shoulders. Most are polite, but they have a job to do and are focused on getting it done. Not Simon Atlee. Simon understood how to connect, and he did this instinctively because he was one of the most caring people I ever met. I learned this about him the first day.

Music is an important aspect of any photo shoot; ninety percent of the time, it's played in the background. When you feel good, when you feel comfortable, you project that, and you get the best pictures. I can work from the whole music spectrum, depending on the mood, except for heavy metal. With some photographers, you shout out what you want to hear as you're posing.

"Can we get some Prince!"

"How about Justin?"

"Let's have Madonna!"

For the model it's the fastest way to get into poses. If it's supposed to be a sensual shot, sensual music is played; if it's happy, happy music is played, and so on. It's a very simple formula but unbelievably helpful for getting in the right frame of mind. Models often take their favorite CDs with them. I love music, but I quickly discovered that Simon Atlee *really* loved music. He knew all the artists, all the songs, and could talk about everything intelligently. He didn't impose his taste; he encouraged the model to make her choices. Simon felt that if a model had what she wanted to hear, she would give even more emotion to the camera. For Simon this kind of consideration extended beyond the selection of music. Before we began the actual shooting, he came over to me.

"Would you like something to drink, Petra?" he asked. "Tea or coffee?"

I couldn't believe it! It amazed me that he would be caring enough to offer to get the model a drink. In England tea is a big deal. Usually, the assistant will ask you if you want it and how you want it—white (that is, with milk) or with sugar or not. Simon was an Englishman, and tea was very important to him. Later, when we were together, I had to learn the tea culture, which I adore. I found it very funny because there are people who put the tea in first and then pour the hot water over it. Others pour the water, then add the tea. Each side thinks it's doing it the right way. Simon told me that there was a saying in England: If she knows how to make a good cup of tea and she knows what "offside" means, it's a woman to marry. The Englishmen, they love their tea and their soccer. On the set Simon would get the tea for everyone; for him there was no high or low position. He connected with all the people on the crew. He was a master of making people feel great. Right away, professionally, there was a comfortable energy between Simon Atlee and me.

On the Freemans shoot, Simon was using, for the first time, a digital camera, which was quite new for the business. Shooting digitally is different. The digital shutter goes *click—click—click*—slow. Normally, with film, it's *clickclickclick*—fast. (Like the way Prague people say "hello" as compared to Moravians, remember?) You have to get used to the digital rhythm because as a model you go with a certain flow, changing your mood and your positions to the tempo. I had to make adjustments for the digital camera, and we were click-click-clicking for a bit of time before I settled into the new beat. The digital camera was attached to the computer, which was great. You could see immediately on the screen if anything was wrong—the hair, the light, the clothes—and you could correct it on the spot. At first, because of the newness of the technique, there were some silly photographs coming out. Then, as we got accustomed to it, the photos became elegant and beautiful.

It was such a pleasure to work with a professional who was full of fun and thoroughly enjoying himself—and looking out for everybody, even people not in the crew. We ordered our lunch, and there were leftovers—which always happens. Usually, the leftovers are thrown out, but this time Simon said, "Let's give the food to the people who live here. It'll make them happy."

We brought the food to some of them, and it did make them happy.

The next day we moved to the second location, a more modern house. That morning I came to work wearing a black off-the-shoulder shirt, a short jean skirt, fishnet stockings, and short boots. I also had on a short jacket and a black mafioso-type hat. (I love hats.) This was high fashion in 2003. I also brought my Sony Ericsson cell phone, which had a wireless earpiece. Simon really was impressed with my phone; he said it was like a James Bond thing.

"Petra," he said, "may I take a Polaroid of you in your outfit with the phone and the earpiece? You look like a very tech sexy secretary."

It wasn't an unusual request. Many photographers will ask to take photos of you in your own clothes in different places before the actual shoot so they can test the light and shade and that kind of thing. If the photographs are any good, they keep them. I posed for Simon and didn't think anything of it. What I found out was, he kept that Polaroid and carried it in his wallet.

The third location was a wine bar, and by this time Simon knew that I ate in a health-conscious manner.

"Do you want to go to the supermarket with me?" he asked. "You can pick out the foods that you want."

We went together and bought food for everyone, including some nice breads as well as carrots and almonds. I enjoyed his company, and we had a good conversation, but that was all.

The last of the locations was an apartment that was decorated in a pinky, romantic style and the clothes were also in this pinky, romantic style. I was really enjoying this shoot; the whole experience was like a fresh breath. By now all of us on the crew were friends and getting quite silly. After the final shot we all dressed up in the Freemans catalog clothes, only we put Simon and his assistants, Toby and Barnaby, in women's clothing, including high heels. I stood behind the camera taking photographs, saying the same words like Simon:

"Okay. Great. Okay. Stop it there. Relax your lips. Okay. Change. Now sexy, give me the sexy look. On the side. Okay, a little bit more from the side. Shake your hair." When you hear these commands out of the moment, they sound very sexual, which they really are not, because we are working our asses off and don't have time to think sexy thoughts.

In catalog shoots there are so many photos to take that sometimes you lose the energy to be creative. Simon never lost his energy or his creativity. He put his heart into each photo. He always tried to make the shot amazing, even if it was only a catalog picture. He was quite demanding, and I liked that, because I am, too. If we take a hundred photos of the same outfit and the photographer says, "Okay, you go change," if I'm not satisfied, I'll say, "No, a few more." Everyone knows I'm like that. Now, if I want to keep shooting, they say, "Oh, Petra, give us a break."

Simon loved his work; he loved taking gorgeous photos. I love my work, and I love helping to create beautiful photos, so in that sense we connected. We had good laughs and there was a nice creative energy working with him, and then it was over. When the shoot ended, I said, "Nice to meet you," kissed him on both cheeks—three times, I always give three kisses—and I left for Paris and Donaes.

Six months later my agent called. The Freemans people really liked what I had done and wanted me again. The agent also said I would be working with the same photographer. I remember thinking, Oh, that's nice.

"They want you to work eight days straight," my agent said.

"No way," I answered. "I'm not going to do more than four days in a row. Tell them I'll do eight days if I get a day off in the middle."

I wasn't being a prima donna. I've discovered that you cannot give a hundred percent for more than four days in a row, and I hate to give less than that. I wanted to be fair to the client and myself. Freemans changed the shoot to four days in Majorca and four days in London with a day of travel in the middle. Traveling is not work for me; it's really rest. When I'm in a plane by myself, I catch up either on my work or on my sleep.

Everything fell into place, and on July 2, 2003, I went to Majorca, and that's when the whole beauty of my life began.

I arrived and checked in at the hotel. As always, I followed my routine—unpacked my suitcase, hung up my clothes, put my cosmetics in the bathroom, and set up my exercise equipment. I carry elastic body bands with me; they're great because they don't weigh anything and you can exercise your legs and arms, your back and your booty. There's no excuse not to exercise, because all you need is a door to attach the bands to. (When I'm traveling, I'll buy two-liter bottles of water and use them as weights.) A lot of the time on location, they don't have healthy foods, so I pack my fruits, almonds, oats, and good veggie snacks. That way I don't have to eat candy bars and sandwiches. As a rule, I don't eat bread unless it's a rye or dark bread. Believe me, if I didn't carry my own food, I sometimes wouldn't find anything to eat at all.

The next morning after I woke up, I did my exercises, had breakfast in the room, and went downstairs to the lobby to meet the group. Simon was there.

"Hello," I said. "Very nice to see you again."

"Nice to see you, too; we're gonna do some gorgeous pictures."

We hugged, and I gave him three kisses on his cheeks.

Among the others on that shoot were Simon's friends and assistants, Barney and Grant, and Mike Chalk, the client. Mike stayed in our lives for a long time; he's still a good friend. That first day we all got into one of the two vans we were using—the other one was for the equipment. Before we took off, Simon explained the rules.

"We'll be leaving every morning at four o'clock," he said. "Everyone has to be on time. If anyone is late, we'll go without you." (This wasn't true; he always waited for everyone.) Every day, the schedule was the same: We started at 4:00 a.m. and returned to the hotel around 11:00 p.m. There were many different locations, and we traveled an hour or more from one to another. It was pack, unpack, shoot, pack, and on to the next location, often three and four times a day. People think that fashion photography is glamorous and chic. It's not; it's brutal. Simply going from one place to another is hard work—but it has the pluses as

well as minuses. And with Simon Atlee, there were definitely more pluses.

Majorca is a lovely sunny island with very dry weather.
Some parts are quite commercial with lots of tourists.
Other parts are raw, with stone houses, beautiful wild countryside, and amazing beaches. We covered most of the island, and there was much laughter, even more than in
London in January. Mike Chalk said it was the funniest and
best trip ever. It was the same for me. My stomach was
hurting from laughing. We were feeding off each other's
jokes and humor, and everything was a perfect fit. Simon
wasn't the only funny man. Grant is like a clown. He's from
Australia and a fanatic Frisbee player. I think his Frisbee
has its own passport. Lots of Frisbee playing was going on
and water fights, too. Everybody was soaking wet and having fun.

One morning Simon showed up wearing a blue T-shirt
with DICKIES printed on it.

"Oh my gosh," I said when I saw it. "I have the same
T-shirt in red. We're gonna have to take photographs
together."

We did, and I still have those pictures of Simon and me,
wearing our Dickies shirts and laughing. Nothing was
going on between us—just good times.

We didn't get much sleep. Simon was working very
hard. He had to think ahead, to find new locations and
map out the trips, but he also had to be in the present and
concentrate on the shooting at hand. Always he was caring
and always so professional.

On the last day, we were driving in the van and Simon

mentioned that he never sent postcards to his mom. At that moment we passed the Cathedral of Majorca, and I took a photograph of it. Later I gave him the picture.

"Send this to your mom," I told him. "I'd like her to have something from the trip." Everything had been very professional up to that moment; this was the first personal touch.

On the last night, we had a celebration dinner at the Hotel Portixol. They have wonderful food; one of my favorite dishes is spinach salad with caramelized walnuts. Delicious! We were at a long table outside on the terrace and having a good time. I have to tell you something to show you how attractive Simon was. One woman on the production team was really into him. "He's got the most amazing blue eyes," she told me. "I could go for him." She was a lesbian! Simon's appeal was so strong no one could resist.

I had noticed his blue eyes back in London, but I was in love with someone and didn't look closer. In Majorca those eyes began to get to me. They were the most incredible pure and deep blue I ever saw in my whole life. I guess I'll never see more beautiful ones, and I'm sure they will be mentioned a thousand times in these pages. We got very silly at the dinner, and a little naughty, too. We played the napkin game, which goes like this: You take a napkin and create something with it, then the next person gets the napkin and creates something else; the funnier the better—things like headphones, a necktie, a crown, a priest's collar, a rose, a penis—and then you have to do a little acting thing. When it was my turn, I made a garter that a bride wears on her wedding day and slipped it on my leg.

We finished dinner and went out to a bar in town. While we walked along, Grant and Simon were taking shots, pretending to be paparazzi. We stayed in the bar for a little while and then I excused myself. I went back to the hotel. I was pretty tired. The next morning I packed up my stuff and got to the lobby at around nine o'clock. I saw Simon and Mike Chalk coming in the entrance; Mike had a bandage over his eye. He walked unsteadily and Simon was supporting him. I remember thinking, Oh my God, they must have had some wild night.

"What happened?"

"It's okay. It's okay," said Simon.

What happened was, Mike slipped and fell and got a bad gash over his eye and had to be taken to the hospital by ambulance. Simon went with him and stayed the whole night. He could have left Mike there with the nurses, but that wouldn't have been Simon. I was very concerned, but I had a flight to catch and both Mike and Simon said I had to leave. They got another plane in the afternoon. Mike told me later that when they got to London, Simon insisted on taking him from the airport to the train station. (Mike lived outside of London.) He could have sent Mike off in a taxi on his own, but that wouldn't have been Simon. Funny, when Simon told me the story, he didn't make himself the hero, but Mike did.

The next day we began the London shoot in Simon's studio. We set up the equipment and started the music. The photo shoot in London was all about Prince. I love Prince. He's incredible. I was getting ready to pose when Simon called out, "This song is for you, Petra."

The music began. It was Prince, and it was "I Would Die 4 U." The emotion of that song went right in me and absorbed me completely. I think that listening to it was the first moment I began to realize that something was happening. Such a strong energy was going between Simon and me. I tried to convince myself that I was imagining it, but something was in the air. On a photo shoot, if someone, anyone, has a pain in the shoulders, back, or neck, I will do massage for them. I saw that Simon was moving his head back and forth and making a circle with it. I asked him what was the matter.

"Just a pull in my neck," he said.

"Sit down," I ordered. "I'll give you massage."

He sat in a chair. I went behind him and began rubbing his neck. I could feel such a force in my hands. After I finished, Simon stood up, turned around, and got down on his knees. He looked up at me.

"Would you marry me?" he asked, quite seriously.

I didn't answer. I went silent.

"Well, Simon," Mike Chalk called out, "she didn't say no."

I was a little scared by the way I was feeling about Simon Atlee. I could control my actions, but I couldn't control my thoughts, and he was constantly in them. Another thing drew me to him. He rode a Suzuki motorbike back and forth to work, and ever since Milan, I was crazy about motorbikes. I even planned to get a license. Just the sound of a motorcycle gave me goose bumps. I thought they were sexy—dangerous, too, but so sexy. On the set I'd hear the whir of Simon's Suzuki, and my heart would race

Love Always, Petra

106

because I knew he would soon be walking into the room. When I told him I loved motorbikes, he said, "I promise, one day I'm going to take you for a ride."

I waited for that day.

It happened on the third evening of the shoot. I had made a date to meet my agent Sara for dinner. We finished work, and I was getting ready when Simon offered to take me. Funny thing, he had a second helmet with him; obviously, he'd planned to give me a ride. I got on the bike and sat behind him. I hadn't been on one in the four years since Milan. I was a little stiff as we took off. Simon told me to hold on tight. I drew nearer. It was amazing to be so close to him. I did nothing, just rode with my arms around his waist, my chest against his back. It felt as though we were flying, the same kind of sensation I got going down the hill on my grandfather's plastic bag sled. We stopped in front of the restaurant. I was sad that the ride was so short.

"You're really good on the bike," Simon told me as I got off. "I couldn't even feel you."

I thanked him and went inside. I was beaming with smiles, and most of the evening I was talking about how wonderful Simon was. Later my friends and Simon's told us that they all saw what was happening. They knew we were falling in love before we did.

For the final London shoot we went to a bar that was empty during the day. We were pressed for time because the bar had to open in the evening. We did one page of the catalog in the morning, broke for lunch, and got ready for the afternoon shoot, the last catalog page. Time was running out, and Simon made a decision.

"We're not going to change the set because we don't have time to relight. We're going to do this very quickly and simply. We're going to shoot straight on this wall, and, Petra, you're going to get in and out of the clothes and give me great beautiful poses—it's all up to you."

Shooting that last page was so thrilling, so exciting, so charged with energy, I didn't want that day to end. I was getting in and out of the clothes so fast because I wanted to spend more time in front of the camera looking at Simon. I waited for those moments that he stepped from behind the lens and came over to check me, especially my hair. Because I'm always shaking my hair, sometimes a strand lands on my shoulder. Simon would push the hair away. I wanted him to come to me, I wanted to look into his eyes, I wanted to feel his gentle touch. I was getting into the last outfit for the catalog, a very sexy, short black biker-style skirt, when Barnaby called out, "Petra, why don't you take Simon's helmet? It goes with the outfit."

This fit right in with the way I like to do things. There are so many pictures to take that people can get bored. Every ten or fifteen shots, I would make funny faces or do funny things, so for each outfit there would be at least one strange photograph sent to the computer. That way we could all get a laugh, and sometimes we actually used those shots. The helmet was on a little cocktail table near the bar. I picked it up and posed with it.

Barnaby called out again. "Simon, put on your bike jacket and take a picture with Petra."

Simon put on his jacket, and we had some pictures taken of us together. It was awkward because of the energy going on between us. Simon was nervous and stood very stiffly. He didn't know what to do with his hands. You can see it when you look at the photographs, or at least I can see it.

After we finished, it was time for me to give everyone presents. I always give presents at either the start or the end of a shoot. I love to give them, and what I love the most is to see the happiness in people's eyes. What I do is, I buy things all over the world, and when it feels right, I give them to certain people. That way my friends get flavors from all different cultures. I bring everything, especially chocolates. Everyone knows I have a thing for chocolates. Every single shoot I bring a box of them. Why do I do it? Around four o'clock in the afternoon everyone gets tired. Chocolate gives you a quick pickup and makes people happy. Usually, I'm not eating them but I enjoy watching the others have them. This time I gave the stylist a wonderful black-and-white photography book about family, and I gave Simon and Grant T-shirts. I forget what I gave the others. They all thanked me and it was time to leave.

I didn't want to say good-bye to Simon. I wanted more time with him. I wanted so badly to say, "Let's meet for dinner." In fact, I was working up my courage to do so when he said, "Would you like to have dinner?" After I said yes (meaning *Yes!*), Simon asked Grant to come with us. I was relieved because I was a bit nervous about what might happen if Simon and I were alone.

With Grant as our chaperone we went to Les Trois Garçons. It's an excellent restaurant in not such a great area, with delicious French food and amusing decor.

Stuffed animals wearing jewelry are all over the place, and antique handbags hang from the ceiling. I sat next to Simon, and Grant sat opposite us. Grant was making jokes and doing a lot of talking. I was leaning a little bit toward Simon. He wasn't leaning back, though; he didn't seem to notice what I was doing, and I guessed that he wasn't as impressed with me as I was with him. Okay, I thought, I'm imagining things. (Later Simon told me that he couldn't believe that I, a supermodel, was attracted to him. He really put me on a high level. I'm not that special, just a normal human being.) We talked about a lot of things. He had such a great outlook on life, and I loved hearing him talk about what interested him, what made him happy. He was full of life and understanding and, of course, laughter.

When it came time to leave, I excused myself, saying I had to go to the ladies' room. On the way I did what I usually do when I'm out for dinner. I gave my credit card to the waiter. I can afford to pay for meals and I like to. In our industry many men, particularly older ones, think that if they take out a girl and buy her dinner, there's a continuation to it. You can't buy me. I don't want anyone to think they own me because they bought me a meal. There's another reason, too. I'm lucky enough to be able to pay for my own dinner, so it's a lot about being equal. By the way, I'm famous for my ladies' room/credit card action. Sometimes when I go out with friends who know my little trick, they'll prebook with their credit cards to make sure I don't pick up the bill.

When I returned to the table, Simon was signing the bill, which was on his credit card.

"You shouldn't do that." Simon laughed. "I invited you to dinner. It was very sneaky, very cheeky of you."

I couldn't do anything but say, "Okay." This was the first time that somebody saw through what I was doing. I was shocked.

We left the restaurant and went around the corner to a little bar. I could only stay for a bit and then I had to go. Grant and Simon walked me to a taxi stand. I got into a cab and sat down. Simon looked through the open window to say good-bye. I looked into his eyes. The whole evening I was looking into his eyes, I couldn't find the end to them. When the cab drove off, his eyes stayed with me. I had his eyes in front of me all the time. I was shaking, and tears were coming. What was happening? The energy was so powerful, and we hadn't even done anything. I tried to think of Donaes, whom I loved, and immediately my thoughts returned to Simon. I had never experienced anything like this before. All I could think was, it cannot be that I won't see him again. It cannot.

When I got up the next morning, my first thought was, I'm going to call him, and later that day I did.

"Simon, this is Petra. I'm at my agency. I have a few hours till my flight. Would you want to come over?"

My voice was getting higher and higher, and I was trembling like I did when I was a schoolgirl standing in front of the class. Simon's answer was brief. "I'll be there in ten minutes."

Ten minutes later I heard the roar of his motorcycle, and I was trembling with joy. I could hardly contain myself. We went to a nearby café, sat next to each other, and drank ice water with lemon. I was looking into his eyes, being hypnotized completely. At one point I reached over and took his hand in mine. "You are such a wonderful man. I am happy I met you."

Simon told me later it was then that he realized something was coming from my side. How funny—we both thought the other wasn't interested. We finished our drinks, exchanged phone numbers, and said good-bye. He roared off on his motorcycle, and I headed back to the hotel to pack. My feelings were a lot different than they had been the night before. Then I had been heartbroken, I wasn't sure I'd see Simon again. I knew after our little meeting, it would happen.

At the airport I went into the duty-free shop to store up on gifts. Justin Timberlake was singing "Cry Me a River" on the speakers. I thought of Simon, and I wanted to cry my own river. I got onto the plane and took my seat. Normally, I would immediately be doing my work on the computer or going through my papers, or reading or writing. I'm one of those crazy people who think the longer the flight the better, because I can accomplish so much in the air. There are no distractions, no phone calls or text messages. This time was very different. I was zoned-out. Everything was slow-motion. I put on the headphones and plugged into the music channel. Of course, it was Justin Timberlake and "Cry Me a River." That song was following me and Simon for a long time. I began crying again. I had such mixed feelings, such crazy emotions. I kept telling myself to breathe deeply, and I almost couldn't catch my breath. What's going on? What's happening? I was so exhausted I fell asleep and was out for the entire flight.

I arrived in New York. Donaes was waiting for me. I don't think that he noticed anything different about me because it was such a hectic week. I had a photo shoot in the Hamptons for several days, and I was preparing a huge party for my twenty-fourth birthday—for four hundred people at Pier 59. It was a lot to organize, and I couldn't do it alone. My agents, my publicists, Donaes, everyone was helping, too many to mention here. There's a Czech saying that "for good people there's always enough room," and I had a lot of good people staying with me: my sister, Donaes, and my parents, who were for the first time in New York. Because I was working, I didn't have a second to be with any of them—not a chance to talk to them, even, which may have been just as well, since I had all these conflicting passions in my heart. I had so much on my mind I felt like I would burst. Simon and I were texting each other all the time. During the shoot I would go into the bathroom and send off a message. One night driving back to New York, I was messaging Simon. I was half-asleep and punching in the letters for two hours. I made lots of mistakes in grammar and spelling, even more than usual. Simon loved my mistakes. Later on, he would help me with the grammar. I wanted to be helped; I still do. I want to learn to speak and write English the best way.

My mom always told me that what we give, we get back, and I believe this is true. I was almost at the point of collapse, but I pulled myself together for the party and put my belief to the test. We live our very fast lives, and we forget things and have to be reminded about what's important. At this moment the important thing for me was having a great party for all my friends, to show them how much I loved and appreciated them. I designed shirts for the party—red tank tops for the girls which said "Love is the key to everything" and blue T-shirts for the men which read "If you fill up your heart with love, there is not space for fear." It may sound a little much for a guy to wear, but it was done in a very cool way.

The party was amazing—lots of dancing, food, fun, and friends. I love a good party, but the truth is, I was just going through the motions. I was exhausted—and apprehensive about confronting Donaes with the story of Simon.

At the end of the evening a motorboat arrived at the pier, and some of us got on and went for a ride around the Statue of Liberty. How beautiful it is, and how especially breathtaking it looks at night. As worn-out as I was, I couldn't help but be moved by the sight of that great green lady. After the party we went back to the apartment, and I flopped on the bed and fell immediately to sleep with Donaes beside me.

When we awoke the next morning, I gathered my courage and poured out my heart. I told Donaes everything that had happened in Majorca and London. Well, really, nothing *had* happened except there was this energy, and if it was there, then it meant something and I wanted to know what it was. I had always believed that Donaes and I would marry and have children. I told my friends that I was confident that he was the one. We had a wonderful relationship. I could talk to him about anything, even, as it turned, about Simon. However, if my relationship with Donaes was the ultimate one, my feeling about Simon shouldn't be there—but it was. I reminded Donaes of what he had said to me at the beginning. "You are very young," he had told me, "and I know that at one point you will go away." At the time, I couldn't understand why he said that; now maybe his prediction was coming true.

Donaes was hurt but understanding and kind as always. He never put an ultimatum to me like, "Don't see this guy!" What he said was, "Go and find out how you really feel." It was so smart, and I admire him so much for having the strength to say it.

That morning we talked for hours and hours and cried about the past and the future. I kept telling him that Simon and I hadn't done anything because I wanted Donaes to know that I honored our relationship. The following day we parted and Donaes returned to Paris.

My next assignment was on the Continent, and I hatched a plan. I called the agency and told them, "I want to make a stopover in London." It really wasn't on the way, but I wanted to see Simon. I called him after the flight was booked.

"Hello, Simon, it's me, Petra. I have a layover in London before my next assignment. Can you imagine? I didn't want to, but they had to book it this way. I have a few hours. Would you like to see me? Would you like to come to the airport?"

I could hear excitement in his voice. "Would I? I'll pick you up with the bike."

I was all pins and needles on the flight. The minute we

landed I went to the bathroom to fix up. I wanted to look my best. I called Simon and told him I was there. He said he'd be right over.

It was August 2, 2003.

How many times have I been to Heathrow airport in London? So many I couldn't even tell you. It's like my second home. There are four separate terminal buildings, and this time, this most important of times, I got mixed up and told Simon the wrong terminal! I called on the cell phone and redirected him. As I approached the exit, I saw him outside standing next to the motorbike. I was wondering, Well, what do we do? Do we say hello? Do we hug? Do we kiss? The sun was shining. (Always the sun shines for me in London, if not for my entire stay, then certainly when I arrive.) I walked through the doors and reached him.

"Hello. Hello." I kissed him on the cheeks three times.

"Thank you for picking me up."

I got on the back of the bike. This time I wrapped my legs more closely around his and pressed my body even closer. We took off. I had such a feeling of energy and excitement and closeness. The wind was in my face, and I was leaning into him; we were as one. It was an amazing, incredible dream coming true, a new life opening for me. I felt it. He took me to the restaurant in Holland Park, the Belvedere. I had never been there. He parked the bike and took off the license plates. (Cheeky boy, he was making sure he wouldn't get a ticket!) I remember ordering some kind of bean salad. I couldn't eat. I think I had two beans. I was just looking at him, staring into his eyes, getting lost in his blue eyes. He wasn't eating much, either; he was nervous. We finished our nonmeal and went for a walk. The sun was shining; the flowers and the grass smelled so beautiful. We walked and talked. It was nice. I loved talking to him. He made me laugh all the time. We sat on the grass by the path. I was lying down, and he was leaning closer to me. I knew he wanted to kiss me. I don't know why, but I turned away.

"Why did you pull back?" he asked so sweetly, tears came to my eyes.

"I don't know," I answered and truthfully, I didn't know. All I wanted was to have him hold me.

He came closer again, and this time I welcomed his embrace. We were in each other's arms for at least half an hour, maybe forty-five minutes, our lips together. It was so gentle, passionate, and beautiful. The longest kiss I ever experienced. We opened and closed our eyes, but we never left each other's arms and our lips stayed locked. I saw people walking by looking at us, and I'm sure they were thinking, Gross! Go get a hotel room.

Maybe if I hadn't been part of that kiss, I would have thought the same thing myself. It is impossible to describe the ecstasy of that moment. Lying there on the grass, with the sun coming through the branches of the trees and dappling our cheeks with warmth, hearing the sound of the wind rustling the leaves, hearing the distant voices of children playing, I felt such a sense of peace and happiness, it makes me weep to recall.

7

Simon Says

2nd August 2003. The moment you came running out of the terminal with that smile. The drive to Holland Park with your legs wrapped around mine. Listening to you talk over lunch at the Belvedere. You not eating anything, me feeling sick with nerves. Lying in the grass . . . smiling . . . laughing . . . enjoying the sun. That kiss!!!

This is the first entry in the tiny blue leather book from Smythson of Bond Street in which Siddy wrote of our first year together—from August 2, 2003, to August 2, 2004. The book has 437 pages with a thought on each page. He gave it to me as a present for our anniversary. We lived a lifetime together in that first year, and that book is my direct link to those blissful days. It is my most precious possession.

That afternoon in Holland Park, Simon and I finally drew apart. I wanted to stay in his embrace, but I had a plane to catch and there was only a little more time for us to be together. We stood up, brushed each other off, and began walking along the path. We held hands, leaned against each other, and exchanged many, many kisses. We waited on line in front of a concession stand, bought some ice cream, and took it over to a nearby fountain. We sat down on the grass to eat. In between the bites, we kept looking at each other and smiling. The layover of seven hours wasn't long enough. I didn't want to go. I wanted to stay and enjoy more beautiful moments. I had no choice; there was a job awaiting me.

We returned to the motorbike and sped off to Heathrow. On the ride, again I put my arms around him, pulled my body as close to him as possible, and lay my head on his shoulder. Energy, such a strong floating energy, was overwhelming everything. I couldn't think. My head was full of the sound of the motorbike, and my arms were full of the sweetness and strength of Simon. At the terminal we got off the bike and said our good-byes, clinging to each other one last time.

On board the plane I was quite agitated. I was totally infatuated with Simon, but I had things to settle. I knew I was in a transitional stage, that I had a decision to make. I had told Simon about my relationship and my conversation with Donaes the morning after my birthday. The thing is, I loved two honorable men, and both of them understood my dilemma.

My loving parents. You can see how terrified my mom was of dropping her firstborn!

Me, age two, in Karvina. My mother insists my hairstyle was quite fashionable.

My baby sister, Olga, age four, and me, age six, at a town carnival. She's Little Red Riding Hood, I'm a blue flower. We're still dressing up, even today!

This is my photo from the Czech Republic Look of the Year, 1996. I was completely shocked to find out that I won!

My first modeling photograph. I had it taken at a passport photo place, and I even made the dress myself—can you tell?

My dearest Grandpa Karel—always so strong and inspiring.

My sweet Granny Anezka—loving and caring, and always looking out for us.

The name Petra may mean "rock," but Olga is *my* rock. She has supported me through the most difficult times.

Siddy's family, and my new English family (left to right): Harry, Mark, Chris, me, Vernon, Jodi, Livvy.

The photo crew from the Freemans shoot in Majorca, 2003. A spark was in the air with Siddy. We worked really hard and didn't sleep at all, but I've never laughed so much on a job.

The Cannes Film Festival, 2004. Strolling on the red carpet together at the amfAR benefit. It was Siddy's first red carpet. He was squeezing my hand so hard I thought he might break it!

I surprised Siddy with a Valentine's Day ski trip in 2004. He considered skiing in Vermont to be paradise, and his amazing blue eyes sparkled more than ever there.

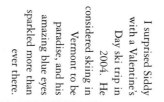

The Dolce & Gabbana party at Cannes, 2004. I was proud to be wearing one of their dresses. I love their style, and they've been very supportive of me and my cause.

Costa Rica, 2003—our first Christmas together. I will remember it always.

Kisses from the llama were sweet, but I preferred Simon.

Chile, September 2004. Our wonderful Chilean friends Señora Audina and her husband. She taught me to make goat cheese, and I reached things on high shelves for her.

Siddy's niece, Livvy, and his nephew, Harry, are addicted to sweets, and Siddy was addicted to them.

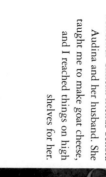

IS A DAY WASTED

Miami, 2004—clowning around as usual!

On this beach in Costa Rica, Siddy's joking made me laugh without stopping for hours.

My oldest and best friend from Karvina, Marian. He lived the dream with me from the beginning.

My angels Leyla and Kamilka. We are always there for each other.

My dear friend, Veronika Varekova, joins me in playing with the little angels at a Czech orphanage.

My caring friend and big supporter, Faith Kates.

Left to right: Lewis, Chris, Ben, Scott, Roosevelt, Gloria, Olga, me, Leigh, and Jamison—my gang of loved ones.

My friends Jeff Levy and his wife, Aileen Atkins, and Sydney. Jeff has been my guide and protector, and I feel lucky to have him looking out for me.

Klara Nademlynska, a famous Czech designer, with me, Tereza Maxova, and Prince Albert at a charity fashion show for the Tereza Maxova Foundation in 2004. This was one of Siddy's and my favorite charities.

Ben and I with my New York friends. These children at P.S. 59 sent me the most uplifting letters when I was in the hospital.

SIDDY'S FRIENDS

Jamie and his fiancée. Siddy would have been best man at their wedding.

Georgie and her daughter Millie. They were so special to him.

Oskar Simon. He was named for Simon, who never got to meet him—but I think Oskar has Siddy's eyes.

...eth and Barnaby, Siddy's loving friends.

...iddy's gang (left to right): Barry, Jodi, me, Ben, Kate, Toby, ...rant, Jo, Sandra, Lauren, Tim. He loved them all so much.

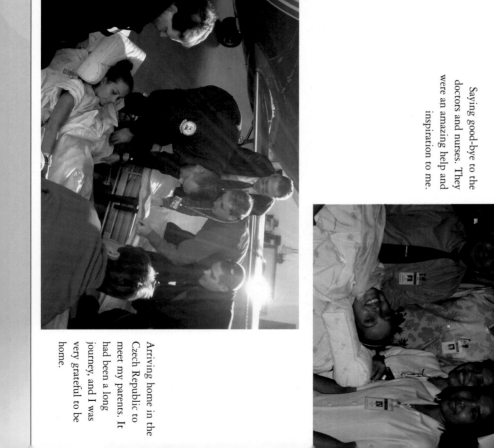

Saying good-bye to the doctors and nurses. They were an amazing help and inspiration to me.

Arriving home in the Czech Republic to meet my parents. It had been a long journey, and I was very grateful to be home.

In the Hat Yai Hospital with my sister and Leigh. They were taking care of me and I was so, so happy to be with them.

Reading, learning, trying to gather knowledge about the tsunami: why, where, and how many... and maybe to find a sign of Siddy.

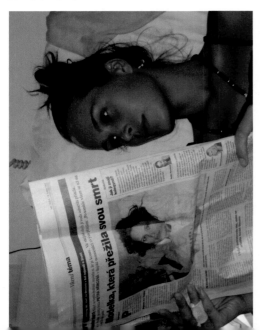

My first steps—wow! What a gift that we don't really ever appreciate.

My spiritual family: Minh Hiet, Master Dang, his wife, Terez, Donaes, Sylvie, Moos, and Moos's mother. The energy work I learned with them helped me to recover emotionally and physically in an amazingly short time. Some people take two years to recover from my injuries. I did it in just three months.

At the construction site for the new school, seeing what we can do to help.

Olga, Karolinka, and Jamison gave me a great deal of support on my trip back to Thailand.

The joy of making new friends.

Roman and me. He's the first friend I got to see after the tsunam

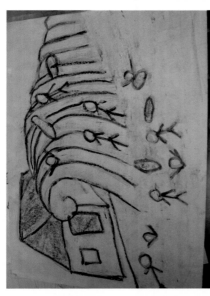

This little girl was born two days after the tsunami, and that is her name, Tsunami. She is a sign of hope.

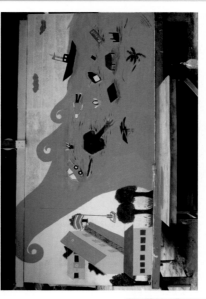

Many children couldn't talk about what they felt, so they drew or painted it.

The painting of this school speaks for itself.

The remains of the Khao Lak Orchid Resort, four months after the tsunami.

Twelve hundred children were orphaned in Thailand after the tsunami. I cry just thinking about them.

I love this picture of Siddy and me. We are connected by shadows here, and forever will be.

When I arrived at the shoot, I immediately texted Simon:

Thank you for one of the happiest days of my life.
Love and more, for my dearest Simey. X X X
[three crosses for three kisses]

I worked for four days, and during that time I was crying and laughing, crying and laughing, hysterically crying and laughing. I couldn't stop. I called Donaes and told him what was happening, how my emotions were overcoming me. I cried over the phone. I couldn't control myself. I was so confused. I loved Donaes—I still love him, he will always be in my heart—but I was helpless before this amazing passion. I was also calling Simon every night and crying over the phone. Simon made me laugh. It was the funniest thing: I was laughing and crying. I kept thinking how all this laughing and crying was going to make me look on the shoot. My emotions went wild. High, low, high, low, everything was so intense.

During the day Simon and I were texting each other. I couldn't wait to receive his messages. I kept escaping from the set and rushing to the ladies' room to see what he had sent, and to send off my answers:

Dreamt with you all night long . . . so, so beautiful. I'm acting like a teenager. I had no idea that it will be so intense. My feelings are so intense. Did you put a spell on me? Thank you for being you. I would love to jump into this amazing river of love, joy, happiness, fun, learning and growing. My heart is filled with love for you. You are making it jump so high, very, very high. Is your heart on a trampoline, too?

His responses were full of his wonderful intelligence, thoughtfulness, and humor. I was learning about him, about his personality, his passion, and those text words are gone forever. That is why that little blue book is so dear to me. Simon also made a huge scrapbook for me. In it are clippings from newspapers, written accounts of special moments, copies of my text messages to him, photographs, and drawings. He was a wonderful artist and cartoonist and clever with words, too. I am thankful that he was so thoughtful because I was not so good about it. I had kept his text messages on my cell phone, but the phone, like everything else we brought to Thailand, was swallowed by the ocean. I have almost no journals of my own and have had to rely on his accounts and observations. I could not have done this book you are reading without Simon. We have written it together.

My renewed energy and passion on the shoot amazed me. I was working quite hard; yet I was happy and excited and so in love. I was all over the place, and people looked at me like I was a crazy woman. I *was* a crazy woman. At first I didn't tell the team about Simon (they knew Donaes), but by the third day I told them, mostly because I couldn't keep it inside but also because I was afraid they would think I was going mental. Once I told the team, I had to tell everybody. Soon I was calling my friends and asking their advice.

"What should I do? I'm so in love. What do I do?"

Everyone was telling me the same things:

"You're overworked. You need rest. It's been too much on you with all the work and the emotions. You had a huge birthday party. You've been working nonstop. You can't make any decisions now. Go to a spa or a retreat for a couple of days. Clear your mind. You'll make better decisions."

Donaes, too, advised me to take time off and then work things out.

"It's okay, Petra," he said over the phone. "Go and make a decision."

I wanted so badly to see Simon. He wanted to see me, too. He kept urging me to come back to London. When I told my friends, their advice was not to go so fast, not to join him until I'd done some thinking on my own. I planned to go to the Czech Republic and on August 9 I sent Simon a message:

I wish I didn't have to go to Prague. I can't wait to fall into your arms. Look into the deepest blue oceans. Feel your energy, feel your kisses on my skin. If you still want to.

I wrote "If you still want to" because, despite the fact that he wanted me in London, I went to the Czech Republic instead.

In Prague I stayed at the Hotel Josef. I had decided to follow the good advice I'd been given and take time off. I got on the Internet and researched spas all over the world, especially Spain. Somehow I couldn't find the right spa in Spain. Actually, I couldn't find the right spa anywhere in the world except for—you guessed it—England.

"Don't worry," I told my friends, "I am going to a spa." Of course, I never mentioned where.

Early in the morning on August 13 I arrived in London on my way to the Grayshott Spa in Surrey. A car was waiting for me. I got in and messaged Simon. He immediately called.

"Guess where I am?" I asked him.

"I don't know. Prague somewhere?"

"No, I'm in England. I'm going to be at Grayshott Spa. Would you like to come see me for dinner?"

13th August. The drive to Grayshott at 130 mph with my heart beating out of my chest. [from Simon's book]

When Simon told me he'd be there, I was so, so happy. It meant there was a continuation, a real one. Yes, we had that kiss in Holland Park, but you can't let everything hinge on a kiss, no matter how wonderful it was. Coming back together would be the confirmation of the kiss and a reaffirmation of our feelings. Simon canceled all his appointments and arrived for dinner that day. Then began the most incredible thirteen days of my life—nothing planned, everything spontaneous and glorious.

I was in room 2, the best room in the whole place, with a four-poster bed and a little balcony, like for Romeo and Juliet, overlooking the gardens. I was up in the room when I heard the sound of the Suzuki. I was out of the room, down the stairs, and out the door to greet him in a heartbeat. We hugged and kissed. I had gotten the name and address of a restaurant from Reception, and we went out for dinner. We ordered the food, but I ate nothing. I filled myself with his presence. I was so happy and so drawn to him. He was happy, too, but a little cautious as well. We sat next to each other at a banquette, and I was trying to hold his hands. I'm a very touchy person; I love the contact. At one point I sat on his lap. I couldn't help myself. I wanted to be near him. I wasn't doing anything naughty, but he was embarrassed. (Oh, Siddy, you were such an English gentleman.)

After dinner we went back to the spa and up to the room. "13th August lying next to you for the first time," Simon wrote in his book. We were just lying next to each other, nothing was happening, but there was such a strong energy all around us like I never experienced—an energy and a calmness, too, as though we had known each other forever. Sometimes you are awkward when you're lying next to someone for the first time. This was so normal, so comfortable; there was no tension, no awkwardness, only a great good feeling.

We stayed at the Grayshott for three days, and each day we felt that we'd known each other for years. We had such a lovely time exploring each other. I learned then that he wore contact lenses—clear ones, since nothing was needed to enhance the color of those eyes. I walked into the room and he was lying on the bed with his glasses on, reading. I loved it. I told him he looked sexy in glasses. He said I was a crazy girl. We were taking lots of massages and treatments during the day and strolling around the grounds in between the activities. The other people in the spa were older;

everybody was looking at us and smiling like people do when they see a young couple in love. They were sweet.

We were so very close, but nothing happened for two nights. How shall I put this? Okay, it wasn't on the first date, but even for me it was fast. Always I would give a hard time to anyone, and yet this time I was the more eager one. Simon could wait. I couldn't. I could not resist the powerful energy. On the evening of August 15 we took our love to the next level.

The next morning we made plans to move on, back to London and then on to Paris, and then . . . well, we'd decide. I couldn't go on the bike with Simon because I had suitcases. I took the car service and set out a little before him. The driver turned on the radio; it was playing Prince, "I Would Die 4 U." At that moment Simon zoomed by on his motorbike. A strange sudden feeling of dread came over me, and I remember thinking, Please, God, don't let this be any kind of message. I pushed the thought out of my brain. It was only a song—the one Simon played on the first shoot, our theme song, nothing more. *I would die for you.* I cannot listen to it anymore.

The first night in London I stayed at a hotel. Simon sent me a beautiful bunch of sunflowers. The next morning I brought the flowers with me to his apartment in Islington, and we spent the next days together there. I loved his apartment. I was more at home there than anywhere else in the world. When I told him how I felt, he said that it was because he was spreading love all over, painting love on the walls.

On the second morning we were awakened by someone ringing the doorbell. It was a messenger. Who could be sending us anything so early? It was a card with a picture of John Travolta dancing in the movie *Saturday Night Fever.* On August 17 we got our first congratulations card. "Dear Petra and Simon, Great news. Have fun. Enjoy. Love, Mike." Simon could not keep our love a secret and had messaged Mike Chalk.

Simon had a little garden behind his apartment, and we'd sit out there and talk for hours. He told me about his childhood, and I told him about mine. I described the mountains and the forest behind my grandparents' house and about the loving way in which my parents looked after Olga and me. We never ran out of subjects, from our backgrounds to our beliefs; our conversations covered everything. As different as our upbringings were, we had much in common, more than we ever thought.

Simon was a great chef, a master of cooking. He could grill tuna to perfection, and his specialty was Sunday roast of meat with roasted vegetables. He introduced me to parsnips, which I'd never even heard of before. I fell in love with them and I made all sorts of smacking sounds when I ate them. The taste was so delicious. Simon was always teasing me that I loved the parsnips, not him, and they were the only reason I stayed with him. Once, when he went out to the market to get food, I began tidying up the apartment. I was vacuuming when he came back. He took one look and said, "Oh my God, I'm marrying this girl."

On the third morning we decided to go to Paris. And we did. We checked into the Hôtel Thérèse and spent the next couple of days taking in the sights. I had a car in Paris, a BMW convertible, and I was driving Simon all over the city, around the Etoile, along the Champs Elysées, and onto the grand boulevards of the Left Bank. We had leisurely breakfasts in the little cafés clustered on the sidewalks, and at night we walked along the avenues. One evening, for the first time, we went dancing together, to a club in the 1st Arrondissement. Simon was shy about dancing with me; he did a little bit but left most of the movements to me.

We decided to drive to Normandy. I wanted to see Etretat, where is the huge rock in the ocean with a big hole in the middle, which so many artists, like Monet, painted. We left the Thérèse and headed west toward the Channel. Driving in the car was all about listening to Justin Timberlake, the same songs over and over. When the Global Positioning System didn't work, we pulled out the maps. Even so, we got hopelessly lost. We were supposed to have a picnic, but we couldn't find a proper place. Late that night I was getting hungry and we decided to stop. We pulled up next to a little cemetery by a church and had our picnic in the car overlooking the tombstones.

Etretat was as wonderful as I hoped. After a lovely lunch in a little restaurant, we went onto the beach to see the rock. The sight of it was as beautiful as I could ever have hoped. I was thrilled to share my first view of it with Simon.

By now, both of us had run out of time. We had to get back to work, Simon in London and me in Mexico for Victoria's Secret. On August 25, when we parted at Heathrow, I gave him thirteen kisses, one for each day we had spent together. Those days were even more precious than I realized. In a year and a half he would be gone.

I never thought I could live this dream. You made the impossible. Every minute of these 13 days was like living with you in paradise. I feel very, very lucky that our paths grew together. I will miss your smile, thoughts, touch, every bit of you.
Love, Petra

8

Wishes

I texted Simon the minute I arrived in Mexico. We were both in the clouds. For him the most important of those August days was the second, when we kissed for the first time. For me it was the thirteenth, when we began our romantic journey. How nice that we chose different dates—this gave us two anniversaries to celebrate. Now we would be apart for a little while, and both of us would be very busy.

After the shoot in Mexico I was going with my friends Kamilka and Leyla to Madrid. I had planned that trip for quite some time, and I couldn't change it, not even for Simon. I was actually looking forward to it. This was something new for me. Never in my life did I go on a trip with girls—I always went with my boyfriend or a big group.

In Madrid all I could talk about was Simon. I must have bored Kamilka and Leyla to death, but they were happy for me. I was glowing with love. As usual, the messages were flying through the air. Simon wrote that he wanted to make a "contract" with me.

"How about twenty-five years?" I wrote back.

"Only twenty-five years?" he answered. "So when I am fifty-nine and with ugly feet you will disappear and leave me. If we do a contract, it is forever. That's my deal."

I have to tell you something about Simon. He had this silly complex about his feet. When he was young, he had some accident on his toes, and they were a bit crooked. His family and friends teased him about them. They said he had trotter's hooves. He truly thought his feet were ugly and did everything to hide them—he never wore flip-flops. His toes were a little different, but I've seen worse. I loved his feet.

After the trip to Spain I returned to London. Sometimes Simon picked me up; other times Richard (my special driver) got me and drove me to Islington. When I was in the car with Richard, I'd text Simon telling him our exact location so that when I arrived, he'd be standing there in front of the open door, waiting for me. I loved that moment—seeing him, his eyes shining and his arms outspread. I would jump out of the car and run into his arms. He was my haven. He was so thoughtful about everything. He knew how much I liked *Pretty Woman* and rented it the day I returned from Spain. The two of us lay on the bed watching it, and I was laughing and giggling like I was a teenager seeing it for the first time. Simon was looking more at me enjoying myself than at the movie. He was happy making me happy.

On Saturday night he took me to a concert in the park in Hampstead Heath. This was the last concert of the season, and there were fireworks. We packed the food (he'd prepared it) in a hamper, put it on the back of the motorbike, and rode to the park. We had a picnic on the grass, listened to the music, and watched the fireworks display. Everything was going so wonderfully well. We were still in a "honeymoon" stage.

Over the next months Simon and I were catching time together as best we could. I had lots of shows and shoots to do, all over the world. Simon, too, was busy, but I definitely was on the faster global track. After a fashion show in Paris I returned to London in October 2003 for a spectacular event, the first "Fashion Rocks" for the Prince's Trust at the Royal Albert Hall. It was a combination of the best designers, the best models, and the best musicians. Each designer had his own performer. I remember Beyoncé was singing for Armani, Sheryl Crow for Tommy Hilfiger, and Andrea Bocelli for Ralph Lauren. Liz Hurley and Denis Leary were the hosts. Simon was taking pictures like crazy. Right after the Fashion Rocks gala, I was part of a TV award show to which I wore a dress worth ten thousand pounds! When we came back from the show, Simon took a picture of me in the dress standing in his bedroom. Once the picture was taken, I got out of the gown and into one of Simon's long T-shirts and a pair of long red socks.

"You know something? I think you look even more beautiful in my old clothes," he told me.

Simon could be with me for London events; he couldn't leave his work to follow me, nor would he have wanted to. It's tricky dating a model, often very difficult for men. They are shoved into the background and have to stand around a lot. Simon was in the business, though, and had no ego problems with my fame; he did have problems with my "workaholic nature." While we communicated continuously through the texting and the telephone, we were apart a lot, and even when we were together, there were real pressures, mostly coming from me and my murderous schedule. Eventually, my nature would become an obstacle.

In November, after the London shows, I went to Prague to appear in a charity show for my friend Tereza Maxova. Like me, Tereza is a model, and like me, she is interested in the welfare of children. The Tereza Maxova Foundation supports orphanages, and every year Tereza invites Czech supermodels to participate in a fund-raiser. Simon was between assignments and came with me. He took many photographs for the gala, but really, he was there to meet my family. Although he never said anything to me, Simon told his friend James that he couldn't propose without meeting my parents. They didn't speak the same language, but I could tell by the way my mother and father were looking at him that they liked him.

Tereza took Simon and me to the orphanages. Prince Albert of Monaco was also with us, and Simon took pictures of him and the children. You can tell a lot about people by how they are with little ones. Simon didn't speak a word of Czech and the children didn't speak English, but they didn't need to—they were all over him, pulling him this way and that, and giggling and laughing. Simon loved children. He would have been a wonderful father. I wish so much that we could have had children together.

Something happened after we returned from Prague. The honeymoon was beginning to be over. I was exhausted, completely drained from all the work and still trying to keep up both my professional and my personal lives. I didn't know how to give a hundred percent to my work and a hundred percent to my life. The relationship with Simon was so powerful and amazing to me that I couldn't bear the thought of not being with him. I needed him, I wanted him, and the minute we were together our souls were united. Yet I couldn't stay with him. A few days, and I was off to the next shoot. The pressure is intense for those in the public eye because our images are constantly before the public; we have to present ourselves as perfectly as possible. We must be superorganized and on top of every situation. At gala events, if you slip up even on the tiniest detail, it can make a huge difference. Maybe something is wrong with your hair or your makeup or maybe your dress is too transparent, whatever—it can be a big problem. The press gets right on it, and suddenly, the newspapers are full of pictures and stories, and you don't want that kind of publicity. Actually, some people do it *because* they want the publicity, that's not my style. Nothing is perfect, but I was determined to try for it. I was constantly striving for perfection and absolutely consumed by my profession. All this was too much for Simon; he didn't like what the pressures were doing to me and what they were doing to us.

"If you don't give time to a relationship, there is no relationship," he told me. "It's just dating."

We talked and talked, and I tried to explain that I didn't know what else to do. I had been on the run since school days when I was going to classes and castings. Over the years, without my really noticing, the pace had accelerated. I guess because I enjoyed my work so much I didn't realize that I had become "all work." Simon and I even discussed separating, and I got scared that we would break up for good. I started to cry, and he started to cry, and both of us were crying like kids. We didn't give in. We stayed with it. I couldn't give him up; I was determined to make my personal life work. I could never have done it without Simon, though; he taught me how to balance my life. Simon thought we should each do a "wish list" concerning our relationship. That is, write down our wishes and then, when they were realized, scratch them off and make new ones.

Simon's wish list was loving and caring. He wanted to make sure that no matter how stressed-out or unhappy we might get, we'd always be able to communicate with respect and compassion. He wanted to share the good and the bad with me, and he promised he'd always be there to listen. Most beautiful of all, he wanted to remember our days in Majorca before we even knew how close we would become. I realized that his list was simply an attempt to get me to put my life into perspective and to teach me, gently and kindly, how to enjoy life more fully. Nothing happened overnight. I began a list, but I had to put it aside—too much work to do. Still, Simon kept after me.

"Find a few minutes to call me, Petra. Not when you're jumping out of a taxi or running off the set into a ladies' room to send a text. Take five or ten minutes in the day to talk to me. And if you can't talk, then send a fax; don't make it something that you're doing while you're doing something else. Give it your full attention for those brief minutes. If you invest the time in the relationship, then the dividends will be good."

Through Simon's wise words I began to learn how to make the balance. His "lessons" were easy to follow because he didn't nag or scold me; often he teased me into relaxing. "You know, Petra, if you take two days off, it's called the weekend."

Gradually, my attitude and my actions began to change. I wasn't simply running from job to job. I made space, for myself and for us. Our phone calls were more frequent and longer. Most telling, I turned down one or two assignments to be with him. I did my wish list, too, only I cannot tell you about it because it was on my cell phone and the ocean took it. Our relationship got better and better, and by December 2003 we were ready to take our first real holiday together.

I had always wanted to go to Costa Rica, and Simon was eager to see it, too. Despite his schedule, he researched the trip and took care of all the arrangements. Whenever we traveled, we shared the expenses, but Simon took care of the bookings. He would be traveling from London, and I from New York, on December 23. We would meet in Costa Rica. Simon got there, I didn't. I missed my plane. The traffic to the airport was so backed up nothing was moving. I got to the gate as they announced that the flight had closed. I tried to sweet-talk them into letting me board, but without any success. I was so upset. I didn't want to let Simon down. I wanted to show him that I could put him before my work. There was one bright spot. I had ordered a digital camera as a present for Simon, and it hadn't arrived in time. I hated the idea of not having a present for him. When I returned home from the airport, the camera was there. At least I wouldn't be going to Costa Rica empty-handed.

I arrived on the evening of the twenty-fourth, just in time for Christmas Eve. We were staying at the Sanctuary Resort and Spa on the west side of Costa Rica. A man from the hotel escorted me to the private residence that Simon and I would occupy, a darling little two-story house. The lights were on, and big lizards were crawling up the outside walls as the man, carrying the suitcases, and I approached the house. The door opened and Simon was standing there. My whole body went *whoooosh*. Every time I saw him after an absence, my reaction was the same. I seemed to deflate. We hugged, and Simon took the bags from the man and led me into the house. Downstairs was a kitchen and bathroom and a sitting area. Upstairs was a hall, bathroom, and bedroom. We went upstairs; on the bed were laid out many beautifully wrapped presents from Simon and his family. Oh my God, I had only one for him!

We went for a lovely Christmas Eve dinner at the main building and then back to our little house. We talked for a long while and fell asleep entwined in each other, like two spoons fitting together. We were a "single bed" couple. Some couples I know like to separate in the night and have their privacy and distance. Forget king-size, queen-size, full-size, they were way too big; we didn't want to be apart for a second. If there were twin beds, we used only one. Many times when we made reservations, we'd ask for a single bed, and almost always the people didn't get it straight. They couldn't believe that two people wanted to be in the same little bed.

Christmas morning we went to a beautiful beach of the most amazing sparkly black sand with white driftwood scattered all around. You could walk for an hour to the right and an hour to the left on that beach and you wouldn't see another person. We got into a rock pool and sat and talked and talked. We were on the beach all day.

That evening after dinner we went back to our little house. I had brought with me a DVD of a Czech fairy tale, the Czech *Cinderella*, which I wanted Simon to see. I turned on the video, and Simon and I curled up on the sofa, his head on my chest. Unfortunately, there were no English subtitles. My eyes were riveted on the screen as I struggled to translate the dialogue. Later Simon confessed that he had fallen asleep even before Cinderella got to the ball.

The next day we did more exploring along the shore

and returned to the rock pool. In the evening we built a fire on the beach. We had taken (I was going to say stolen, but really, I don't think it was stealing since we were paying clients) some chicken breasts from the hotel at lunch, and now we grilled them on sticks. After the fire died down, we curled up together and slept on the beach, our sandy single bed.

The following morning we drove for seventeen hours to the Rafiki Safari Lodge in the Savegre Valley in central Costa Rica. Here we stayed in a tent with a wooden floor, which, unlike my grandfather's tent, or even his house, had a built-in bathroom! Such a lovely tent. We did bird-watching. There are more than three hundred species of identified birds in the Savegre Valley, and people come from all over the world to see them. We went white-water rafting. The guides told Simon to be careful, but he was thrown around and banged his butt on the bottom of the boat.

The days were active, the evenings quiet. Simon was teaching me how to play backgammon, but mostly, we talked and talked. On the night of December 31 they built a huge bonfire, and along with other guests, we sat around the fire, eating and talking. There was no champagne, but I didn't need it: I was drunk on conversation. Siddy and I never ran out of things to talk about. This was our first New Year's Eve together, and our last.

The next day we went to Quepos in the south and stayed, from January 1 to 4, in a one-story wooden house with the bedroom, bathroom, and kitchen all together. I taught Simon how to bake oat cookies in our little stove;

he loved to eat them as much as he loved to bake them. We would get food from the hotel, fish and vegetables and good things like that, and bring it down to the private white-sand beach. Our days on the beach were spent playing in the water, lying on the sand, and reading. Oh, and laughing, always laughing. He made me laugh so much I had to hold myself in one position so I didn't pee in my bathing suit. He was so silly, so funny, and so tender and caring. How caring? Before I came to Costa Rica, I had cut my hair and dyed it black and then changed it back to brown and put in extensions. In the water and in the sun my hair became impossibly knotted. I put off brushing it, but the time came when it had to be done. I got some conditioner and went at it. It really hurt! I had tears in my eyes not only from the pain of pulling at my scalp; I was also mad at myself for letting things go too long. I was so frustrated. Simon came inside and saw me struggling.

"What's going on?" he asked.

"I can't get these knots out of my hair," I cried.

"Here, give me the brush," he said. "I'll do it."

We went outside and sat down on the beach. Simon began to brush out my hair. He went section by section, first putting on the conditioner and then gently and patiently brushing the strands until they were free. It took him two hours to get out the knots. So kind, so gentle, so loving was my Siddy.

Another beautiful thing happened. Simon was a smoker when we met and had been smoking during the time we'd been together. In Costa Rica I immediately saw that he wasn't smoking. He told me he had been going to a hypnotist for the past few months to kick the habit. He had never said a word about it, and now he was a nonsmoker.

"How could you kiss me?" he joked. "It must have been like kissing an ashtray. How could you be with me?"

"Because I love you," I told him.

The truth is, I believe that when you love somebody, you love them for who they are and you are taking them as they are and not trying to make them do what you want. It's a matter of respect. I didn't want him to smoke, but it was his wish to. Until he decided to stop, I accepted it.

We left Costa Rica on January 5, 2003, and flew to New York City. It was the first time we would be in New York together. I had to go straight from the plane to pick up my dress and to get my hair and makeup done for a charity event. Simon joined me later; he looked so handsome in his suit and tie. At the benefit, they auctioned off a dinner date with me to raise money. Simon bid; he didn't win, but he pushed the price up!

The Costa Rican holiday had brought us much closer. It was kind of a test. When you are falling in love, the first thirteen days can be a "just for the moment" thing, but being together for two weeks in one place is different. We were learning more and more about each other, and from that time, we knew we had something special. Passion can go, but Simon and I were made for each other. We were soulmates.

9

Miluji Te

When Simon and I returned from Costa Rica, we got the best "anniversary" present you could imagine: our first assignment together as boyfriend and girlfriend. The shoot, once again for Freemans, was in Cape Town, from January 17 to 22. The soulmates would be working mates once again. In our business, models and photographers may date each other, but the relationships don't often last. In Cape Town the others on the team could see that Simon and I weren't just dating; it was obvious to everyone that we were in love. They were happy for us; even so, Simon and I were trying hard not to do too much kissing or cuddling in front of them. We didn't want to make them sad that they didn't have their other halves along—but oh, the joy of being together, working together, and coming back to the same room together. We'd lie down on the bed and listen to our favorite songs, especially Al Green singing "Let's Stay

Together." When I hear it now, it makes me sad and happy at the same time.

Cape Town was five days of hard work and bliss. After the shoot we returned to my apartment in New York. Wouldn't you know the wonderful time in Cape Town would be followed by a little trouble? This was our second bad moment. I was having difficulties with someone who worked for me. I relied on this person, but other people didn't like the way he did things. I had to admit he *was* doing things in not such a nice way. I am loyal; I didn't want to fire him. I can't bear to fire anyone. I was so torn I couldn't think straight. I was weak and confused. Simon tried to help me. He told me that I should get rid of the guy and stop obsessing. He wanted me to realize that it's important to know when to let go and move on. I got upset and we were having what I think is called a lovers' spat. Then, one afternoon, in the midst of a soul-searching, we heard "Let's Stay Together" over the radio. It was a sign. I let the other guy go and stayed with Simon. I wish all problems could be solved with a little help from Al Green.

In February I made a Valentine's Day surprise for my Simey. (That was my nickname for him until Mike Chalk said it sounded like "Slimy.") Simon was a skier, really a fantastic skier. I never learned to ski, but I knew how much he loved it, so I arranged a long weekend in Stowe, Vermont. Simon was beside himself with happiness. In Vermont, while I did my work in the morning, he'd go off to ski and return at lunchtime with his blue eyes shining. He was so happy. In the afternoon we took massages and treatments, and in the evening we sat by the fire in the lodge. Simon wrote in his book:

The fact that you took me skiing even though you couldn't, was one of the most amazing gestures anyone has done for me.

I didn't think it was such a big deal. We were together, and he was doing something he really loved. What could be better?

During the winter and the spring of 2004 we traveled back and forth between New York and London. In New York I worked a bit, but our pace was leisurely. We spent the days exploring the city; we took long walks, we went to museums and art galleries. In April we had a chocolate Easter egg hunt in my apartment. This was new for me; we don't have egg hunts in the Czech Republic. I think it's a splendid tradition. In London we cruised around on the motorbike, popping on and off to go to stores or to take walks in the park. Simon also organized trips around England to visit castles. Because I told him of my childhood love of them, he introduced me to the English versions of the haunted ones. Whether in New York or London, Simon cooked dinner for me and I made breakfast for him and served morning tea the way he liked it—a splash of milk and one spoon of sugar.

Every moment we spent together was full of life. Even the smallest things were the most beautiful—getting on and off the bike, sharing our homes, cooking dinner in both cities, having tea together. I had never experienced anything like this. It was pure joy and love.

In March Simon introduced me to his family: his mom, Chris Oxley, his stepfather, Vernon, his sister, Jodi, her husband, Mark Hansard, and their two children, Livvy and Harry. How Simon adored those kids and how they loved him back. I discovered that the family called him Siddy. Soon I began to call him Siddy, too; it seemed natural. Meeting his mother, I fully understood why Simon was so wonderful. In fact, they were all wonderful, as warm and loving and welcoming to me as anyone could wish. They became my English family; they will always be my family.

The Cape Town experience had been such a joy that Simon and I wanted to continue to work together, and even before we left South Africa, we began brainstorming. I have to say here that once he helped me to get off the workaholic track, Simon became my greatest supporter and inspiration. Confident that I had learned to balance things, he willingly invested his time in my career and helped me in my business. It was mutual; I looked out for him. We really complemented each other on many levels. We could be silly, sophisticated, philosophical, spiritual, passionate, you name it, everything we did together clicked. Our goal was to come up with something creative that would benefit children. Finally, in May, after tossing around ideas, we got it. We decided to do a calendar with me as the model and Simon as the photographer. We planned to do it on off-hours at the same time as we were doing our regular assignments. It wouldn't have stopped us, but I don't think either of us realized the amount of work it was going to take.

11th May 2004. To Simon from Petra: Just one thing, miluji te (that's Czech for I love you). I'm so excited about our little baby calendar. But we have to keep love and work separate.

When you're working with someone, you can get so drawn in you forget to be boyfriend and girlfriend. I was excited but aware that doing the calendar might challenge our relationship. I was a little concerned that we might have trouble. It was a needless worry. In all, there was only one disappointment. We wanted to donate the proceeds to UNICEF, but they couldn't use it—the calendar was too sexy and didn't fit their image. I understood their position completely and I didn't blame them, but still, I was hurt. We offered the calendar to amfAR, which helps children with AIDS and is not as restrictive as UNICEF in terms of "correctness." They welcomed our gift, and Simon and I were proud and happy to sign over the profits to them. Dolce & Gabbana provided outfits for the calendar; they've always been supportive of me.

May 2004 was a period of intense work, intense but oh so enjoyable because we were working together. We began shooting (all digitally) in a beautiful country house outside of London on a freezing day in May—typical English weather. I put on a bathing suit, got into the pool, and turned blue; it was bloody cold. After the shots I jumped out of the water and ran into the bathroom, where I turned on the hot water and stood shivering under the shower. I

143

came out still numb and heard someone say casually, "Oh, the pool is heated. Didn't anyone turn on the switch?"

During the shooting Simon and I were invited to an amfAR dinner in Cannes during the film festival. We decided to go and to use the opportunity to get some photos for the calendar on the Riviera. Cannes is crazy during the festival. The hotels are bulging with people, and everyone is running from one event to another. Actually, I should say driving, not running. You have to have a car to get around. We didn't have a car and needed one to take us to the amfAR dinner. At gala events you can't walk to the red carpet or even take a taxi; you've got to make your entrance stepping out of a fancy limo.

This would be Siddy's first red-carpet appearance. I had this incredible red dress from Dolce & Gabbana, and, of course, I had to spend my time prettying up for the big moment. While I was having my hair and makeup done, Siddy arranged for the car. He called and told me to get dressed and meet him in front of our hotel. I walked out and found him waiting for me in the back of a vintage Cadillac—not the requisite black, but a beautiful blue. (I learned that this car had once transported President John Kennedy and Marilyn Monroe—I don't know whether it was at the same time or not.) Everywhere we drove, people were trying to look at us through the windows. "Who is there? Who is there?" they were asking, all because we were in that blue Caddy.

Simon and I arrived at the dinner and, for the first time, walked the red carpet together—such a thrill for me and for him. I was sort of used to such things, but Siddy was absolutely gobsmacked. I think he was most excited about talking to Jerry Hall. The amfAR dinner was a great event. Liza Minnelli and Sharon Stone were the hosts and organizers.

I learned something useful that evening. There was an auction, and Sharon Stone was one of the auctioneers. She knew many people in the audience, and during the bidding she'd call out to someone by name, "What about you, Jack? Aren't you going to bid?" In June of 2005 I was invited to a fund-raising dinner for the Thai tsunami relief. At dinner I was introduced to a charming gentleman from Italy. When the auction began, I used Sharon Stone's technique and called out, "Signor So-and-So from Italy, I know you want this item." Signor So-and-So laughed and bid two thousand dollars more.

The morning after the dinner, we shot the rest of the calendar. That evening we attended a Dolce & Gabbana party and the next day returned to London.

Finally learning about what you do and how I can help however small it may be. Going to amfAR with you in the red dress. The most beautiful girl I've ever seen in my life. How much fun we had together and then getting to take you home with me . . . finally relaxing now that we have got the calendar done.

The calendar was a consuming project. Simon was at it all the time, spending evenings on the Internet looking through magazines and Web sites and then shooting me between his regular assignments. He was so eager to make it perfect. Once the photography ended, there was even more pressure: choosing the pictures, airbrushing them on the computer, and then putting them together. Each of the twelve scenes was very different. We also included a collage of informal photos so people could see the process. Simon captured me like nobody else had captured me before. The trust between us came out in the photographs themselves. I trust other photographers, of course, but with Simon and me so close, it brought us onto a different plane. We poured ourselves into that project, and I believe the results were worth it. The calendar was a big labor of love. Now it's a memento of our love.

So many things were crowded into our brief time together, and, like the calendar, each has its own particular significance. I don't want to forget any of them. Some are too personal and belong only to me, but others I can share. As much as I adored motorbikes and as much as I loved riding around with Simon on his Suzuki, I reached the point where I was a little scared about him on the bike. He was a great driver, but he did go fast. Late in April I brought my car over from Paris. Right after that, Simon's motorcycle was stolen—for the third time in two years! The next day he got a call from the insurance company saying that his motorbike had been totaled in a fatal accident. This time Simon didn't replace it. His mom and his sister were happy, because they'd always been afraid of the motorbike. There were two things that Simon did while he was with me that pleased his family: He gave up the motorbike, and he stopped smoking. They credited me, but really, it wasn't my doing. I never pushed anything on him.

The last week in May, Simon and I were briefly separated when I was invited to be a judge at the Miss Universe contest in Quito, Ecuador. How could I refuse such an offer? Simon had an assignment at the time and insisted that I go. What a whirlwind event that was! I flew in Donald Trump's private plane along with him and his then fiancée, now his wife, Melania, and some of the other judges, including Bo Derek and Emilio Estevez.

Donald Trump was not at all what I expected; he's a very kind and caring man. I was amazed because I thought that someone in his position would do his own thing and remain apart. Was I wrong! He couldn't have been nicer. I was traveling with one of my publicists, and both Mr. Trump and Melania kept asking if we needed anything or if they could get anything for us. It was also amazing to see how he was making very important decisions on the go; often people in his position have to be in their offices to make sure of certain things before they make a judgment, not him. I was very busy on the plane going over the rule book for the judges and highlighting the major points. Trump saw me and smiled as if to say, Well, she's doing her homework.

Everything about the contest was exciting. I only wish I'd been able to see more of the country. The plane ride home was fun, too; Trump's son joined us, and he and I talked to each other in Czech (his mother is from my country). The only thing missing on the trip was Siddy.

Late in June, for my birthday, Simon took me to Great Fosters, a beautiful hotel outside London. I was flying into Heathrow from a shoot, and he was to pick me up at the airport. He said he'd be waiting outside. I went through customs, got my bags, and proceeded through the doors. Standing at the curb beside their limousines were liveried drivers holding up signs for their clientele. One of the drivers had his hat pulled down low over his face. I almost kept going and then I saw his sign. It read "Petra Nemcova." I looked again at the driver; it was Simon all rigged out in uniform. I could not stop giggling on the ride to Great Fosters. My God, Siddy, how you made me laugh!

They didn't have a single bed for us at the hotel, but everything else was perfect, especially the lovely garden, which had only two colors of flowers, white and lavender. Oh, and such delicious food and special cheeses. Simon said he could live on bread, cheese, and wine. Sometimes, when I look back, I wish that I had relented a bit about not drinking. Siddy loved wine, and I could have enjoyed this part of his life with him. We never did because I was so strict with myself. A small regret, but a regret nonetheless.

When we were together, Siddy and I created our own world, a special place that we occupied. Whenever stress overtook us, we'd talk about coming back to our "bubble." On August 2 we were bubbling over with joy. It was our first anniversary. Remember, we had two of them, and this was Simon's choice. For the second of our first anniversaries, August 13, Simon came to visit me in Lisbon, where I was working. We spent the day on the beach, and I organized a beautiful dinner in a small restaurant on the hill overlooking the city. That night we had a single bed.

In September we were looking for another place to unwind when my agent Leigh called and told me that they'd like me to go to Santiago, Chile, for a big annual fashion show. Each year, a supermodel is invited to attend. Naomi Campbell had been there, and now they were asking me! Since they sent two tickets, Simon and I thought this would be a good opportunity to get some R&R. Simon had been in Chile in the Atacama Desert on a shoot and said it was one of the most amazing places he'd ever seen. He couldn't wait to go back.

We arranged to fly to Santiago a few days before the fashion show and fly directly from there to Atacama. During our two-hour layover at the Santiago airport, we watched a group of children, dressed in native costumes, dancing and singing in the main terminal. They were so talented and so adorable. Simon took many pictures and befriended one little boy. Simon actually let the boy take the camera and shoot pictures of his friends. I have those photographs, and every time I look at them, I'm thankful that we had that special trip together.

We took a small plane to Atacama, and as we neared the desert, we could see the amazing textural changes in the terrain. The different layers have been altering since the Ice Age, and you must see this topography to believe it.

When we landed, we were picked up and taken to the Explora Hotel. The hotel is integrated with the landscape, so unusual and so beautiful. There was much to explore. The Atacama landscape is amazing, from volcanoes to salt flats, from blue lagoons to geysers, from unending desert to ocean beaches. It is a timeless place of incredible tranquillity. Nothing is rushed, and Simon and I found exactly what we needed, the chance to be in our bubble.

Every day was an adventure. We went on exploratory trips, and one of the best was to a remote sheep and goat farm owned by Señora Audina and her husband. I actually learned how to make goat cheese. Señora Audina taught me. Everything is done by hand, everything. First you milk the goat, and then the milk is left to thicken for a day or two. When it's ready, you reach in the bucket, grab a hunk in your hands, and squeeze until all the water is gone. You take what's left and put it into a metal ring on a large stone. You press the cheese into the ring, and when the ring is full, you sprinkle it with salt and put a clean stone on top to weigh the cheese down. I was so proud when Señora Audina presented me with the results of my labor. Of course, the cheese should have been aged, but Simon and I gobbled it up when we returned to the hotel. It was delicious, and I made it myself.

The evenings in the Atacama were just as magical as the days. The sky is so full of stars it takes your breath away. We looked at the heavens through a telescope, and I saw a nova being born. It was awe-inspiring to be so close to nature, and both of us were transported by the entire experience. When the time came, we went back to Santiago and the fashion show, which was fun and glamorous, but what I'll always remember about the trip to Chile is the miracle of the Atacama.

10

Confession

Okay, it's confession time again.

Everything was wonderful between me and Simon, really wonderful. I had learned the balance, I was happy in my professional and personal lives, and yet there was a cloud hanging over, something about which Simon knew nothing. I didn't know myself how dangerous a situation I had gotten myself into. Remember I said that I was never anorexic or bulimic—that was the truth. I never starved myself or threw up to keep skinny, but I did do something, and I started doing it a few months before I met Simon. After we'd been together for a while, he became aware that something wasn't quite right. For a long time, he kept a watchful eye on me, without actually saying anything. Finally, in Chile, he took charge.

We stayed in a gorgeous English-style hotel in Santiago. The first day, we went to the hotel restaurant and had a beautiful meal. Then it came time for dessert. Simon loved desserts, especially cheesecake. The waiter brought us the dessert menu and I looked. I always look. Just by looking I get a kind of taste. Actually, my way of tasting and getting the flavors was by kissing Simon. That's the best diet—no calories but so delicious! The waiter asked what we wanted, and Simon ordered a blue cheesecake.

"And for you, lady?"

"Oh no, not for me." I laughed. "I don't eat desserts."

"Well, if you were eating dessert, what would you choose?"

I looked closely at the menu.

"I would have this fruit-date thing. But if I was really going to be wild, I'd get this chocolate brownie with chocolate sauce."

The waiter went off and returned with the blue cheesecake *and* the chocolate brownie. I had to taste it. I took a little baby spoon and began to nibble at this thick chocolate dessert. I closed my eyes and made all these *mmmmmm* sounds as I chewed. Simon couldn't believe me.

"Is it so good?" he asked.

"Better than orgasm!" I cried.

After that meal I eased up and allowed myself to take little bites of different things. I thought I could get away with it because I was doing something else, too, something I believed would protect me from gaining weight. I got into the habit innocently enough; really, it had nothing to do with dieting, although I eventually discovered that I had stumbled into a practice that is often used in connection with losing weight. When you travel as much as I do, your system can go crazy—especially the digestive system—and I was always constipated. To help the situation, I used to drink an aloe vera juice, but the juice had to be refrigerated, so I couldn't take it with me on my travels. I got laxative capsules that contained not only aloe vera and flaxseed oil but a lot of other not-so-beneficial ingredients. The capsules were very, very strong, and I was taking them every day. Those pills took everything out of me. Right after going to the bathroom I felt drained of energy, like a zombie. I could barely stand up. Sure, I'd recover after a while, but in the meantime I was absolutely wasted. I felt really "lighter," and in my stupid head I thought that meant I was losing weight. I wasn't; I was messing up my stomach and my digestion.

Simon noticed that I would disappear into the bathroom for long periods, and when I came out, I was listless. He never nagged me; he just asked if I was okay. Finally, I told him I was taking medicine that was good for me. But Simon was convinced that the medicine was bad for me. Without making a fuss, he began to research it on the Internet. He sent me the results and talked to me about what the implications might be and of the potential dangers. When we were together, he'd talk a little about it, then he'd switch the subject to something else. Then he'd come back to it again very casually. He never said I had to stop taking the pills; he simply guided me away from them. He always knew how to strategize. He had incredibly sharp common sense.

Without saying who it was for, he got the name of a doctor in England from his mother. (Thank you, Chris.) I met with the doctor. He told me that what I was doing was both dangerous and futile. He explained that, since the calories had already been absorbed by my body, all that the laxatives were doing was taking away the nutrients; that's one of the reasons I was washed-out. He also told me laxative abuse can lead to kidney failure, irregular heartbeats, and worse, heart attack. Taking them this way could be fatal. The doctor suggested that I wean myself off the pills by substituting a natural fiber in their place. I did, immediately. Thanks to Simon, I began a new, clean regimen. Ironically, I took the very last pill in Thailand, a few days before the tsunami.

Part III

11

Saved

*H*ello, hello, how are you, miss?"

I pulled the damp T-shirt off my face. I had no idea how long it had been since my two rescuers left. My last memory was of sending energy and praying for everyone to be safe. I must have fallen asleep. Now six men were standing around me, three of them Thai and three of them Swedish. One of the Thais wore a fluorescent vest and seemed to be in charge. He may have been a policeman.

"Thank you for coming back. Thank you."

I smiled up at the men. They smiled back. Their faces were so beautiful. The man in the vest motioned to the

157

others. They had brought a yellow plastic water mattress with them, and quickly they surrounded me—one stood at my head, one at my feet, and two on each side of me. They started to lift me onto the mattress.

"No, no, no!" I shrieked.

It would be painful, but there was no other way to transport me, and once I was on the raft, my body would be cushioned by the water. Realizing this, I clenched my teeth and nodded for them to go ahead. As gently as possible, they slid my body onto the mattress. I was flat on my back with my knees drawn up to my chest. I could no longer put my legs out. They dressed me in the shorts and T-shirt and then began pushing the mattress through the water.

One of the men went ahead and shoved aside the rubbish. I couldn't help crying out whenever we hit any kind of bump. We reached the hotel; it had been badly damaged by the tsunami. The men attempted to lift the mattress out of the water and slide it over a huge mud pile. I screamed for them to stop. Again, I had to endure the pain. I motioned for them to go ahead. I wish I had fainted.

They carried me to the second level of the hotel and put me down on the floor on top of a brown blanket. The place was filled with men, women, and children; some were lying flat, while others were slumped against the walls. Many people wandered aimlessly around the room; another group was looking for loved ones. There were no doctors and nurses. Everyone was trying to help, but nothing was organized. People were coming by offering medicine, mostly aspirin. They were not professionals, just survivors who were giving what they had to others.

I looked around, and my heart leaped with joy when I saw a young boy walking around the room. I recognized him as a Swedish child who had been at the Orchid Hotel. He stood out because he had a prosthetic arm, which didn't seem to get in his way at all. He was very mischievous—you could just see it—and he was always smiling. The last time I had seen him was in that split of a second when I looked out the bungalow window and caught sight of him jumping into the pool. Unbelievably, he had survived. I was sure, too, that Simon had survived. He had to be somewhere, maybe looking for me, or maybe injured and in need of care. I was sure he was alive and that we'd find each other.

People were walking around asking questions about their loved ones, if anyone had seen them. Whenever anyone approached me, I asked if they knew of an Englishman named Simon. A woman said she heard there was someone by that name in another hotel. It made me even surer that Simon and I would be reunited. A Swedish man came by to ask how I was doing. "I can't find my wife or my children," he told me. He gave me one of those plastic flotation rings that children wear when they go swimming. "This was my little girl's. Please take it. You can use it as a cushion." He was so kind and so brave. During this frightening time, people like him were paying more attention to the fate of others than to themselves. I wanted to do more myself, but the only thing I could do was give those who came over to me as much information as I had. I couldn't move.

It was sunset when they began transporting people to

the local hospital. When it was my turn, I started shaking my head at the men who came to get me. I said I couldn't be lifted. One man left the room, cut a door out from its frame, and brought it back. He and three other men took hold of each corner of the blanket I was lying on and in one motion lifted me. I was cradled in the blanket, my legs pulled up, my arms clutching the white plastic ring, as they placed me on the door. They carried me down the stairs and out onto a path covered with mud so slick they were in danger of sliding. If they slipped, I'd go right off the door into the mud. A few spots were so slimy they had to put down planks to step on. Many people were walking around us. Some were going to the hospital; others were just walking away from the ocean. Those like me who couldn't walk to the hospital were driven.

We reached a small van which had two seats in the front. Gently, the men slid the wooden door onto the back of the van. People were crowded around me. It's hard to believe, but some of them had to be stopped from bringing suitcases. How could they take up precious room like that? I was lying in the middle of the van with my legs drawn up. I couldn't move them even a millimeter apart. You must believe me when I say that I am a pretty brave person and I was undone. Any movement at all was agony. I had thoughts that maybe I wouldn't be able to walk again, but when those thoughts came, I would say, Okay, even if I can't walk, I'm alive. My life would change for sure, but I was alive!

The van began to move. I looked back toward the ocean and saw the huge crimson ball of sun sinking into the water. I have never seen such a bloodred sunset. It was my last image of Khao Lak.

The trip to the hospital over the rutted remains of the road was like a death ride. I begged the people sitting next to me to hold my knees together. They did, but sometimes they had to let go to help themselves, and when that happened, my screams came involuntarily. We arrived at the hospital in Khao Lak, and attendants came to get me. They carried me in my blanket into a large room. It was like a war hospital. There were no beds. People, battered and bleeding, were lying next to each other on the floor. Blood was everywhere. The screams never stopped. I was put down on the floor, and a man came to check me. He looked over my broken body.

"What is your name? Where are you from?" He wrote down the information on a card and put the card on my wrist. It looked more like a suitcase tag than a hospital bracelet.

"Please," I said, "please, do you have some painkiller, please?" I was begging.

He gave me a morphine injection. Normally, the morphine should last for about three hours. Those first days, the pain was so powerful I was lucky to get relief for half that time. The attendant told me that they would come and take me to be X-rayed. There were so many injured people lying around that the doctors and nurses couldn't keep up.

I lay there for a long time until a young man came over and started talking to me. His name was Eylam and he was from Israel. Eylam had been on vacation with his girlfriend,

Carma. The two of them were on a bus going to Khao Lak when the wave hit. They were lucky enough to break a window and swim out; most of the people in the bus weren't so lucky. He and his girlfriend were unhurt. They could have left but decided to stay and help the injured.

"Is there anything I can do for you?" he asked me.

I was concerned about his taking time to help me rather than others more injured. Eylam assured me that he'd helped a number of people and would have time to help more after me. I agreed to take his kind offer.

"I've been lying here for a long time," I said. "Maybe you could ask if they can bring me for the X-ray."

He went right off and soon came back with two men wheeling a gurney.

"Is there anything else?" Eylam asked.

"Please, can you keep my legs together while they take me?"

Again I was lifted on my blanket and placed on the gurney. The pain was horrible. Eylam held my legs together and walked alongside as they rolled me to the X-ray. All around was chaos, but the people working in the hospital were smiling and bowing and saying things like, "Don't worry, we're going to take care of you."

In order to X-ray me, they lifted my butt and put a plate underneath. They slipped another plate under my back so they could get a picture of my lungs.

"Please, my legs, I can't move them. Please, can you help? Can you hold them together?" I was always saying the same thing.

They took a sheet and tied it around my legs to keep

them from separating. It made a difference. They wheeled me out of X-ray and then into a room where there were beds. My blanket was still under me, and once again I endured the awful process of being lifted and put down. Nurses came over to attend me. First they cut away the shorts and T-shirt. I wanted to keep the shirt because I thought I could find the man who gave it to me, but they took it away so quickly I never got a chance to read the writing on it. They cleaned me with damp cloths. I couldn't look at my body. Because of internal bleeding, my stomach was so swollen it looked like a soccer ball, a huge soccer ball. They catheterized me and put a white hospital gown over me. When they finished, they smiled, bowed, and left the room.

In the bed next to me was a Thai man. He had lots of tubes running in and out of his body. He spoke a little English and asked me what my name was and where I was from. Both of us were in great pain, but so thankful to be in a safe place. He told me that he had lost everything; he didn't know what had happened to his family. He feared the worst. I told him what had happened to Simon and me and that I was worried but certain that Simon was okay. After we talked for a while, he reached down and took off a chain from around his neck; on it was a small figure of the Buddha.

"Take this," he said, reaching over and putting the necklace on my bed. "He will protect you now."

I honestly believe this was the last material object that this man had, and he gave it to me. I took the necklace and told him that I would treasure it. I do. I cannot tell you how many times I witnessed little and big acts of generosity from complete strangers—many who lost so much themselves but put their own sorrows aside to help others. I know that for every deed of goodness I saw, there were thousands more, and not just in Asia. All over the world, people were reacting the same; they wanted to help. The tsunami was a horrid tragedy, but out of it came a triumph of humanity.

A doctor entered the room and walked over to my bed.

"Do I need an operation?" I asked. I was afraid what the answer would be.

"Your pelvis is broken in many places," explained the doctor, "but it's a stable fracture and we think it better not to operate."

"Are you sure?"

"Yes."

I was so happy to hear this—so happy.

That night, the evening of December 26, I got maybe two hours of sleep. I was glad to be alive, but at the same time, the pain kept me awake. Whenever I closed my eyes to try and sleep, the image of that horrible wave of black water came before me and frightened me into consciousness. I called the nurses all night to ask for more morphine or tablets. They didn't ignore me, but they couldn't give it to me because they didn't have enough. In the morning the king of Thailand sent emergency supplies to the survivors in the hospital, a cotton bag containing clothing and various other necessities.

Eylam and Carma reappeared. They were so sweet and caring. I couldn't get over the way they continued to stay on instead of going home. They talked to me, and it made me feel better, especially since they really could speak English. I told them about Simon and asked them please to see if they could find out where he was. I also asked them if they would try to phone my family. I gave them Olga's number. I so wanted to speak to someone I loved.

I had no way of knowing that at this very moment a network was forming. My friends are all over the world and many of them don't know each other, but when I sent out the group e-mail for Christmas from that little Internet café in Khao Lak, it listed the addresses of my family and friends. Even though they were strangers, they immediately began e-mailing each other to find out if anyone had heard from me. Then they began organizing. From Thailand to New York to London all of them were going without sleep in their frantic efforts to find me. Olga, my friend Jamison Ernest, and others, were desperately tracing my whereabouts through my credit card charges. Faith Kates cut short her holiday, packed up, and brought her family back to New York City, where she was on the phone for twenty-four hours straight. My friends Karolinka Bosakova and Roman Hajabac were in Bangkok and also trying to track me down. Lewis Black was systematically calling his contacts all over the world. Simon's friends, Benedict Redgraves and James Purnell, flew to Thailand and were searching for him in hospitals. Everyone was involved.

On December 27 a helicopter arrived to take the seriously injured to another, better-equipped hospital, in Hat Yai. I was supposed to go on the first flight, but I thought that since I didn't need an operation, they should take others whose condition was more critical. When they returned for the second flight, they told me I had to be on this one. I dreaded the thought of being transported because I knew it would be excruciatingly painful. My knees remained drawn up and tied together with a sheet, and I was still lying on my beautiful filthy blanket. They brought the gurney to my room and placed me and my blanket on it. I could not keep from crying out at every move as I was put in the ambulance and driven to the airport. When they tried to put me on a stretcher to get me onto the helicopter, I lost it.

"No. No. I can't do this! I have to have support."

Someone was smart enough to put a wide belt around my pelvis, and then they got me, and my blanket, on the helicopter. A television camera actually recorded this, and the footage, which I haven't seen, shows me screaming my head off as I'm being lifted on the stretcher. There were eight patients including myself on the flight. A doctor and a nurse looked after us. It was supposed to be an hour flight, but it was more like two, and as bumpy as you could imagine.

We landed in Hat Yai, and once again I had to be put on a gurney (I wonder why it's called a gurney) and brought to the hospital. I could see it was a better-equipped hospital. Right away, they took me to X-ray, where I was photographed from different angles. The Hat Yai doctor had the same wonderful report as the Khao Lak doctor: I had four stable fractures and I didn't need an operation.

I was put in some kind of emergency room, which was nice and big, with curtains around the beds. The nurses were incredible, so kind; I especially remember little Chanya, whose smile was so sweet. They took soapy sponges and, without lifting me, gently cleaned my face and chest, my soccer-ball stomach, and my arms. They were especially tender when they washed my legs. Every day I was there, they washed me and always with such kindness. I felt clean even though I was still lying on my dirty blanket. By then I was off the catheter and I had to wear Pampers like a baby. It was quite embarrassing, but I'm sure it would have been worse in another country. Somehow the Thai nurses made me feel okay and not horribly embarrassed. I was still asking if there was any word of my English friend, Simon Atlee.

On December 28 a nurse came in the room and handed me a Czech passport. I looked at the photograph; it was Roman Hajabac. When he and Karolinka discovered where I was, he came immediately; she arrived a little bit later. I told the nurse to bring him right in. I cried when I saw him. His was the first familiar face I'd seen since the tsunami. Roman became like my bodyguard and was on two telephones at once trying to coordinate everything.

The phones rang nonstop; it was like a tsunami of phone calls. Everyone wanted to talk to me and I wanted to talk, too, but it was very difficult to carry on a coherent conversation because I was so weak and so full of medicine. One of the reasons the phones rang nonstop was the time difference between the countries. The middle of the night for me was midday in New York and early morning in Europe. The press called, too, at four in the morning, and I have to say some of them weren't so nice, asking all sorts of inappropriate personal questions. Early in the morning of the twenty-eighth a call came from New York. I was sure it was Olga, so I took it. It wasn't; it was a reporter from the *Daily News*. Fortunately, he was a very nice man, and I was happy to be able to speak to someone.

The next day I was transferred to a private room in the children's section of the hospital. By this time Eylam and Carma had reached my sister in New York, and Olga called. I was so happy to hear her voice. We were talking a mile a minute. I was relieved to hear that she was coming over to be with me.

At the end of our long conversation, as we were saying good-bye, I tried to reassure her. "I'm okay, really," I said, "only I don't know where Siddy is." The minute I said it, I began to cry. The first time I had shed tears. I was so worried about him and so concerned for his family. I couldn't imagine what his mother and sister were going through. I wanted to be able to talk to them to tell them not to worry, that everything would be all right, but I didn't know myself where Siddy was.

Roman arrived after Olga's phone call. He was staying in a hotel next door and came every day to be with me. I asked him if anything had been heard from Simon. He told me that many people were searching for him. I was good about it because I believed that with so many people looking, he would be found. My main concern was that Siddy might have some kind of amnesia and be unable to identify himself.

Faith Kates had contacted Leigh Crystal, who was vacationing in India, and Leigh arranged to come to Thailand to be with me. Olga came on December 29, and dear Leigh arrived on December 31. I remember their faces when they walked into the hospital room, such incredibly moving expressions of joy and sadness at the same time. Olga told me that after they found out where I was, Faith told her she would be picked up in half an hour and be taken to the airport for a flight to Bangkok. My poor sister barely had time to pack a toothbrush. She was so rushed that only when she got on the plane was she able to reach Roman. She was talking to him when a flight attendant came over and told her to turn off her cell phone immediately. Olga looked at her and broke down into tears. Everyone was feeling the strain.

Olga and Leigh were with me for the rest of my stay; they slept in my room on hard little benches which weren't big enough to hold an adult, especially a 5'10" adult like my little sister. They took such good care of me, and the three of us really bonded. We played cards and talked and spent quality time together, including the evenings when they were sleeping on those benches. Very little English is spoken in that part of Thailand, and every day was a challenge for Olga and Leigh—just to buy food in the store was a test. They told me about all the children in the hospital. I couldn't visit them, so I asked Olga and Leigh to buy them little presents. One day, while they were out, the wind came up and made loud, frightening noises, just like the ones I heard in Khao Lak. I was terrified that something had happened to my sister and Leigh and that they wouldn't be back. I was sobbing when they returned.

The nights were hard. I would wake up screaming, and

Olga would come over to comfort me and hold me. Over and over, I kept thinking, Where is Siddy? Leigh told me, much later, that she was very worried because I didn't talk about him. I know I didn't bring him up because I wanted to believe one hundred percent that he was okay. I thought if I didn't say anything aloud, it would make it happen. Leigh knew this wasn't good. She brought up his name and asked me about him. She wanted to know what had drawn us together. So I began to talk about Siddy and I talked and talked and it was such a relief.

I was on intravenous drips and having all different blood tests. I also was a little woozy from the morphine; I had to have it. My legs were still tied up, and my stomach was getting even more distended. I had a CAT scan, and couldn't anything. I started crying and I couldn't stop. It was the first time I was crying because I felt sorry for myself. I must have been on the machine for a day and a half, and it was horrible. The machine made awful noises, and the tube was bringing up all sorts of disgusting stuff, draining the poisons out of me. It was painful, too, but my stomach started to go down.

When they did a follow-up CAT scan, they saw that all the bleeding in my stomach and a hematoma in my kidney had been reduced to a small spot of blood in my lower left abdomen. Olga was in the computer room when the doctors were looking at the images; amazed at what they saw, they called her over. Olga peered at the image.

"What's this, the brain?" asked my sister.

"No, it's the liver," said the doctor.

He showed her other images, shaking his head in disbelief.

"It's unbelievable how quickly your sister has recovered.
This is amazing. How is it she is healing so quickly?"

Olga told the doctor that I was simply using energy, con-
centrating it on myself and sending it out to others.

A couple of days later I got a big surprise. Donaes came
to visit me. He had been vacationing in Thailand and contacted me as soon as he learned of my whereabouts. It was
so good to see him.

Leigh and Olga learned that a huge amount of money
was being offered for my photograph. Someone said it was
as high as a quarter million dollars! I couldn't believe it.
Photographers were trying to sneak into the hospital to
snap photos of me, and guards were positioned to keep
them out. We decided that, rather than have strangers
profit from my picture, we would take a photograph and
give any money to UNICEF and Save the Children. Leigh
took the picture, and the photo was sent around the world.
(The picture was great, and people wanted to know who
took it. They thought it was the work of a professional photographer. I told Leigh she could have a second career.) In
the picture I'm smiling. I really had a serene feeling, like
there was a light within me that I wanted to shine everywhere. Look, my smile seemed to say, how wonderful it is

to be alive. In fact, I was starting to feel a bit better. The tube was out of my nose, and although my legs remained up and tied together, the bed was electric, so I could change my positions. Eventually, I was able to move my legs a little bit apart and then to put them down and up. In the Thai hospital, that was all I could do, put both legs down.

Faith kept calling. She was checking with the doctors in New York and relaying their recommendations. Based on their advice, she told my sister to keep massaging my legs to keep the blood circulating. Olga was constantly rubbing my feet and my arms. The calls kept coming. I spoke to my mother and father, who wanted to come right away to Thailand. I said no. I ached to see them, but I knew it would be too hard for them. I would be too worried about them, and I had to concentrate on myself. When they insisted, I almost gave in, but I caught myself and said, "No, Olga is here. I will see you when I go to the hospital in Prague." I am so glad that they listened to me. My friends were calling, practically nonstop. It meant a lot to me to hear from loving friends, but I still hadn't heard from my beloved Simon.

Doctors were coming and going, checking on me all the time. I was getting better for sure, though I was still being fed intravenously. On the fifth day in the Hat Yai hospital the nurses stole my blanket. No, I'm kidding. What happened was this: I had settled into a daily routine. I was on drips for a long time, being fed intravenously, and every morning I was getting morphine injections and having blood taken. Then the nurses would wash me. They were so gentle and so nice and they were always smiling—but they wanted to take my blanket and wash it. I protested until finally I told them okay. They removed my amazing security blanket, cleaned it, folded it, and returned it. I have never opened it again, but I will keep it always.

I don't like to keep talking about pain; still, it was so much a part of my experience I can't avoid it. Despite the morphine and other drugs, nothing could completely block the constant hurting. As bad as the physical pain, I also suffered night terrors. When I closed my eyes, I would see the swirling, rising waters, and whenever there was a loud noise, I became terrified because it reminded me of the crashing sounds of the tsunami. Banging noises terrified me more than anything else. I was strong, but loud sounds completely unnerved me.

On December 31 I was in agony all day. They gave me as much medication as they could; it wasn't enough. Around 11:00 p.m. Olga and the nurses called the doctor to ask what they should do. He was at my bedside within half an hour. On New Year's Eve, 2004, the incredible Dr. Tamarad came to my rescue. He asked me to describe the pain, to tell him what I was feeling; when I finished, he thought for a while and then spoke.

"Petra, sometimes pain seems like it's a 10 on a scale of 1 to 10, but it really may be only a 4. Pain isn't that big; our minds make it bigger. What you must do is focus on something else, not the pain. Think about objects, or people, or nice situations, or things that you would like to do. The pain will get easier and go down. Stay cheerful. Don't drift into sadness. When you do that, you go down. Stay happy, and when you do, you will heal faster."

Such simple advice about the power of the mind, and I followed it. In fact, this visualization technique is what I'd always done with my energy work. If I wanted something to happen, I pictured it happening, which helped me to achieve it. In the past it had been for things like being a nicer person or picturing myself being helpful to others. But I had used it when I was in the palm tree. To give me the strength to hold on, I visualized myself full of strength and able to search for Siddy.

Now I began to picture all the wonderful people in my life. I was a little girl again and I saw my parents. They were giving Olga and me a bath in the tub, cleaning us and washing our hair. I saw my grandfather and the beautiful forest behind his house. I saw my grandmothers, my aunts and uncles and cousins. I thought about all my friends who cared about me and who were so kind. I could see their smiling faces. I thought about all the people in Thailand who were so giving; but most of all, I thought about Simon, and my mind was flooded with beautiful memories. I thought about being reunited with him and how there would be an even stronger bond between us because we had lived through such a nightmare. It would bring us so close that nothing would ever bring us apart again. I fell asleep dreaming of my Siddy, and the next day, for the first time in a week, I had no pain. I went off the morphine and the pills. I began controlling everything with my mind.

Beginning on January 1, every day was a little victory. I could move my legs apart from nothing to five centimeters. I still kept them drawn up most of the time because it was more comfortable, but I could put them down if I wanted.

My beautiful sister washed me every morning; she was my private nurse. On January 3 the Thai nurses put a basin on the bed and washed my hair, which was thick with mud. My first shampoo—what a glorious feeling! I have pictures of me with clean wet hair. The speed of my healing process amazed the doctors; they called it a miracle. I was skin and bones—probably in Milan I would have been ordered to lose a few pounds for Fashion Week. I was fascinated watching the scars on my body fade. Almost all are gone now except for one on the back of my right arm, a small one on my left forearm, and a couple on my stomach. They are not worth talking about.

After three weeks I was ready to move on. I needed to get to a hospital where they could further assess my condition. Most of all, I needed to get walking again. My friends were pushing me to go to a hospital in New York; I wanted to go to the Czech Republic. I wanted to be with my family. Arrangements were made to fly me from Thailand to Prague. I could not change planes, and since there were no direct flights, the insurance company provided a plane. We were leaving late at night, and all the nurses and doctors, even the ones off duty, came to say good-bye. Olga and I were flying to Prague, Leigh had left that afternoon for New York. Dr. Tamarad and the head nurse rode in the ambulance with my sister and me. The doctor told Olga to make sure that I didn't drift into sadness. I felt so strange about leaving Thailand, happy and sad, happy to be going home, and sad, even sadder, to be leaving Simon. There was still no news of him, yet I remained hopeful.

When we arrived at the airport and drove onto the tarmac, one tiny little plane was standing there, the smallest plane you ever saw.

"Oh my God," said my sister, "I just hope it's not that plane. I just hope it's not that plane!"

Of course, it *was* that plane.

12

Home

The plane took off with a pilot, a copilot, a doctor, a medical assistant, and my sister and me. This was a really little plane with a long way to go and barely enough room for all of us. I was in a stretcher bed on one side, and the others were across from me. I felt so strange; I didn't cry because I was happy to be going home, and yet the sadness was there. I worried about Simon. I worried that I hadn't thanked everyone in the hospital enough. I worried about all the people affected by the tsunami, and I worried about how long it would take me to get back to Thailand and help them with my own hands to rebuild. This was a driving force for me, and from the very beginning, I was making plans for my return. Thinking about it made me want to get well and strong.

I slept a lot on the flight. I know we made stops in India, Iran, and Turkey to refuel—little planes have little tanks—

but the flight was smooth and I was comfortable. (I can't speak for my sister.) I did have to be helped to change the position of my legs. Later I learned that the doctors were very worried about my being in the air for so long. To prevent thrombosis, I was given injections to thin the blood and my legs were encased in "sexy" elastic stockings. We didn't want photographers when we landed in Prague, and to throw the press off the track, we released misinformation about our arrival time. The pilots were smart. We landed and they went directly to a hangar, not a gate. I was put into an ambulance and driven off. Nobody got any pictures. My mother and father were waiting at the hospital and were overcome with joy. For once, Czechs were showing their emotions. My mom was so excited; she thought it was like being in a James Bond movie.

"We tricked them!" she cried when she came into my room.

We hugged and kissed, and there was so much happiness, not so many tears, just smiles and love. I was already strong when I saw them, and that's the way I wanted it.

Now began my long time of recuperation. I was checked over by X-rays, MRIs, CAT scans, general surgeons, orthopedic surgeons, gynecologists, and psychiatrists; everything and everyone got a chance to look me over. Basically, I was fine; I just had to remain in bed and wait for the bones to heal. My father stayed; he slept in my room and took care of me, carrying bedpans back and forth. My mom was working; she came on the weekends and took over.

After a few days a rehabilitation nurse began to work with me, and I started to exercise a little bit. First I did weights with my arms while lying in bed. I had these over-hanging pulleys, and I would pull myself up to strengthen my arms. The arms were okay, but the challenging part was my legs. I couldn't lift them off the bed because I still couldn't open them much. Each day, I would push them apart a little more, and I began to turn my body a bit. It felt so strange. I had been on my back for twenty days and I had always slept on my tummy, except with Siddy; we would sleep on our sides together like two spoons. Before the tsunami I could never sleep on my back; today I can.

I have to say I didn't have a quiet recovery. The press was always around, and people were trying to get to me by bribing the nurses. The phone rang all the time. People were protecting me, still it was not such a good feeling to be hounded, but I so appreciated all the messages of good-will I let the other stuff go.

Very shortly, I was back on the e-mail. Like I've said, I'm a real techie, and I love the gadgets. I was so moved by all the e-mails and letters I received. I tried to reply to every-one. (Thank you, thank you, if you didn't hear from me.) I felt good when I was in the Czech hospital, but they were being supercautious. They let me stand up on the first day, which I begged them to do. Two nurses held me, and I can't tell you what an amazing feeling it was to be *on* my feet. That was it for a while; I didn't get on them again for two weeks, and then I was able to stand up with a walker.

Even though I'd built up my muscles with the exercises on the bed, I was exhausted after a few minutes of standing in the same spot. The next time, I took a step or two, and still, I was exhausted. It's strange, you walk all the time, and you never think about it. Then you don't walk for a long time, and you have to think about it—a lot! You have to give all your energy into moving one foot in front of the other. I was putting great pressure on my hands, gripping and pushing down so hard on the walker that I had to wear cycling gloves so I wouldn't get blisters. I graduated to crutches and walked along the hospital corridor. I remember saying to the rehab nurse, "I can do more; I can do more." And she would say, "Don't rush, don't rush." I wanted to get well fast, so I could go back to Thailand.

January 20, 2005, is a date I'll never forget. Twenty-five days after the tsunami, I took my first shower, assisted by my special nurse, Olga Nemcova. How wonderful to stand under the beautiful clean water and have it flow all over my body. This was a great moment.

Every day, I read the papers, searching for any piece of information that might lead us to Siddy. When I began reading the papers, I realized the full magnitude of what had happened. I was getting stronger, but I don't know if you can ever be strong enough to take some things. In the papers I learned about the "trafficants," people who abducted the lost and orphaned children, stealing them from the streets, and even from the hospitals and shelters, and offering them, in the best-case scenario, for adoption on the black market. Most were sold as sex slaves or used to harvest organs. For such people I have no words, only utter contempt. The horror is, it's still going on. The more I read, the more anxious I was to go back. I wanted to find Siddy. Time was passing and still, occasionally, there would be a story about someone who survived, someone who was found and reunited with loved ones. I prayed for that miracle for Siddy.

I had lots of visitors. People came from all over, so many friends and family members. I was happy to see everyone. Veronika Varekova arrived with a pot of chicken soup, which she had made. It was delicious. Can you imagine, such a beautiful person and a good cook, too? (Maybe I cannot acknowledge everyone individually right here, but I do thank you, all my angels, from the bottom of my heart.) Jodi and Mark came over from England. They had called to find out what they could bring. I asked for some of Siddy's T-shirts. They brought the shirts, some photographs, wonderful presents from the children, Simon's old winter jacket, and a special gift and note from Chris. We talked about Siddy. I could tell that they had less hope than I did, but they spoke positively. I knew they didn't want to upset me. I continued to try and think positively. After they left, I put on one of the T-shirts and the jacket; it was like having Siddy's arms around me. I opened the present from his mother. It was a gold ring. In the note, she wrote that she knew Siddy would want me to have it. I sobbed when I read it.

I continued to recuperate. At night I would lie in my bed listening to healing music to put me to sleep. The music was so beautiful, powerful, and cleansing I would cry; it was such a pure crying, almost peaceful. A psychologist came to see me. He thought I was coping well and helped me deal with one big problem. Anything that resembled the kinds of noises I heard during the tsunami still terrified me. I would jump out of my skin when I heard a sudden crash. The doctor said my reactions were understandable, the noises were triggering a response.

"When you hear the sounds, Petra, don't try to ignore them, analyze them. Just say to yourself, Okay, that bang is a book falling off the shelf, or maybe someone dropped a baking pan. If you identify the source, then you can deal with it. Don't try to stay out of it. Analyze it and you'll move on."

I took his advice and it worked. Noises haven't bothered me for a long time. The doctor also told me that I might have some kind of reaction six months and one year from the date of the tsunami. I might even be physically ill but that, too, was normal. I was very aware of the date on June 26. I got through it and I'm sure that I'll be able to handle December 26, too. It helps when you know what to expect.

It was mid-February when I went outside for the first time. I couldn't go on the crutches because I wasn't stable enough. I was with my dad and my friends Lauren Gold and Lewis Black; they pushed me outside in a wheelchair. It was snowing; I wanted to hold a snowball. My dad made one for me and put it in my hand; I threw it at Lewis. It was so lovely to be outside.

Lauren brought me a gift, a silver locket on a chain. Inside the locket was a picture of Simon on one side and one of me on the other. I put it on. All the time, I would open the locket and look at his face; his blue, blue eyes were serene, smiling. Siddy, where were you? A strange thing happened. I took a shower and forgot to remove my necklace. I panicked and clumsily opened the locket latch; the inside was soaked. The photos of Siddy and me had come away from the sides and were stuck together; our faces had merged. I was sad until I thought, Well, now we are one forever. A couple of weeks later I opened the locket and was amazed to see that the photographs had melted away and both sides of the locket were coated in a beautiful shade of blue, a blue the color of Simon's eyes. I know it sounds impossible, but I promise it's true. By that time, although I wouldn't admit it even to myself, I didn't have much hope left of looking into those eyes again.

I left the hospital late in February and went back to Karvina. I moved in with my mother and father. So many times in the past I had wanted to come and stay with them but could only drop in for a quick visit on my way to somewhere else. Now I really was home. That was one of the good things that came out of my experience, and it was something that Simon, more than anyone else, would have appreciated. I was connecting, really connecting, with my loved ones. One thing, I didn't allow myself to be too sad or unhappy around others. I felt that I owed it to them to keep up my spirit so that I didn't bring them down.

Every day, my health improved and I got better and better on the crutches. By the first week in March I thought I was well enough to do an interview with Diane Sawyer. I wasn't totally up to it, because I was still emotionally and physically drained. But I wanted to do it. I wanted to give people the strength not to give up in the face of tragedy. The second week in March I went to Prague for an interview with *Vanity Fair* magazine. Patrick Demarchelier took the accompanying pictures. This would be my first real "photo shoot" since the tsunami. I checked into the hotel and was getting ready to join the writer and my friends Veronika and Tereza for dinner when the telephone rang. I thought it was one of them calling. It was Jodi.

"Hello, Jodi, how are you? How is everybody?"

There was a pause, a terrible pause.

"Petra, they found Simon's body."

I couldn't speak. Some part of me heard Jodi saying something about memorial services and not to worry, that they wouldn't schedule anything until I was well enough to fly there.

"I'll be there," I said.

I asked about Siddy's mom, and the children and some of his friends. Jodi answered all my questions. Just before we hung up, she said, "Petra, the authorities told us that the only thing they found on Simon's body was some sort of cloth bracelet. They're sending it to us. We thought you might want to have it."

The second she said it, I saw it. I saw Siddy untying the bracelet and putting it on his other wrist. All I could do was sigh.

"Yes, yes, thank you, I would like to have it."

"It will be here for you."

We said good-bye and I put down the phone.

I took a deep breath. In a way, I was glad no one was with me; it gave me time to think. My mind was whirling. I said I would be there for a memorial, but the doctors had said I couldn't fly for at least three months; it was too dangerous. I vowed I would go no matter what.

Ever since the disaster, I had tried hard not to think about some things, but they wouldn't go away and now they surfaced again. Why was I alive? Why was Siddy gone? And, the most awful thought of all, was: If we hadn't gone to Thailand, he would still be alive. In some way I couldn't help feeling responsible. I had told others about my feelings of guilt, and all of them said the same thing. It was simply Siddy's time to go. I take comfort in the thought that what happened was beyond anyone's control. As I thought more about it, I realized that deep inside, I didn't want Siddy's body found. I wanted continuation, not closure. I knew he wasn't coming back, but without tangible proof, I had something to hold on to. Now all I had was the bracelet.

In tears I reached for his little blue book, which is always with me. I began leafing through the pages. Sentences jumped out at me. "You are not only the best girlfriend in the world but the best model in the world and possibly the cutest girl on the planet." And there was a little sketch of the world, and me standing on top. "Happy Anniversary, my angel, this has been the happiest year of my life." "You are the kindest and most honest person I have ever met." "I love the look of excitement on your face when I take the roast vegetables out of the oven or when I mention the word barbecue." "You are my north, my south, my east, my west, my daily wear, my Sunday best. My sun, my moon, my stars above, my reason to be, my only true love."

You know what? Reading what Siddy wrote made me cry and laugh in the same moment. I could hear him saying, "Stop sobbing, Petra. Get over it and be happy." I know that's what my beautiful blue-eyed boy would have said, and knowing this has given me not only the courage but the will to go on.

Epilogue

The holiest of all holidays are those
Kept by ourselves in silence and apart;
The secret anniversaries of the heart . . . .

—H. W. Longfellow, *Silence*

On May 19, 2005, five months after I left, I flew back to Thailand. Always in my heart, I knew the healing process could go only so far without my revisiting the place of my greatest sorrow *and* my greatest joy. I love the Thai people; I wanted to see them again. I love their country; I needed to return. I was given the gift of life in Thailand; I had to find a way to help.

I wanted especially to help the children, to establish a charity that would fund the rebuilding of schools and provide professional psychological help through special support groups for the little ones who had lost their families and were all alone. Helping is not so easy to do even when the desire is strong. I tried to set things up quickly, but it takes time to establish a nonprofit foundation. In the meantime the people, the children, they are suffering. I did what I could to get things going, but nothing would happen for many weeks. Okay, I thought, if I cannot act right away on a big scale, I'll do something on a small scale. I think this is a good way for all people to think.

Not everyone can afford to give a lot of money, but we can do things in other ways. A smile, a handshake, a gentle touch, sometimes a simple act of kindness can bring as much immediate relief as a check for a lot of money. No cash was involved when I was rescued from the palm tree. I learned from tragedy that everything can change in a split second. What is beautiful can turn ugly; what is benevolent can become vicious; and what is living and loving can be swept away. It's too bad that it takes a catastrophe to make us realize how precious is every moment of life and how quickly it can be gone. The tsunami was a terrible experience, but all experiences, good and bad, make us grow. They give us a chance to improve, to put meaning into our lives, and to think of others.

On that flight to Bangkok I was thinking of the others and of the events of the past few months. In March, I had gone to Siddy's cremation and memorial service despite the doctors' warnings. They hadn't wanted me flying because there was still a risk of thrombosis. I told them I was going, no matter what the risk. I worked extra hard to make myself fit enough to travel. My parents were going to come with me, then my dad got sick and my mom couldn't leave him. They didn't want me to go myself, but I insisted; nothing could stop me. Besides, I argued, Olga was flying in from New York and she'd look after me; she was used to it.

I was on my way to a memorial service and yet, oddly, I was excited about returning to England, eager to see my friends and my English family. I flew into Heathrow. The minute I got off the plane, I inhaled London's special scent. You know, each airport has its own unique smell. I can't describe it in words, but I promise, if you blindfolded me and brought me to a terminal, I could tell you exactly where I was, just by my nose. The terminal doors opened. I maneuvered myself through on my crutches and walked out in front of the row of drivers.

For a moment I faltered. How many times had Siddy been waiting for me? How many times had I rushed out the door into his arms? I saw my dear driver, Richard, coming toward me. We embraced. I was crying and so was he. "Come on, Petra, let's get out of here." Richard spoke gruffly and treated me tenderly. I knew he was embarrassed to have me see his tears. He loved Simon, too.

When we arrived at the house, I was a bit nervous to see Chris; it would be the first time since before Christmas, since the tsunami, since Simon had gone. She was so welcoming and so brave; truly, her strength made me strong. I hugged and kissed everyone. I felt at home.

The cremation was private, with family and close friends attending. Afterward, we toasted Siddy with his favorite drink, Slippery Nipples (equal parts sambuca and Irish Cream liqueur). Even I had one—actually, two—and I got a little tipsy. (Remember, I don't drink.)

Two days later the memorial was held at the Forest School chapel. The former school chaplain, who knew Siddy, conducted the service. It was beautiful and simple.

Siddy wasn't very religious. There was no formal reading or anything like that. People just spoke about him, and his favorite music was played in the background. I couldn't speak—it was too much for me—but I listened with joy as his friends and family talked about all the attributes that made Siddy the magnificent person he was. One friend called Siddy an emotional genius, perceptive and honest, who believed in you more than you did yourself. He told of how Siddy would happily share moments of triumph but was right there to pick you up in defeat; how he'd tell you when you let yourself down or tried to deceive yourself. "You could place your hopes and dreams with Siddy, and he would take care of them." There was praise and there was humor—there had to be humor. Mark Hansard said that the rumor was not true that he married Jodi so he could get to hang out with her brother. Another friend read a selection of postcards Simon had written to his niece and nephew. So full of fun.

The service ended, and we left the chapel to the sounds of Stevie Wonder singing "Another Star." Plans were made to scatter Siddy's ashes on all the continents—on the Atacama Desert in Chile, on the outback in Australia, on Cape Town in South Africa, on New York City, and I even arranged for a friend to bring them to Antarctica. In England there were a few destinations, including the Arsenal soccer stadium (he loved that team), and before I returned to the Czech Republic, I went to Holland Park and spread his ashes on the very spot where we had our first kiss. It seemed like no time had passed since then, and now I was bringing his ashes to Thailand to scatter on the beach at

I t took us twenty-six hours to reach Thailand, and almost all that time tears were in my eyes. My friends Karolinka and Roman, Jamison, and my sister were with me. We stayed overnight in Bangkok and on May 22 flew to Hat Yai to visit the hospital where I had been lovingly looked after. It was a big celebration with a welcoming luncheon. In the crowd I saw Dr. Tamarad coming toward me.

"How are you, Petra? How are you doing? Are you well?" he asked. He was so calm and peaceful like always. His daughter was with him and he introduced us. Then he gave me a present, a book of sayings of the Buddha. I owed *him* so much I could not believe he was giving me a present.

After the lunch we went to the hospital. I had pins and needles in my whole body. How strange to *walk* through those doors, to *walk* into my room. All the time I'd been there, I was on my back—on a bed, on a gurney, on an examining table—never on my feet. It was such a different perspective now. The nurses and doctors were the same, kind and smiling. We went to the children's ward and *gave* out candies and little presents. The children were so adorable and yet so tortured. One little girl didn't move,

Khao Lak. I was wondering how I would feel. How would it be to see again the beautiful beach where Siddy and I walked that last morning, to see the Orchid Hotel, or whatever was left of it, to see the palm tree that sheltered me like a mother? Such thoughts were running through my head as the plane flew into the sunset.

didn't talk, didn't even blink. She stared at nothing, or maybe her eyes were still seeing the wall of black water. Can she be helped? I don't know, I only know I want to do everything in my power to bring the light back into those eyes, the eyes of all those battered children.

May 23. We went to the little island of Koh Samet. It is so lovely, so lush. We played Frisbee on the beach, and I actually went scuba diving. I knew if I didn't do it then, I might never do it again. Oh, and such a silly thing happened. Karolinka and Roman were trying to buy some trinkets, and, of course, you always bargain in Thailand. They were talking to the merchant when I marched over and looked at the price tag. It read four thousand baht.

"I was here last year," I said to the Thai gentleman, "and you were selling these for three thousand baht, and that is all that we will pay."

Karolinka and Roman started laughing.

"What's the matter with you two?" I asked. "You should thank me; I'm bargaining."

"Petra, he was asking two thousand baht. You bargained up!"

⸂

That evening after dinner on the beach, I lay down on the sand and looked up at the sky. The stars were looking down at me, the same stars Siddy and I looked up at together from so many beaches around the world. I thought about him, about the way he lived his life, the way he connected with everyone, the way he made every day count. I thought about all that I learned from him—to take time to be with those you love, to let them know how much you care, to enjoy life to the fullest, to care for and love everyone and everything. "A day without laughter is a day wasted," was Siddy's favorite saying, and never was a day wasted with him. I found solace in remembering his mother's words read at the memorial—how he did more with his thirty-three years than most people do with ninety. She was right.

The next day, I returned to Khao Lak.

Rebuilding was already under way, but many scars remained evident, huge holes in the ground where once had been buildings, and the scattered skeletal remains of what had been sweet little homes. Those are the visible scars; the hidden ones are more frightening. The lives of millions of people around the world changed because of what happened on December 26, 2004, and all too soon, few will remember while thousands go on suffering; that is the way of the world. While we are going on, they're still struggling. I know this firsthand. The tsunami was the second monstrous upheaval that I have witnessed. I was not injured in the terrorist attack on New York City on September 11, 2001, but I was there. I saw with my own eyes the second plane smash into the World Trade Center. I saw with my own eyes the towers collapse into smoldering ashes. I saw fear and horror etched in the faces of people around me. I know how hard it is to rise up and move forward, to make good come from the bad. Disasters, natural and otherwise, have the power to destroy and yet they also have the power to create a new and better world by bringing people together in a common cause. That is why I wrote this book.

I wanted to put a face to a catastrophic event, to tell one story out of many so that we will continue to think of this hideous disruption of life and do everything possible to help these people rebuild.

I found my way to the Orchid Hotel and headed toward the ocean. Palm trees were scattered around, but I honestly could not be sure which was mine. It didn't really matter. I saw one tree with a scarred trunk and new growth already appearing in its crown. It could have been my tree. I went over to it. I had brought flowers. I knelt down and placed them at the base of the tree. I put my palms together and bowed my head. Around my wrist was the cloth bracelet from Chiang Mai. I am still wearing it. I got up and walked onto the beach and down to the water's edge. I looked out at the horizon where the cloudless blue sky met the calm blue ocean. Suddenly, I was overcome with rage. I kicked at the water with all my might, screaming, "Damn you! Damn you!"

"Damn who, Petra?" I could hear Siddy laughing.

The rage left me. There was no evil here, no monster, no avenging god, just fate. If I learned nothing else, I discovered that before nature we are all the same, whatever country we are from, whatever the color of our skin, whatever God we worship, rich or poor, we are one. Nature does not discriminate. I discovered that I had come back to Thailand to pay my respects not only to all those who had helped me and to all those who suffered and died but also to nature,

Epilogue

the source of life. We cannot change the past, but we can make a difference in the future. I look forward to the future because, whatever happens, I bring to it beautiful memories of the wonderful man I lost. He was the most precious thing in my life, but life goes on, and whatever good I can accomplish on this earth, I will do for both of us. I took out the small urn I had carried with me, and as I emptied Siddy's ashes into the sea, I could hear him say, "Okay, Petra, get on with it."

I will get on with it, Siddy, I will do all I can to help those who are in need, and I'll do it with love always,

Petra

xxx

All of Petra's proceeds from the sale of this book will be donated to the Give2Asia®/Happy Hearts Fund.

For more information on the fund, please contact:

Give2Asia®/Happy Hearts Fund
465 California Street, 9th floor
San Francisco, CA 94104-1832
USA
phone (415) 743-3336
fax (415) 392-8863
www.give2asia.org

KITCHENER PUBLIC LIBRARY
3 9098 01145366 8

FIC Burge

Burgess, A.
Byrne ; a novel.
Kitchener Public Library
Main-Fiction

BYRNE

ANTHONY BURGESS

BYRNE

A NOVEL

CARROLL & GRAF PUBLISHERS, INC.
NEW YORK

Copyright © 1995 by the Estate of Anthony Burgess

All rights reserved

First Carroll & Graf edition 1997
    Second Printing, October 1997

Carroll & Graf Publishers, Inc.
19 West 21st Street
New York, NY 10010

Library of Congress Cataloging-in-Publication Data
    Burgess, Anthony, 1917–1993
            Byrne / Anthony Burgess. — 1st Carroll & Graf ed.
            p.   cm.
        ISBN 0-7867-0456-X
        I. Title.
    PR6052.U638B96   1997
    823'.914—dc21   97-17247
                                                                    CIP

Manufactured in the United States of America

To you and you and you.
Also you.

'Prudence, prudence,' the pigeons call,
'Scorpions lurk in the gilded meadow,
An eye is embossed on the island wall.
The running tap casts a static shadow.'

'Caution, caution,' the rooks proclaim,
'The dear departed, the weeping widow,
Will meet in you in the core of flame.
The running tap casts a static shadow.'

'Act, act!' the ducks give voice.
'Enjoy the widow in the meadow.
Drain the sacrament of choice.
The running tap casts a static shadow.'

F.X.E.

CONTENTS

Byrne

a novel

Anthony Burgess

ONE

Somebody had to do it. Blasted Byrne
Pulled out a bunch of dollars from his pocket,
Escudos, francs and dirhams. 'Let them learn
If they've a speck of talent not to mock it
But plant it and expect a slow return.
I whizzed mine skywards like a bloody rocket.
Tell what they call a cautionary tale.
Here's on the nail. Expect more in the mail.'

He thought he was a kind of living myth
And hence deserving of *ottava rima*,
The scheme that Ariosto juggled with,
Apt for a lecherous defective dreamer.
He'd have preferred a stronger-muscled smith,
Anvilling rhymes amid poetic steam, a
Sort of Lord Byron. Byron was long dead.
This poetaster had to do instead.

Some lines attributed to Homer speak
Of someone called Margites. 'Him the gods
Had not made skilled in craft or good in Greek.
He failed in every art.' Against the odds
His name survives. His case is not unique.
He should lie with forgotten odds and sods,
But still he serves to nominate a species
And lives while Byrne is mixed with his own faeces.

Byrne's name survives among film-music-makers
Because the late-night shows subsist on trash.
His opera's buried by art's undertakers,
His paintings join his funerary ash.
He left no land. 'My property's two achers,'
Stroking laborious ballocks. As for cash,
He lived on women, paying in about
Ten inches. We don't know what they paid out.

Handsome enough, there was no doubt of that –
Blue-eyed and with an Irish peasant's stature,
His belly flat, it never ran to fat;
Possessed of quite a punch whose crack could match your
Boundary-winning slam; lithe as a cat,
With two great paws, a natural outfield catcher;
Not that he ever wasted time on sport
Save only for the amatory sort.

The Irish are peculiar, no doubt:
They prefer drink to women. Nightly splurges
On whiskey, pints of plain or creaming stout
Serve to inhibit their erotic urges.
Seed-spending's peccative, but seed will out,
As Dr Kettle said. The Irish clergy's
At one with booze in locking semen in,
Though holy wedlock will annul the sin.

Byrne was no Rechabite by any means;
Drink was for him an aphrodisiac.
A foreign substance in the family genes
Burned up this Byrne alone. Long ages back,
When restive Erin was a redhaired queen's
Pain in the arse, the Spanish took a crack
At heretic England with their proud Armada,
Striking her navy hard, but that struck harder.

6

God's wind blew and they scattered, and some scattered
To Ireland's coast. When they had dried their doublets,
Survival seemed the only thing that mattered.
They swilled their buttermilk from peasant goblets
And, vowing they would never more be battered
By wind and wave, said, with a Spanish sob, 'Let's
Resign ourselves to pigshit, peat and mud,
And tickle these mad Irish with our blood.'

The Spaniard darkly shone from Byrne's complexion,
Though this was tempered by his mother's colour.
She was a Liverpudlian confection,
With Wales and Glasgow brightening the duller
Pallor, and a half-hazy recollection
Of sourmilk skin upon a Nordic skull, a
Tobacco-chewer's beard, half-grey, half-flaxen,
Proclaiming Dutch or Dane or Swede or Saxon.

Since Ireland was all England's, Irish reason
Said England was all Ireland's, and it showed
In July barbering or, at any season,
Setting down rails or mammocking the road.
O'Connell preached his demagogic treason:
The English harrow crushed the Irish toad;
Freed, though not freed of economic panics,
Ireland would not use England as an annexe.

The County Mayo Byrnes were not political:
They only wanted to be free to eat.
Their situation wobbled to the critical
Each harvest time. Pigs were forbidden meat
That paid the farm-rent to the parasitical
Absentee landlord. Over smoky peat
They munched their murphies, stirred their rancid stirabout.
Poverty was the one thing to confer about.

Old Peter Byrne could not say: 'This is my land.'
So when the blight killed the potato crop,
He spat upon the stones, then cursed awhile and
Announced that Liverpool was their next stop,
A Celtic port in John Bull's primary island,
Where other Byrnes already ran a shop
That catered to the poor's nutritive needs
By selling wormy cabbages and swedes.

The vegetable Byrnes sent off the fare,
And then the seasick vegetableless,
Hearing the Cunard sirens blast the air,
Settled to chronic urban shiftlessness,
Except for Kate, who, with a dancing flair,
Cavorted at the Empire in undress
And fired the fancy of a cotton broker.
Her brother Pat became a Cunard stoker.

Another brother came like Christmas sun
When Byrne the father thought his wells were dry.
His wife's fertility had months to run
Before the menopause should bid it fly.
It seemed to him that what the Lord had done
Was like the dayspring flashing from on high.
His knowledge of the Bible being dim,
He did not think of Ann and Joachim.

It was coincidence that made them christen
The fruit of this late coupling Sean or John.
Paternal pride made rheumy optics glisten
Behind the mended glasses they had on.
It brought the country past alive to listen
To lullabies culled from a time long gone.
But, like Saint Joseph, he'd a certain doubt
About his wife the nights that he was out.

She was a pretty woman, with a figure
Whose slimness was a fruit of malnutrition.
Her eyes were like a doe's, though rather bigger
Because her face bespoke her past condition.
Was someone tupping her with cash and vigour?
She spread a table rich for the position
Of a mere Mersey Harbour Board nightwatchman.
The swine, he thought, could hardly be a Scotchman.

But Father Leary brooked no contradiction
About the unitary fatherhood.
Paternity was but a legal fiction,
And God was good, particularly good,
As was made clear from scriptural depiction,
At fertilising. Earthly fathers stood
Stuck in a kind of foster-parent's groove:
True fatherhood's a thing you cannot prove.

Catholic, of course, and good as Catholics went,
She crossed herself at thunder and forked lightning.
Hearing the sacring bell, she duly bent,
Ate fish on Fridays and went in for tightening
Her corset by eschewing stout in Lent.
The hellfire doctrine she found rather frightening,
But didn't fancy hymning the Almighty
Paraded in a chilly cotton nighty.

Young John grew up a pagan like his dad,
Even more pagan when his dad was dead.
The Christian Brothers schooling that he had
Assailed his rump but passed beyond his head.
His sister was, though long gone to the bad,
Good at odd hand-outs, so his mother said.
Pat stoked away and sent home half his screw.
They managed: Merseysiders sometimes do.

John had a treble voice so sweetly piercing
It quite belied his boyish heathen heart.
Old ladies, when they heard the little dear sing,
Could not forbear to let the teardrops smart.
He got a great audition. They said: 'Here, sing
This *Agnus Dei* – see, the solo part.'
And that was in the massive polyhedral
Holy of holies, Liverpool Cathedral.

He sang and sang, inspiring holy love,
But not averse to dirtying his hassock,
And then he'd give another lad a shove,
Who would shove back, being no Sacher-Masoch.
Then, after rendering 'Wings of a Dove',
He'd wipe his snotty snout upon his cassock.
The Choirmaster did not appear to mind,
But he was growing deaf as well as blind.

During his sweetly vocal pre-pubescence,
John got a post that could be termed sub-clerical.
A shipping firm paid for his daily presence
Dogsbodying. And now the youthful lyrical
Gift had to go. To mock his adolescence,
The larynx squeaked or boomed. But, by a miracle,
Singing, while tidying his master's desk,
He found he'd turned into a young de Reszke.

Well, not quite of that heavy smoker's metal.
Say John McCormack, who became a papal
Count, gifted with a mistier, milder fettle,
Or syrupy, like drippings from the maple,
Or sensuous-soft, like stroking a rose-petal,
Whose songs would be the repertorial staple
Of Irish airs or such innocuous salads
As bland recitals of Victorian ballads.

John had, in fact, one of those tenor voices
You only find among the sons of Erin,
A sugary warbling flute just like James Joyce's,
Whose talent didn't get him anywhere in
The singing business. Still, he had two choices:
Butchering English was his other care. In
All honesty I'll give my verdict. This is:
He should have sung and not spewed up *Ulysses*.

John Byrne, not John McCormack, couldn't write,
Except fair copies of the company's letters,
But he would take his voice out every night
In temporary remission from the fetters
Of clerkly slavery. In the smoky light
Of pub or club or parish hall he'd get a s-
-Mall recompense for singing out his soul
In Tom Moore's words, set to the tunes he stole.

One Christmas he sang solo in *Messiah* –
With 'Comfort ye, my pee-eople' etcetera.
He saw a dark-haired mezzo in the choir,
And a few days after he'd properly met her a
Fleshly affection in them both took fire.
They kissed and colled in parks and fields and, better, a
Warm bed, her own. There's danger, I suppose,
In singing sacred oratorios.

Here name was Sybil (Delphic prophetess:
The etymology meant nothing to her).
She was the sort of girl whose comeliness
Lies less in shape than sensual allure.
There are such women, often drab in dress,
Who give out thermal signals. Pure, demure,
They show, even when singing in a choir,
The lineaments of gratified desire.

Her parents were, for two nights, out of town.
When she and John wrenched their glued parts apart
No admonitory hagiographs gloomed down
Of Holy Family or Sacred Heart
Done in the Dublin style, thick-coated brown,
The piety more potent than the art.
Strict C. of E., she found it fun to doubt
God's seeing eye. Besides, the light was out.

Her father was a partner in a company
That specialised in oranges. They made
A decent profit, and they used to dump any
Gone putrid on to factories that paid
Not by the gross but by the sodden lump. Any
Orangy rot will do for orangeade
Or marmalade. They shipped them from the Bosporus.
The old man was illiterate but prosperous.

He did not much object to John Byrne's wooing
His little Sybil, and his literate spouse
Guessed what her giggling girl and he were doing
In the back parlour. Yet true love allows
Something more solid than mere billing, cooing,
Cuddling and kissing, petulance and rows.
But stern Victoria at this time was regnant,
And it was awkward when a girl grew pregnant.

Still, Sybil's mother's folk came from Glamorgan,
Where pregnancy was an engagement ring.
Accordingly she did not play the Gorgon
When Sybil blurted out that very thing.
The wedding would be now, with flowers and organ,
The bride in lying white, and John could sing
After, if not quite during, his own wedding.
Then there could be decorum in their bedding.

12

The father yielded to the nuptial knot
As fathers, pushed by mothers, always do.
John's dolled-up sister, best-man brother (hot
From stoking) looked, his snivelling mother too,
Uncomfortably alien in what
Was, in their native Irish papist view,
A church that God Almighty scowled upon.
This was no marriage. But it was to John.

It was, as well, a genuine advancement,
For Sybil's father fixed him with a place
Among the oranges. This citrous chance meant
Another insult to the Irish race,
According to John's brother, an enhancement
Of Williamite schismatical disgrace.
He'd wrongly smashed the fruit into a symbol;
His sense of history would fill a thimble.

So orange-fragrant John came home each day
To a mortgaged house, exiguous but clean,
Out of the noisy town, near Crosby way.
Sybil served up the Liverpool cuisine
– Lobscowse with oranges for afters, say.
He sang, she sang, they both sang; in between
They pedalled joyfully the nuptial cycle
And soon their son appeared: they called him Michael.

So Michael Byrne, the figurative bastard,
Entered the world smugly legitimate.
His father's seed had prematurely mastered
The conjugation of the verb 'beget',
But now forgot it. In that prim and plastered
Nest out at Crosby Michael was sole pet,
A kind of cuckoo-ego unsurprised
That later eggs should be unfertilised.

The Crosby bells clashed in this century
While Michael howled at cutting his first tooth.
A clash between his true biography
And what he swore was the untarnished truth
Is soon resolved. He loved mendacity
Especially when spelling out his youth.
And though his heart was all too glibly crossable,
Some of his tales are proved to be impossible.

For instance, he alleged that he was seated
Not far from Arnold Schoenberg on the day
That *Pierrot Lunaire*'s screams were first excreted;
He lent his fists to the ensuing fray,
Flooring a *Polizist*, was badly treated,
Then kicked out of Vienna right away.
A lad of thirteen? Such a lie is manic
(This was the year that ice struck the *Titanic*).

And then, upon the twenty-ninth of May
In the year following, he burst a fist
At the Théâtre des Champs-Elysées
When those who cheered were cracked by those who hissed
And vice versa. That well-known mêlée
Was in *Le Sacre*'s cause. Byrne would insist
That he'd kissed Diaghilev, also Nijinsky
And (the rhyme's unavoidable) Stravinsky.

Clearly a passion for the sonic art
Was something that his father's voice bequeathed.
Above the rhythm of his mother's heart
The foetus heard it long before it breathed.
Erotic soarings of a tenor part
Would soothe his gummy twinges when he teethed.
But he was destined to be less than awed
By songs like 'Come into the garden, Maud'.

In nineteen-twelve and -thirteen he was merely
Taking piano lessons at his school
(Protestant, secular – the terms are nearly
Synonymous). Though known as the school fool,
He won high-pissing contests and was dearly
Attached to heating up his somewhat cool
Female coevals with a slap and tickle;
He jerked his gherkin too, apt for a 'pickle'.

His father sang the tenor solo (badly)
In Elgar's famed *Dream of Gerontius*.
His son was there to listen, not too gladly,
Moved, though, against his will, by all the fuss
Of a huge orchestra careering madly
Through a next world weirdly euphonious.
He loved the tuba, trumpets and trombones,
Which smote his very scrotum with their groans.

He gained a chance to slide and lip and spit
Himself when, still a boy, he joined a band.
The war was on. He was not part of it,
Merely a junior munitions hand,
A teaboy really. John Byrne did his bit,
Serving the king of his adopted land,
Meaning he joined the Roosters, sang, wenched, boozed,
And oiled a rifle that he never used.

The trombone's a descendant of the sackbut:
Its music, solemn, martial, crisply clear, is
Produced by sliding forward and then back, but
You have to lip out the harmonic series
In something like an oscular attack, but,
In a young boy like Byrne, the action wearies.
An adjunct of the adult life is missing:
One needs the muscular panache of kissing.

The Industrial Revolution, Britain's pride,
Began, as we all know, in Lancashire.
It had a strong demotic cultural side:
Lest counter-revolution start to rear
Its snarling head, a salve was pre-applied
Whose safe cathartic properties we hear
In choirs that belt out oratorios,
And factory bands. Byrne played in one of those.

He played outside it too. At seventeen,
He put a Catholic Bootle girl in pod,
And, to avoid the inevitable scene
Of outraged parents crying out to God,
He swiftly packed a toothbrush and some clean
Shirts and, of course, the horn with sliding rod
(Both symbols of his sexual bravado)
And fled, like Nanki-Poo in *The Mikado*.

His mother, when she found him gone, was stunned.
There was a visit from a police inspector:
He'd taken nearly all the picnic fund
Entrusted to him by the band's director.
She howled, she was not far from moribund;
The news could hardly otherwise affect her.
His father came home with the armistice,
But neither got much pleasure out of this.

The gods of art were spitting on their palms,
So one might fancy, ready to create
A small creator who, unblessed by qualms
About the teachings of the Church and State,
Regarded prayers and penitential psalms
And all that truck as a sheer opiate.
Oscar had said art was above morality
Till the State buggered him for his rascality.

16

But national ethics, or what passed for it,
Had dumped some millions in the Flanders loam.
They whom the bombs banged or the bullets bit
(Trombonists were among them) had left home
For good, and some left places in the pit
Of the once famous Ardwick Hippodrome.
Here Byrne, though an apprentice still, got paid
To melodise, fart bass-parts, and glissade.

It was all conjurors and dancing dogs,
And veteran sawers of a girl in half,
Arthritic troupes that clumped about in clogs,
Comedians who never raised a laugh
Except in sentimental monologues:
Nobody ever sought their autograph.
But a soprano, once of the Carl Rosa,
Enabled Byrne to bud as a composer.

A faker really. Guinness on the brain
Had made this ageing warbler grow forgetful:
She'd left her music on the Sunday train.
The Hippodrome conductor was regretful,
But singers always gave the band a pain.
The pianist, asked to improvise, was fretful.
Byrne said he'd hammer band-parts out if she
Would name her songs and also name the key.

He named his price, of course. He knew about
The double-stops on fiddle and on 'cello.
He'd read a book by Ebenezer Prout
And one by Higgs, both published by Novello,
And Stainer's *Harmony*. He had some doubt
About the pertinence of the old fellow,
Who said you could use that chord but not this chord.
The war had sanctified the use of discord.

He cobbled band-parts for 'The Holy City'
And Zionised the apocalyptic words
With little Jewish motifs, rather witty.
And for 'Down in the forest something stirred' 's
Banalities he introduced a pretty
Garland of rather Beethovenian birds.
The singer got the bird and he the blame:
She railed and roared but paid him just the same.

Public rebuke determined him to harden
An ego hard enough. He drank the cash.
The band played 'In a Monastery Garden'
And his trombone farted with dare and dash
The opening bars of 'Colonel Bogey'. 'Pardon,'
He belched, then passed out, falling with a crash
Into a drum, and drowned the solo flute.
That night he literally got the boot.

It was as well. His landlord's youngest daughter
Was two months late, she'd told him, with her menses.
The Bootle family was still breathing slaughter
(He wrote home, in abeyance of his senses,
Got that and, other, news). In short, he caught a
Vision of condign hell for his offences.
The thing to do when life seems all a-topple is
To run and hide oneself in the metropolis.

He played outside the London Underground
And found that coppers rather added up.
He paid his doss-house rent with a brown mound,
Ate saveloys, drank gin from a cracked cup,
And coughed a lot when wintertime came round.
The sad demeanour of a homeless pup
Along with a defective embouchure
Gave him, to lonely ladies, some allure.

18

A Lady Boxfox dragged him from the snow
And gave him welcome, warmth and wine and dinner,
The widow of an impresario
Who, when less prosperous and therefore thinner,
Patronised, without paying, Savile Row.
His suits exactly suited our young sinner,
Who showed his gratitude, or so he said,
By playing the trombone for her in bed.

There was a visit from a poor musician
Who taught in St Paul's School in Hammersmith.
His name was Holst. The German preposition
'Von' he had never been too happy with;
The war had forced him to its abolition.
Despite his Scandinavian kin and kith,
He was as English as Canute the king:
The English can make English anything.

Strange that the names of English-born composers
Should often sound (Delius, van Dieren) foreign:
Holst, Rubbra, Finzi, Elgar – names like those, as
Though the native stock skulked in a warren
Shivering at Calliope's bulldozers.
McCunn, true, rather overdid the sporran.
That Handel was staunch British to the end'll
Still be denied by Huns who call him Haendel.

Holst had composed *The Planets* some years back.
Byrne knew it, and he knew that the trombone
Had been Holst's instrument. There was a smack
Of fellow-feeling therefore in Byrne's own
Orchestral fantasy *The Zodiac* –
Twelve movements rising by a semitone
To come full circle. Byrne saw strange conflations
Between the key-ring and the constellations.

His lady took top-hatted Byrne to Goodwood.
Elgar was there, his sharp eyes on the course.
He couldn't help, but even if he could, would
It much avail? Music was a resource
Dumb to the English. Wait – Sir Henry Wood would
Air it perhaps. Look at that blasted horse,
Come nowhere, so much for the bloody favourite.
He groaned a groan but somehow seemed to savour it.

A baronetted masochist, thought Byrne,
Who'd slogged at art and fed his pearls to swine.
The English were determined not to learn
How to arrest their cultural decline.
Well, here's a David that will overturn
The assumptive glory of the Philistine.
Art, if it's pure, is hardly worth the candle.
They'll take it if it's seasoned well with scandal.

Wood, though reluctant, took *The Zodiac*,
And though the players found it fairly hard,
They tore it off with bulldoggish attack.
This was, of course, a summer Promenade.
The noise took the conservative aback,
But others cooed at it as avant-garde.
There are always intellectuals around
Who praise the incompetent as the profound.

Throughout the twenties, Byrne made little money
Out of an art deliberately dirtied
– *Absonderungstoffe* with a smear of honey.
His jazzed-up *Crucifixion* was asserted
To be foul blasphemy, and far from funny
Rabelais choruses that more than flirted
With the erotic and the lavatorial.
Would Mozart have liked this for his memorial?

Byrne found a theme in the *Decameron* –
The story of the devil put in hell –
And made a one-act opera. When put on,
In private though, it went down far from well.
The guests arrived, they gawped, and then were gone.
Not even postwar laxness could compel
Huxley, the Sitwells to find elevation
In naked howlers miming copulation.

And Lady Boxfox frowned her discontent.
She was not subsidising sweet sublimities;
Her protégé's pseudo-aesthetic bent
Was not for smooth silk or for flowered dimities.
She should have known the way his talent went
From his bed-prowess. Some men's sexual limit is
The pit. Its rage can find a counterpart
In how they mangle, tear, and rape their art.

And she was getting old, hence had suspicions
That Byrne clandestinely sought younger flesh.
For women, sense of smell, not intuition's,
The way to seek out perfidy, enmesh
The sinner in the guilt of his admissions.
She caught off bedward Byrne a whiff of fresh
Juice of arousal and cheap scented stuff.
The maid brought morning tea. She sniffed. Enough.

There was a screaming shouting snivelling trio,
With many a vigorous percussive burst
(Smashed vases, clanged Benares ware), a Cleo-
Patran storm alone for Byrne the curst,
Who cursed more loudly with Antonian brio.
He checked that he had pounds enough impursed,
Saleable silver. Baggage overflowing,
He slammed the door. He knew where he was going.

There were three sisters, not of Chekhov's breed,
Who lived in opulence off Berkeley Square,
All handsome girls, very well off indeed.
Their father, a dead Bradford millionaire,
Had left them everything but had decreed
The matrimonial act would strip them bare,
Ensuring that no idle wastrel would
Waste what he'd gained through sweat and bloody blood.

Bizarre condition! But they did not mind,
Since casual love sufficed. With Byrne's incursion
Into their household, they were pleased to find
One lover was enough, a rare perversion
Of patterns of the matriarchal kind.
Seraglios, whether Arab, Turk or Persian,
Are dreams of virile omnicompetence
Unratifiable by waking sense.

One of the sisters, Polly, painted prettily
And loved the ejaculative squelch of oil
In thick impasto that she'd learned in Italy.
Byrne left his hard compositorial toil
To wrestle with this craft, though rather grittily:
His vital function was, it seemed, to soil
(A twofold term implying health and tilth).
His paintings, in a double sense, were filth.

They chiefly showed the organs of coition,
Sometimes at rest, more frequently in action,
With hints of many a perverse position
Implying inadmissible infraction
Of copulatory laws. His exhibition,
Subvented by the girls, was an attraction
For amateurs of smut and not of painting.
The gallery was full of ladies fainting.

The London police, however, did not faint.
They clomped into the show in blue-clad torrents
And closed it down. In Parliament some quaint
Ruskinian terms expressed the State's abhorrence.
The same thing happened later to that saint
Of sexuality, the dying Lawrence.
Byrne felt the arrow of the martyrised.
He rather liked it, and he was surprised.

He did not like, though, in the local bars,
The nudge and leer of topers who suspected,
Except for more arcane particulars,
The nature of the life that he'd elected.
Aesthetic martyrs ought to kiss the stars,
Rejoice in being totally rejected,
And work away like disregarded beavers,
Unsubsidised by Harriet Shaw Weavers.

He left, but left behind a pregnant sister,
Granting to the triunal sisterhood
A task they realised should not be missed, a
Chance to do the maternal cause some good,
Anticipating later feminist a-
Ssertions that the male's sole function should
Be the provision of spermatozoa:
Show him that function, then show him the door.

The century had just passed thirty-one.
The Nazis, soon, would hog the floodlit stage.
But a more lasting movement had begun,
Possibly beneficial to the age.
Although the talking cinema has done
Great harm to the mimetic heritage,
In Chaplin's view, we must bow down to what
Progress decrees, whether we will or not.

23

Progress decreed Britain should join the rush
To fasten speech to faces on a screen.
The stories were a sentimental mush,
The ladies' accents genuine Roedean,
The gentlemen's a kind of thespian plush,
Unless a Cockney comicised the scene.
These British films were not well understood
By British ears attuned to Hollywood.

Byrne went to Elstree for an interview
And ended writing pseudo-music for
An Admiralty-subsidised *ragoût*
About the Navy's readiness for war,
With stiff-lipped skipper and a comic crew
Whose harmless booze- and punch-ups when ashore
Did not appear to lessen anyone's
Brisk readiness to rally to the guns.

With 'Rule Britannia' and the Sailor's Hornpipe
As *données*, all this frivolous sub-art meant
Sitting and dutifully grinding corn, pipe
In mouth and gin at hand in his apartment,
Often until the crack of queasy dawn (pipe
Of Tennysonian birds). And this new start meant
A new leaf, life, willingness to atone, a
Search for stability, a fresh persona.

He married Brenda Brown, who worked in make-up
– A cosmetician: God was not much more
(*Kosmetikos* from *kosmos*) – keen to take up
Domestic calm he once had thought a bore.
She was a decent girl who did not rake up
Harsh details of the life he'd lived before.
Happy in Morden, mortgaged, half-detached,
He fertilised her eggs. They duly hatched.

But during the long months of her gestation
He ground out music you can sometimes hear
In late-night films whose moral orientation
Speaks of a wholly alien biosphere –
Marriage without apparent copulation,
A Boy Scout code, social cohesion, mere
Euphemism, coiffured accents, desperate tedium,
Black versus white (appropriate to the medium).

Twins came while he wrote drone-stuff for some trash
About clan conflicts on the Scottish border,
A total failure, but it earned him cash.
And now three brothers with the surname Korda,
Who introduced Hungarian panache,
Preserved the industry from rank disorder
With quite a simple formula – i.e.
Make movies moviegoers want to see.

The Kordas were not insular – pelagic,
Thalassic rather in their visual vision.
They waved their Magyar wands, conjuring magic,
But were unwitting causes of perdition
To Michael Byrne. The technical term 'tragic'
Can be applied with absolute precision
When a man's inner but quiescent flaws
Are lashed alive by an external cause.

For Alexander Korda dreamed a drama
About the life of a tempetuous *diva* –
Tosca's *décolletage*, Brünnhilde's armour –
Whose voice attacked men's gonads like a cleaver,
The star to be a very *schöne Dame*
By name Maria Prauschnitz. She would weave a
Web to attract and finally enmesh
With diabolic pheromones of flesh.

25

She flew from Germany, gorgeous in furs
Against the fancied chill of late September.
There was one presence only – it was hers,
All fire, fire like the fifth night of November,
December Regent Street. As spring's scent stirs
The worm, she stirred the seed of every member
Of the small party Korda had convened
To meet her. Byrne reverted to the fiend.

She had survived abortions and miscarriages
As well as alcohol and drug excesses,
The ravages of four disastrous marriages
– Her fault – and yet with bright Teutonic tresses,
Teeth dog-clean, glorious body, there at Claridges
– The suite was one for shahs, sheikhs and princesses –
She shone, an icon of rich appetite,
A Nordic apple tempting men to bite.

But it was she who bit, bit till men bled.
She plucked, as from a male seraglio,
Byrne, to be borne unquestioning to bed,
There to be eaten with intensely slow
Rapacity till famine should be fed,
Then (*zum Befehl*) ordered to dress and go,
Discarded like a match or walnut shell,
The normal service of a good hotel.

She reckoned without Byrne. Byrne was a devil
Whose horns had been retracted for too long.
He bore her bodily to a deadly level
Where she was eaten, beaten like a gong,
Ox-roasted, in a blood-red reeking revel
Made to shriek sounds impossible to song
(He it was roared and crammed her opera house)
Except perhaps the *Salome* of Strauss.

She did not like the script that Korda proffered,
Scorned his associates as *Judenscheiss*,
Scoffed at the cash proposed to be uncoffered,
Naming a totally *unmöglich* price,
Wished to fly home on the next flight that offered,
Then, after alternating fire and ice,
With Korda in a most unwonted dither,
She limousined away. And Byrne was with her.

Aye, he is gone, seduced by his own glands
And a voluptuous Wagnerian vista.
Like the Commendatore's, see, her hand's
Immovably on his, a petrine fist, a
Faust. And he only partially understands
What life awaits beyond the German mist a
Speedy Lufthansa craft is butting into.
Think of the *Zukunft*? It would be a sin to.

Enshrouded, then, in a Teutonic mist
(*Mist* being dung in German), he's removed
From granting to a frank obituarist
The chance to list the actual and proved.
He's turned to matter for the fabulist,
A kind of Pan, hided, horned, haired and hooved,
Living with humanoids somewhat dissimilar,
Like Hitler, Goebbels, Goering, Hess and Himmler.

Maria Prauschnitz had a sumptuous dwelling
In Grünewald: it looked down on the lake.
Herr Rosenthal had needed little telling
To quit, rush the conveyance, also take
A sum absurd by the known rules of selling
And not to argue, for his comfort's sake.
The Nazis, at that time, did not abuse
The basic *Lebensrecht* of German Jews.

And, at that time, the swastika'd regime,
Compared with the Bolshevik cacotopia,
Had, to the world outside, a saner gleam,
Happier, healthier, even scented-soapier,
So Byrne's expatriation did not seem
A dubious one. The Führer's cornucopia
Of friendly undertakings, fruity, meaty,
Led to an Anglo-German Naval Treaty.

Yet Byrne could not forbear at times to wonder
Why State and Party should be unified:
The horseman in the saddle, the horse under
Were not a centaur. When he ceased to ride,
The horse would still be there. This was a blunder,
And when he made it conversation died
At gaudy parties where the Party boozed.
Joe Goebbels heard him and was not amused.

Shown Jewish blood beneath a microscope
And Aryan ditto on a neighbour slide,
Byrne said his mentors didn't have a hope
Of driving home a haemal Great Divide.
You had to drug yourself with Nazi dope
To see what seeing, damn it all, denied.
They're both the bloody same. The mentors hissed
And sent him to a Nazi oculist.

And Byrne refused to see how Jewish science
Could differ from the pure blue-eyed variety.
He argued: The enquirer puts reliance
On observation, not on racial piety.
Take Einstein, with his rational defiance
Of Newton and the whole damned Royal Society.
How the hell has his Jewishness impaired
The formula $E = Mc^2$?

Of course, his German was a sad affair,
Although he had an all too living lexis
In bed beside him, in beds everywhere.
But, as we know, the *Wörterbuch* of sex is
With absolute appropriateness stripped bare
Of such Hegelian wool as still perplexes
Students of philosophic German patter.
Gestapo cellars are a different matter.

Maria sang in *Carmen* and *Aïda*,
Die Meistersinger, *Tosca*, *La Bohème*,
And, to make merry her beloved Leader,
The Merry Widow. Everywhere her tame
Wild incubus the burning Byrne would feed her
Love (*love?*) unstained by shyness or by shame
And limitless in its varieties.
Her inexhaustibility matched his.

But he was much more than a sex machine.
His mistress, vamping Goebbels, soon secured him
The chance to write some music, crisp and clean,
To satisfy the guardians of the pure dim-
Witted doctrine of the foul obscene
Semitic threat. Mendelssohn, they assured him,
Dirtied Puck, Oberon and Bottom too
With all the black excretions of the Jew.

So, for the showing of *A Midsummer
Night's Dream*, Byrne wrote what was considered Aryan.
Carl Orff, who sniffed disdain at this newcomer,
Told Goebbels that the man was a barbarian
Who jointed notes like an unhandy plumber.
So he replaced him. In his unitarian
Heaven the happy Felix heard a lack
Of talent. Never mind. He'd soon be back.

Carl Orff's the sole survivor of the Nazis'
Conception of an Aryan aesthetic.
As soon as *Carmina Burana* starts, he's
Heard to be a phthisical diabetic;
Rich only in Teutonic grunts and farts, he's
Confounded the intoxicant and emetic.
And yet the ingenuous cherish every note
Instead of wishing that they'd cut his throat.

Byrne shrugged. He started writing a bravura
Opera based on Cleopatra's death,
Exploiting all Maria's *tessitura*,
With a high F before her final breath.
His hand had never, so he thought, been surer
In this her birthday (was it fortieth?
Fiftieth?) *Gift*, no, *Gabe* – was that right?
Yes. *Gift* meant poison, figuratively spite.

There was as yet no spite and little poison
In this, their sexo-musical ménage.
Byrne liked the German life, all brutal joys, an
Alpdrücken in a sensual camouflage.
Maria sometimes played with SS boys, an
Expected swelling of her entourage.
A goddess is, by nature, half a whore,
And Byrne required some semen for his score.

A heavy task, but there was light relief
In the Germanic ambience, boisterous, brash,
Torchlit parades and pogroms, guttural grief
In emigration queues, the smash and crash
Of pawnshop windows by insentient beef
In uniform, the gush of beer, the splash
Of schnapps, the joy of being drunk and Aryan,
Though Hitler was a teetotalitarian.

And Goering's weekends were a pagan riot,
With tough boar that his hunting parties shot.
Eviscerated stags reeked in a pie at
Which gormandisers gaped then scoffed the lot.
The Marshal's grossness publicised his diet,
But he was *künsterlich* as well. He'd got
Into his ringy paws a tawdry hoard
Of loot so vast the visitor grew bored.

Byrne was a foreigner, but it was felt
He was an adjunct to the Master Race.
His blood was right: he was a Saxo-Celt.
His voice proclaimed, an unambiguous bass,
The known resources just below his belt.
His German grammar was a foul disgrace,
But Byrne had his excusers and defenders:
Even the Führer could be weak on genders.

Moreover, England being called *Das Land
Ohne Musik*, Byrne was a kind of freak,
A singing starling or pink elephant,
An anglophone composer, quite unique.
Maria praised him as a *Musikant*,
Admitting, though, his counterpoint was weak.
Carl Orff assumed that Byrne would come a cropper, a
Jew who presumed to write a German opera.

Goebbels, in fact, had dug out the libretto
From dusty long-discarded juvenilia.
His cobwebbed attic was a kind of ghetto
To which, with an admitted necrophilia,
He stole to read, confirm and not regret. *O
Qualis artifex?* No. Too long familiar
With failed aesthetic power, he found it grander
To be the Minister of Propaganda.

31

His Führer's talent too was even littler
Than his. What if the aspiring architect
Had grown to be Herr Doktor Adolf Hitler,
An urbifactor, earning world respect
For soaring towers? No, nothing could be brittler
Than Adolf's dreams of what he would erect
– Sufficient for the whole Wehrmacht to enter –
Out there, the universal Civic Centre.

The poet as acknowledged legislator,
The trumpet also, singing men to battle,
Would soon shoot Shelley as a bloody traitor
And butcher other democrats like cattle.
The poet sees himself as a dictator,
But the dictator as a poet. That'll
Suffice, I think, for those who'd love to mix
Aesthetics with pragmatic politics.

The opus had its première in Berlin.
The Egyptian queen, a Jewish stereotype,
Seduced the Aryan Antony, and in
Her toils of grace, or her disgraceful gripe,
He sank into a slough of ethnic sin.
Maria was a wonder, rotten-ripe,
Capricious, sensual, serpentine or shrewish.
Her rivals swore that she was really Jewish.

The black-clad Roman chorus bore the swastika
On the triumphal banners they held high.
Antony perished by the traitor's law – stick a
Cyanide tablet in your mouth and die.
Egypt's destruction was near-holocaustic, a
Hint of what would be coming by and by.
The music pleased (it was not *nouvelle vague*)
Even the Führer, sparing time from Prague.

After this operatic consummation,
The already long liaison could not last.
Her enemies found sound documentation
Of Jewish ancestry. Agape, aghast,
She sought, in Himmler's high administration,
A uniformed protector, in whose past
Disreputable atoms lurked she knew about
But the hierarchy didn't have a clue about.

Byrne was alone, then, in a foreign city –
No, *he* was foreign, an exotic soul, and
Sat on the Ku-Damm with a cup of gritty
Cold coffee and an ersatz sausage roll and
Felt the authentic budding of self-pity.
That was the day Hitler invaded Poland.
He'd not been following the daily *Zeitung*.
He heard the news with wide eyes and a dry tongue.

A young man in the British Consulate
Informed him there was going to be a war
And he, though a long-term expatriate,
Could not expect to stay there any more.
Gather your goods and passport, do not wait,
Take train and ship to England. But what for?
Byrne wondered. 'England's rather more exotic
Than Germany, and – am I patriotic?

'No, I'm a son of Erin.' So he went
To Ireland's embassy to be assured
That strict neutrality was the intent
Of Ireland's government. Then he endured
A long wait for the Consulate's consent
To grant him a green passport. This secured,
He sat upon a bench inside the Zoo
And wondered what the hell he'd better do.

Now, from this point, like camels in the zoo,
We look upon a Byrne grown greyly distant.
He lived on Mühlenstrasse, Number 2,
But other vital facts soon grow resistant
To probings from embattled me and you.
Such talent as he had remained persistent
In wresting marks and pfennigs for a living.
History damns. Can we be more forgiving?

There was a Joyce (the ignorant said James)
Who quacked upon the Nazi radio,
Sneering at London going down in flames,
Spewing triumphalism, as we know.
'Regard,' said some, 'these two notorious names.'
(Mad Ezra's was the other.) 'Don't they show
That rampant modernism in the arts is
Soil for Fascisti, Falangists and Nazis?'

Now Byrne, the archives tell us, had the choice
Of spouting lies in his attractive brogue,
But he preferred a more impersonal voice,
Letting his flow of music disembogue
In major keys that seemed to cry, 'Rejoice.
Poland is crushed. And France. And soon that rogue
Elephant Britain and its Empire must
Tumble detusked and sobbing to the dust.'

The question is: Can music really speak?
Music is merely notes, all self-referring;
The articulative faculty is weak;
Music means rather less than a cat's purring.
The fact that E flat clarinets can squeak
Will hardly make them murine. So, in stirring
The listener's blood with crash and upper partial,
Is not a march a march, abstractly martial?

The situation grew more problematic
When German radio one night announced
A bass trombone concerto, acrobatic,
Scintillant, solemn. British listeners pounced
On Börn, composer, soloist. Emphatic
Newspaper leaders truculently trounced
Such treachery. 'We'll see the dastard swing.'
Meanwhile the BBC diffused *The Ring*.

There was no problem, no problem whatever
When Byrne or Börn took as a choral text
A passage from *Mein Kampf*. It was not clever,
Though some thought it ironic. It annexed
Motifs from Wagner in a coarse endeavour
To symbolise Teutonic muscles flexed
To kill the Jews, enslave the Slavs, and make
Six of the seas into a German lake.

His muse was silent after Stalingrad,
Save for some neutral children's *Weihnachtslieder*,
Settings of folksongs, neither good nor bad,
A funeral march for brass. The Allies freed a
Racked France whose anti-Dreyfusards had had
A hand in the *Letzte Lösung* but could plead a
Wretched enforced *devoir*, then crossed the Rhine.
Some looked for Byrne, but could not find the swine.

Byrne had, in fact, with little or no trouble,
Just taken refuge with the neutral Swiss –
Well, partly neutral. Always see a double
Aspect in disengagement such as this,
For even when the Ruhr was well-nigh rubble
Switzerland got its coal. The artifice
Of bleak indifference to the evil deed
Is justified by economic need.

And this explains, no doubt, the accommodation
The Swiss contrived with Nazi genocide.
The limit placed on Jewish immigration
Was, with a British Irishman, applied
When Joyce (for Joyce was Bloom) sought his salvation
In Zürich out of France fresh-occupied.
'The Jewish quota's full.' All Joyce could say
Was, so we're told, *'Enfin, c'est le bouquet'*.

Ethics and politics – ay, there's the rub.
Byrne, neutral Irish, could, as we have seen,
Live with the Nazis, in the very hub
Of infamy, morally not unclean
So long as he was silent. But the nub
Of his neutrality is seen to lean
On music's being dumb, hence undidactic –
A hypothetical defensive tactic.

Byrne got to Basle. A punished railroad system,
A purloined truck, abandoned, took him there.
A Germany in ruins hardly missed him,
So – *Sauve qui peut*. This was his own affair.
Though punitive invaders now would list him
A wanted man, Swiss bankers did not care.
He paid in gold in Zürich, quite a lot. It
Would have been rude to ask him where he'd got it.

We can see Byrne, smug with his Irish passport,
Sitting in cafés on the Bahnhofstrasse,
Puffing his Ormonds, sipping from his glass port,
Sherry, that gentian liqueur, seeing en masse a
Decent industrious race that could not grasp or t-
Est on the nerve-ends what had come to pass – a
Plunging of the real Europe into hell.
They'd had no history since William Tell.

No Alberich, though with his *Rheingold* banked,
He swived the insipid daughters of the Rhine
Or ladies of the lake, and then he cranked
The engine of a marital design.
He sought and found a *Witwe* – God be thanked,
Still young, Swissly attractive, on her vine
The grapes of what a billion-building zest
Had led to early cardiac arrest.

Reader, they married. After such collective
Villainy, what was bigamy to Byrne?
She did not trust him, but she scorned detective
Devices to dig up, unturn, and learn
The secrets of a soul perhaps defective
In Swiss morality. Still, Byrne would earn
His keep by, as the Swiss expression said,
Plying the fifth of five bare legs in bed.

A Northerner, she had the *Drang nach Süden*,
And so they set up house by Lake Lugano
To bask in Thyssen territory, Eden
With Adam Börn the snake, although there are no
Strong proofs of casual dalliance, indeed an
Impulse to sing *Là ci darem la mano*
To odd Zerlinas by Ticino's water
Only occurred when he had sired a daughter.

For, to give Byrne his due, he was a maker,
A natural father far more than a wencher.
Quite often the paternal urge will take a
Form that ignores the marital indenture.
Byrne was a bastardiser, not a rake, a
Creator, procreator. The adventure
Of art's not for the rubbered amorist.
Remember Byron, Balzac, Wagner, Liszt.

A minor artist with a two-stringed bow,
Byrne was encouraged by the southern light
To paint again, set up a studio,
Prime ample canvas and resume the fight
To show what no one really wished to know –
Sex, not in pornographic black and white,
But in bright hues – the rod's monstrosity,
The opposed pudenda and their rich pelosity.

Such paintings could not be exhibited,
For Trudi Börn spoke an emphatic *Nein*.
But one huge canvas, quite Guernican, did
Get private showing. Colour, contour, line
Crude but appropriate, it raised the lid
On the enactments of the Nazi swine,
Thickheadedness and thievery and thuggery
All symbolised in panoramic buggery.

After the *Corriere del Ticino*,
The *Corriere della Sera* ran
A brief report. Over her glass of vino,
Brenda, his true wife, visiting Milan,
Saw the name Michael Börn, brooded, could see no
Real reason why this should not be the man
Who'd left her nursing Timothy and Thomas
And forced her to a prosperous life of commerce.

By God, she would confront him at his villa,
Probably bigamist, certainly traitor
To her – to hell with country. Being no killer,
Merely a deadly cutthroat operator
In the cosmetic trade (name and sigilla
Would gain a certain fame a little later),
She'd merely break and bash, belt wounded cries out
And end by scratching (yes, by Christ) his eyes out.

And thus I would explain a gaping gap
In this, his brief but bestial biography.
He ran right off the European map
And learned a rather more outlandish geography.
He'd talent (recognisable) to tap,
But often changed his name with his topography.
Still, whether in Ashanti or Assam,
He's near-locatable: *Cherchez la femme*.

And, while you're at it, *cherchez l'art* also,
If you can call it that. For Byrneish trickles
Came out, with static, from the radio
In regions where mosquitoes bite, heat prickles,
Humidity is high and spirits low,
Concupiscence sporadically tickles,
And white men go to pieces, as we've seen
In overlauded trash by Graham Greene.

Byrne fled, it seems, in the late nineteen-fifties.
I visited Brazil in the mid-sixties
And in a Rio bar one day I sniffed his
Departed presence. For he had affixed his
Daubs to the wall in payment, no mere gift. His
Other bestowals toddled, for he'd mixed his
Blood with the octoroon proprietress's –
The swarthy blue-eyed fruits of his caresses.

I interviewed the Sultan of Brunei,
The richest magnate in the universe,
And heard that a Tuan Byrne had once been by
Running up debts and fighting drunk and, worse,
Smashing a certain *tungku* in the eye
And impregnating an *istana* nurse.
He left an anthem that was sometimes played
When the whole sultanate was on parade.

And in Chicago, in a low bordello,
I spied a dirty painting on the wall
Which mocked the sexual prowess of Saul Bellow
In detail which I don't care to recall,
A daub in mustard, chicken fat and Jell-O.
Libelling major artists, after all,
Portrays, betrays the doer, not the done to.
There was no calumny Byrne wouldn't run to.

This minor artist could be truly nasty
When sneering, leering at the real creators.
Knighthoods for services to pederasty
And CBEs to verbal masturbators
Were, naming names, among the slights he passed. He
Averred that earldoms only went to traitors.
A painted child of dirt, he stank and stung,
Daubing with digits dipped in his own dung.

You should by now be mildly interested
In me, who wear the obituarial robe.
Clearly no poet, all I ever did
In wordcraft was to prick and pry and probe
As an inferior pressman, salaried
To race for scandal round the spinning globe.
Byrne was good garbage for my garbage bin,
But usually got out when I got in.

Why choose this agony of versifying
Instead of tapping journalistic prose?
Call it a tribute to a craft that'd dying,
Call it a harmless hobby. Art, God knows,
Doesn't come into it. Poets, high flying,
Don't need these plodding feet with blistered toes,
Old-fashioned rhymes, prosodic artifice
Essential to an effect such as this.

Remember how I told you at the start
That Byrne himself commissioned me to fashion
A verse obituary. His own sub-art
Called for sub-art, not bardic skill and passion –
Base to the base, low low. A subdued heart
Beat with a carnal lust he'd learned to ration,
A late attempt to mortify the flesh.
I met him in a bar in Marrakesh.

What year was that? He didn't seem too old,
Tired rather. After a pink gin or three,
Fragmentarily, haltingly he told
Some of his tale. I wondered: why to me?
Two Berber lads with skins of tarnished gold
Came in. His sons. No, not sons. I could see
A change of sexual tropism. 'My boys.
I prefer women, but these make less noise.'

Where had he been? In India and Malaysia,
Contracting casual marriage. In Japan,
Like Pinkerton, he shacked up with a geisha,
After a Shinto ceremony, ran
Bangkok *kedùnkadìng*. All South-East Asia
Gained a lopsided view of Western Man
From Byrne, who relished his exotic cup
And wrote some music, though he tore it up.

Bull-charger, also silent-footed stepper,
Like Gauguin, he'd left paintings in Tahiti,
But not been made a syphilitic leper,
Placed his impress, all Celtic, boggy, peaty,
On girls' hibiscus, ginger and red pepper,
Quite unpolluted by a marriage treaty.
Marriage? A bed where two put twenty toes in.
Why should the church- or lawman stick his nose in?

I mentioned treason, but he merely shrugged,
Said something about signs, then dourly drank.
I didn't understand. The drunk, the drugged,
The overtly sodomistic sweated, stank.
The historic as the real – it beckoned, tugged,
Then shrugged like Byrne. Its fingers shrank and sank
Into the beer-slop. History is not tactual.
The factual is different from the actual.

Then 'Africa' he said. 'That's where we are,'
I said, sensing that was not what he meant.
He did not mean a mean Moroccan bar
Pitched on the bright edge of that continent.
A mirror of the Côte d'Azur was far
From what he meant. And far from where he went,
Yearning for mastication from the mouth
That chomped the jungle half-way to the south.

Chad, Mali, Côte d'Ivoire – where did he go?
A younger son bore documented proof
That Byrne had sired him in the place we know
As Happy Valley, under a red roof
Of Kenya. In his accent there would glow
Aristocratic gilt – a lilt, aloof,
Learned from his mother, who had walked with kings
But died of drink and drugs and other things.

One truth we know: two artefacts emerged
Ex Africa. Buffalo hides were sewn
To mock a canvas, and some impulse urged
The manic Byrne, with feathers, hairs and bone
And stone-ground paints, to craft a scene that surged
Junglelike, tenebrose, screeching. It was shown
In Cape Town but was soon incinerated.
It stated what had better not be stated.

The other work was musical, a setting
Of passages he'd taken from *The Heart*
Of Darkness, Mistah Kurtz's death begetting
A nightmare vision very far from art,
Since sounds should not be bistouris for letting
Black blood and ripping bones and veins apart.
Brian, his son, said that the opus swarmed
With screams and howls and could not be performed.

I leave his story here. *Assez. Es ist*
Genug. Basta. I think that Byrne is dead.
None left alive are going to insist
On heaping obloquy upon his head
– Failed artist but successful bigamist,
Thief, fornicator, traitor. I have said
Enough. I'll need a little time to find
Details of those poor sods he left behind.

Why did I do this? Further subsidies
Never arrived, but cash was not my aim.
A bastard, in no metaphor (that's his
Chief attribute), I spoke my mother's name.
He leered and said, 'My own paternity's
A possibility. I'll take the blame.
Be generous in your turn, do what I ask.
Think of a filial not venal task.'

The fascination of the reprehensible
Is my true driving force – was, I should say.
There's no defending of the indefensible,
No armature to strengthen feet of clay.
Wretches like Byrne are far from indispensable,
A single puff will blow their dust away.
Paronomasia is a needless joke:
He needs no fire to turn him into smoke.

TWO

I'm bedded down, it seems, in this hard stanza;
I cannot rise and rinse myself in prose.
Once, in an army cookhouse, with the pans a-
Wash in spuds I'd peeled, the thought arose
That I was a mere adjunct. (See, that man's a
Spud-peeling fist, no more.) So I suppose
I'm now an iron pen penning the ironical
Filial sequel: Father Byrne, his chronicle.

The technique should be much more novelistic,
Occasionally even microscopic,
Hairs and moles noted, if my masochistic
Adherence to this form allows – myopic
Close peering, and close listening to linguistic
Tropes in the thrall of an ephemeral topic –
What Booker fiction gives you every time,
Though never iron-corseted in rhyme.

My hero's a genetic violation
Of all his father stood for. He's a twin
Whose twin we'll meet some pages hence. His station,
The sacerdotal one, abhors all sin,
While Byrne the father made it his vocation.
He has small vices – cheap cigars and gin,
Whether of London, Cork, Bombay or Plymouth. He
Was christened, as you may remember, Timothy.

47

November thirtieth, feast of St Andrew.
He limped from Green Park tube. The air was tepid.
Unseasonable warmth possessed the land. Rheu-
Matically wincing but intrepid
He made for Curzon Street. His bare right hand drew
A hanky out, to wipe. Westward, a lepid-
Opterous sky, filigree, polychrome,
Called secretaries, sparrows, salesmen home.

The icecaps were fast melting, were they not?
The poles were yellowed with a filthy shroud.
Dirty the London sunset too, but what
Sumptuousness. The sackbuts cried aloud
In pageant, gaudy fabrics all aspot
With grease insoluble. An age endowed
With the dry cleaner's blessing made mad sport
With a crepuscular mock-Tudor court.

His left foot winced. The hallux nail, ill-cut,
Assailed the neighbour toe with a shrewd nip.
Did that toe have a name? He thought not, but
Knew his nine fingers had. Five gripped his grip
(Sensible term, American). His gut
Tensed as he passed a glottal fellowship
Of earringed louts shaved bald, swastika-belted.
Ice stood for order. Order too had melted.

He was not yet one of the feeble old
On whom bagsnatchers preyed. But, fifty-five,
Five feet six inches short, greyish, rolled-gold-
Framed-spectacled, an inner self alive
Enough, the fleshly shell though dull and cold
Without the ictus needed to survive.
Even if he'd dressed clerical, not laic,
He knew dog collars weren't apotropaic.

48

Whether that dress, vestments, collar reversed,
Was now to be legitimately his
He could not say – a thing to be rehearsed
In the long vigil of festivities
Named Advent, now beginning. If I'm cursed
Or blessed with death of faith, he thought, that is
A firm imperious signal that I must
Take better care of my decaying crust.

He reached his Mayfair target unmolested.
A hill of plastic bags proclaimed a strike.
His numb left foot disturbed a rat that nested
Inside a soup can. Someone's pedal bike
Distorted to surrealism rested
On old wet *Sun*s. With rictus of dislike,
Detaching shoe from shit, he danced it clean,
Then rang the bell of Number 17.

With his left thumb he pressed again that bell,
Born with no left ring finger, therefore slightly
Deformed, deficient. When his calling fell
Upon him like an enemy, quite rightly
The bishop had his doubts. He said: 'Well, well,
Nine fingers, nine, sufficient but unsightly.
Hands meant for handling the heavenly host
Should be equipped with ten of them at most.'

Priestly recruits, like those to the SS,
Should glow and grow in physical perfection.
Why, since perfection granted an excess
Of most unpriestly urges? The election
Of holy eunuchs should receive a yes
From the Lord God, who scorned the male erection
When, with his logos blueprint, he decreed
Insemination with no need for seed.

49

Dorothy came. He sketched the joky blessing
She much preferred to a half-brother's buccal
Kiss. The hall light-bulb had a most depressing
Low wattage. Mould and stalish honeysuckle –
The sempiternal smell. A more caressing
Odour – vanilla seemed somehow to truckle
To stern black chocolate she was always chewing
Through days and nights of ardent televiewing.

Her ragged crimson velvet viewing chair
Sat too close to the screen. That patient ray
Bit to the bone, they said. One of a pair
Whose twin held videocassettes – here TDK,
BASF, Fuji, Quasar, and there
Slept Sony, Maxell, Kodak. Briskly they
Were swiped by her to join those on the floor,
And on the mantelpiece were many more.

'Bibliomorphs,' he said, when seated. 'You
Need shelves and shelves and shelves and shelves.' But she:
'The cataloguing's slow, and labelling too.
Yukari helps.' 'Where is Yukari?' 'Tea,
She's making tea. You're late.' 'That's all too true,
The train was late. A long delay, you see,
Near Watford Junction. Their delay, not mine.
Something or somebody thrown on the line.'

Five of the eight bulbs of the electrolier
Were dead, one flickered. She seemed not to mind,
For all the light she ever needed here
Came from the TV screen, at present blind.
'And how is Manchester?' 'I rather fear
The Holy Name is going to be assigned
To mosquedom. The multiple muezzin's call
Reigns in a town where there's no rain at all.'

He peered at Dorothy in the dim light.
Celibate like himself, though for a lack
Of what was termed libido. Sixty. Sight
Focused on worlds within. Hair dyed bold black.
A demure dinner dress that once was bright
Near-orange, frills of dirty lace. A slack
Sack bosom, ample though, from which depended
Smeared spectacles whose legs had been ill-mended.

Rattling approached. Yukari, dressed in shorts
And FUCK YOU T-shirt, bore a kind of tray
Equipped with two unfolding short supports.
Tim felt relief: tea in the British way,
A big brown pot, a milk jug, cakes of sorts –
Ricecakes. She munched a raw fish canapé.
'Ikaga des' ka?' Western-eyed, she eyed
And munched and 'Always very good' replied.

A jasmine odour reeked from the weak tea.
Dorothy took one sip, then a cassette.
'This came as a surprise, this you must see,
Hear rather,' and with ghastly deftness let
A boisterous teenage nonsense scream its glee,
Soon quelled. Then static danced a minuet.
A cinematic logogram came on:
Eros-Film, with a firing cupidon.

When Foes Are Friends. This was the spotty title,
The music nautical and shrill and rough.
The credits came, a names-unknown recital
With Michael Byrne, composer. 'That's enough.
A tolerant world. A posthumous requital,'
He said. She said: 'It's early morning stuff,
Meant, I suppose, for empty-headed laughter.
Harmless. It's not the harmless that I'm after.

51

'I want iniquity.' Tim said: 'I know.'
'Law fish?' 'You know I hate it.' 'Nagasaki.
You there once.' 'Nagasaki. Even so,
I hate it.' 'Hiroshima too. The black i-
Niquity,' said Dorothy. 'A foul show
Of sin. The boot in. Racial hatred. Paki-
Bashing is in the dictionary. Rape
And torture. The whole world's in rotten shape.'

'More tea?' Yukari offered. 'Pardon me,
Deeply regret, and do not mean offence,
But as to tea not much strength.' 'Ah. Strong tea
Not good thing. Like that thing. You got no sense.'
Stink of his cheap cigar assailed. And he,
Inhaling deeply, said: 'You're right, and hence-
Forth I must watch my body, must I not?'
She nodded, chewing. 'Only one you got.'

'Are you still going to your English classes?'
'Big time waste. Evening work at Mr Wu,
It Chinese restaurant. Serve drink, wash glasses.
Is run by Japanese.' Probably true,
The time waste. 'I go light the boiler gas. Is
Bath time.' She left with table. How she drew
Him back – the Nippon mission, flowering cherry, money
Scant, a much more leisurely tea ceremony.

Dorothy said, with sudden urgent fire,
'This is important. Proof of immortality.
Don't smoke.' He went on smoking. 'You require
Reverence. I see.' 'I'm reporting actuality.
Joan Etheridge. Her heart stopped. Someone by her
Recalled her to the state they call reality.
Dead for the one split second, but was hurled
Into the world I call the real world.'

'Do tell me more. But not much more,' inhaling.
'She said,' she said, 'it wasn't like a dream.
A great grey hall, a counter with a railing,
Giggling girls. And there was a long stream
Of people moving, a loud hailer hailing.
You joined one team or else another team.
A screaming infant had to leave its mother.
It went in by one door and she another.'

'Just the two doors? No purgatory, limbo?
'Don't scoff. They beckoned her, but then she came
Back to this world.' Dorothy, arms akimbo,
Stood glowering. 'What do you want then – smoke and flame,
Angels with harps? *Maria e il suo bimbo?*
(They don't use that word right here. It's the name
They give the infant Jesus,' she said brittly.
'I ought to know. I spent a month in Italy.')

'Religion deals in faith,' he said, 'not proof.
And if my faith goes, this kind of banality – '
'That's the whole point,' she said. 'Rain through the roof.
Spit, rubbish. Bureaucrats' inhospitality,
Fag-ends on which some oaf had stamped his hoof,
A summing up of daily factuality.
Then immortality.' 'I'm tired,' he said.
'Wrap up your rhymes. I'll lie down on the bed.'

'Wait,' she said sternly. 'Have you made your mind up?'
'I have the whole of Advent to decide in,
But my last sermon was a sort of wind-up.
The Ultimate we usually divide in-
To the eternal three. But we may find we're lined up
To face eternal nothingness to hide in.
So we must worship zero – faith, no hope.
That negativity won't please the Pope.

'I'll live by begging you for the odd hand-out.
I won't. I'm joking. You need every cent
For videocassettes. I have a plan (doubt
Occluded, faith a lie) to pay the rent:
Working on holy TV scripts. Demand out-
Weighs supply, I think. That series went
Down rather well. It had a Spanish backer.
St Francis Xavier's thumbscrews in Malacca.

'I look to Robert Southwell for my bread.'
'Him I don't think I know.' 'I'm not surprised,
There's no cassette about him. Southwell bled
And screamed from frightful instruments devised
For Tudor Jesuits. When almost dead
From hanging, with his balls and guts excised,
He saw his heart. I rather feel for him.
He grants an aromatic pseudonym.

'He was a poet too. Perhaps you know
"The Burning Babe".' 'Horrors are no new thing.'
'This was a holy metaphor, to show
Christ as an infant but incendiary king.
Anyway, Robert Southwell has to go
Tomorrow for some gentle bargaining
With two Americans, who'll hear my line
On a filmed life of Calvin, the foul swine.

'What they propose could, I suppose, come under
The heading of a moral entertainment,
Like what, thanks to this electronic wonder,
You try to justify the world's arraignment
At Nobodaddy's court with – daily plunder
Of sempiternal horrors. Human pain meant
But little in the Gulf War's visual grammar, a
Big feast of death to feed the cinecamera.'

54

She said: 'It's horror, horror all around.
Pornography, locked in this cupboard here.
I wouldn't want that garbage to be found
By young Yukari.' He said: 'Have no fear.
The nerves of Nippon are all overwound
With overwork. Pornography's a mere
Device to them to get their nerves unlocked.
Yukari, I assure you, won't be shocked.'

'The point is this,' she finally confided.
'There has to be eternal chastisement.
That means eternal life.' 'A bit one-sided,
All stick, no sugar. Listen, we're all sent
To one big bedroom, Hitler undivided
From John the Twenty-Third, the innocent
And guilty, raped and rapist, with no cup
Of tea or orange juice to wake us up.'

He climbed the stairs to rest. Her television,
At rest too long, excreted into rock
That sounded like a motorway collision,
And then some politician's poppycock
And counter-cock pop-popping with derision.
They had to leave the house at seven o'clock
To see a show composed by their half-brother
And then to hear from him something or other.

Two frames were on the landing: Bradford bully
Bloody well bursting with his bloody brass;
Then the three daughters, features somewhat woolly,
Gazing with awe at daisies in a glass,
Painted by Polly, who had far from fully
Mistressed the killing craft, but let that pass:
A dull memorial to three unmade maids
Blown up in Florence by the Red Brigades.

Dorothy saw them as a triune mother.
They'd been unable to legitimise her,
But their joint legacy was a sort of smother
Of hungry love. She should have had a wiser
Load of investments, for some voice or other
From the next world had tried to pauperise her.
Still, though debarred from jewels, Jags and jets,
She'd not need to recycle her cassettes.

He found his room. The linen was unchanged
From his last visit, fifteen months ago.
There was that dried emission. One thing strange d-
Eclared her new obsession: a brief row
Of video recordings was arranged,
A kind of breakfast menu, as to show
A choice of Afghan rapes and Kurdish sorrow
To guarantee dyspepsia tomorrow.

He doffed his shirt and took his shaving gear
Into the bathroom. Steam. Yukari, clean,
Soon to be cleaner, lay in the water. 'Here.'
Western-eyed, illubricious. 'What this mean?'
He wore no spectacles and had to peer
Into the blaring porno magazine.
She read and frowned, raising a little ripple.
He had to bring his sight to her right nipple.

'It says that man is being pedicated.
The picture shows it, no need for a text.
You understand?' Unshaky hands gyrated
The razor handle, fixed a new blade; next
He aerosoled his cheeks with cream and grated
His tough beard off, embarrassed, somewhat vexed.
A priest should be impervious to shocks:
A bathtub was a wet confession box.

The Japanese saw aqueous immersion
As purely social, with all sex expunged.
Still, as the girl dripped out, a strong incursion
Of male resentment grew erect and lunged,
Her pedicable arse a wagged assertion
That he was neuter furniture. He plunged
Nine fingers in to splash his face and swore.
'True, I'm a priest, but also less, or more.'

Yield to response, pursue her dripping bareness?
Would she object? But that neat body seemed
Forbidden territory. Vague awareness
Of something in those Western eyes unsteamed
His lustful own. So like his own. In fairness
He must discount that, since the whole world gleamed,
Was hirsute with, was odorous of fair women,
A beckoning bare bath for him to swim in.

Yet, on the concourse of Grand Central Station,
You could meet someone met in Hyderabad
Twenty years back. Promiscuous copulation
Sowed perilous seeds. True, he had always had
A sense, by virtue of his ordination,
That women were his daughters, sisters. Mad
Semantics. Think: Greek incest had been banned,
They argued, to let family land expand.

Yukari had responded to an ad
Of Dorothy's, two years ago: 'Assistant,
Light duties, evenings free.' She said she had
A Western father, fled to somewhere distant.
Student of English, yes, but very glad
To stop, too dull. Probably unresistant
To proffered mistressships, but tired of these:
Why come to London to please Japanese?

Japan had won the war. The rising yen
Shone like an alien sun in sunless England,
With surplus yen exporters, bowing men
In hotel suites, condemned to travel single and
Happy to contact native flesh again.
There is a point where cultures will not mingle and
Bare bodies built on beer, beef, chops and cheese
Nip the concupiscence of Nipponese.

He smeared some aftershave called *Mansex* on,
Nudging his way into the secular scene.
Her high heels clacked, a door slammed. She had gone
Off to help serve the Cantonese cuisine
As rendered by the Empire of Nippon.
Still, the same ideograms spelt out Chow Mein.
(He sat to clip his toenails, brown and brittle,
Dressed in his vest and pants, panting a little.)

He mused on history and responsibility.
Did it have some to us, or we to it?
Whose history? There was a crass futility
In the big abstract monster, composite
Of unrecorded lives, with glib facility
Moulded by swine like Hegel to make fit
Doctrines of an emergent superhuman
Ultimate shining but tyrannic numen.

History as race. His Irishry was myth,
Although his English mother used to rail
Especially when first confronted with
His statement that he'd found the Holy Grail
In Papistry. That Irish kin and kith
Had got at him, she'd rail and even wail.
'That,' he would say, 'dear mother, is half-witted:
No culture is genetically transmitted.'

His twin, at the same school, in the same form,
Had known no like flush of the soul's awaking,
A language boy. Her language had grown warm
When he learned German. They knew why. The braking
Of her vituperative engine, the stilled storm
Of prejudice had much to do with making
Her products' name in Europe. Foreign commerce
Told her that they spoke foreign, just like Thomas.

He, Timothy, had studied at Maynooth,
Appalled at first – bog Irish ignorance,
And chauvinist perversions of God's truth.
He showed himself half-Irish in a sense,
Though hearing Irish phonemes as uncouth.
He modified his speech inheritance
(Pure Thames, or impure) to a diction fit
For a Britannic high-class Jesuit.

He now was nothing. Mother sometimes spoke
Of hating God, an allomorph of Byrne.
This ought to please her shade. Off with faith's yoke,
But she'd cast off all motherly concern,
Nursing her ailments among foreign folk,
Those of Antibes. Her flat, she let them learn,
Was on the rue Pasteur, where too a sort of
Catholic pen had scrawled, rather well thought of.

Really, he thought, he'd none to hurt or please. He
Was not betraying middle-aged parishioners
Who brought their secular sorrows, for the breezy
Brotherly Father Benlowe's cheery mission, as
Most had made clear, had rendered calm and easy
The shepherd–sheep relation. In addition, as
He'd dropped all doctrine, sin got not a mention,:
And God himself was trundled off, on pension.

History, then. He was not opting out of it.
He aimed to earn his living from demotic
Dramatic travesties thereof, no doubt of it.
St Stephen's martyrdom and crude erotic
Grapplings could share a soundtrack, just about. Of it,
The craft, he thought: I'll bow to a despotic
Technology indifferent to narrative,
Its visual values absolute, not comparative.

He put his shirt on. Carelessly he knotted
His only tie, one he had bought in Dublin
In '82, centennially allotted
To James Joyce junketings that caused some trouble in
Circles that said Joyce had defiled the unspotted
Image of Erin. Whorled Brancusi bubble in
A green pea soup, meant to be Joyce's soul
Or, not dissimilar, a cold ham roll.

He went downstairs, where Dorothy said, 'Look.'
He sat, he saw. The TV cameras panned
On Pakistanis and a burning book.
Not new news. Yes, it was. 'It must be banned,'
A Bradford Muslim leader yelled. He shook
An English Dante. 'Both the Prophet and
His son-in-law have blasphemously been
Traduced. This is heretical and obscene.'

'But,' said the Chief Librarian of the city,
'Alighieri died in 1321.
No pressure brought upon our Watch Committee
Can force a mere sectarian writ to run.
He's an established classic. It's a pity
Mohammed is in hell, but what's been done
Can't be etcetera. Liberalise yourselves,
You Muslims. Dante stays upon our shelves.'

'Stay is the word,' said Timothy. 'And shelf,
If that.' Disquiet struck him, somewhat dim
But definite, for Thomas, not himself –
He wondered why. Dorothy poured for him,
Also for her, some Claymore, from a well-f-
Illed cupboard. Airport double malt. 'Here, Tim.'
'*Sláinte*. What do we drink to?' She was lost in
An instant's thought, and then she said: 'Jane Austen.'

She? Dorothy was totally without
Book-learning. Potted drama on TV?
Idealised unviolence? How about
Old Boney? Admiral Austen. War at sea.
The Grand Porte. Captive Christians shelling out,
Delaying forced conversion. Let it be
Indefinitely delayed. The hypocrite.
Christians and Muslims did not change a bit.

With blind skill she arranged a fresh recording,
(A red clock span, lights darted like a gecko)
Thus fixing, *in absentia*, some rewarding
Survey of dying rain forests, a dekko
At child abuse for afters. All this hoarding
Of pain (he drained his dram). Umberto Eco
Had artefact speaking to artefact,
Cold epilogues to follow man's last act.

'We go?' 'We go.' It was not hard to get
A taxicab in Mayfair. As they drove,
They saw, though Advent hadn't started yet,
A London glistening like a golden grove,
Even in streets where signs proclaimed TO LET,
The town all Danaë to coruscant Jove,
Excited crowds, like waiting for a war.
The driver merely ground his gears and swore.

Dorothy paid, and Timothy could see at a
Distance that her tip displeased the cabbie,
Entering first the coruscating theatre.
He saw a well-dressed crowd, while he was shabby,
Many, though not so many as there'd be at a
Smartish first night. Dorothy too looked drab. He
Was given stall seats, rather near the back,
Also a summons to a midnight snack.

Half-brother Brian's musicals were notorious.
He had four running now in the West End –
This; *Brother Judas*; the somewhat inglorious
Queen Thatcher; then a heterogeneous blend
Of Wagner, ragtime, raga, rage, dysphorious
Sex called *Wasteland* that did not quite offend
The Eliotians and amused the gallery.
It made some money for the widow Valerie.

Reading about the hell of Tom and Viv,
Tim half-believed that Brian could adapt
Even *The Critique of Pure Reason*: sieve
The tome into pure Kant, who, rapt, unwrapped
The Categorical Imperative
As medicine to a Europe tyrant-trapped.
The present opus was *The Time Machine*. It
Seemed to divert the thousands who had seen it.

The distant tinkling of a tiny bell
Somewhere along Tim's cortical corridor
Now tintinnabulantly tried to spell
A message, that, some sixty years before,
This project had been broached. He could not tell
By whom, but heard faint music. Brian's score
Erupted now and drowned it with its clamour.
Sitting, they yielded to generic glamour;

The glow of floats upon the silvered curtain,
Waved baton with a light upon its tip,
Orchestral glow-worm lamps, the briskly certain
Drum-thump, bass-bong, warm as a Gruyère dip,
A brass growl, saxophonic squirt and spurt, an
Insufficiency of strings, as always. Whip
Aside the tabs: *fin de siècle* décor:
A rather young Time Traveller takes the floor.

'Observe me trace,' he sings, 'this triple space,
With up and down and then across, and then
Across another way, but there's no place
To accommodate the simple question *When?*
If time's a true dimension we can pace
Or race or chase both up and down – again,
Again, again. Though you look dubious, I'm
Prepared to go off cycling through Time.'

Too many guests, too many servants, but
Structurally justified in a sung chorus,
Danced too, with skirts provocatively cut
Right to the thigh. 'Whatever lies before us,'
They chant and prance, 'must keep its door tight shut.
Whatever's past is past.' They sing some more as
The chronic argonaut (a protonym
Of Wells's own) mounts and the scene grows dim.

But, West-End-like, the engine coruscates,
And, by some trick of holograms, is seen
High overhead. A near-nude dance of dates,
Brilliant in darkness – 1617,
Then 1500, and so back, gyrates
To reach – harsh braking on the Time Machine –
To 1321, *anno felice*
For Dante, paradised with Beatrice.

But no felicity in this Middle Age
That howls aloud now with the injunction 'Die!'
Plague-stricken peasants limp about the stage,
Though stylised dance-leaps rather give the lie
To their professed debility. The rage
Of clerics, landlords, villeins, serfs rides high.
All fingers point in superstitious ire to
A lissom girl they've started setting fire to.

'A witch! A witch!' But 'No, I'm not!' she yells,
Her limbs and bosom glowing through rent stitches.
And then a bishop's tenor tone propels
The truth about all women being witches,
Save one. *Save one? Save all!* They clang the bells.
The fire, as voices reach their topmost pitch, is
Fast spreading, and she screams. The scene's obscene.
But then the god arrives on his machine.

Unpinioned, she is pillioned, and they ride
('The Devil, Devil!') to the Victorian era,
Or mean to. See the Middle Ages glide
Into the past – but no. 'Damn it. I fear a
Fault – a blown valve. It can be rectified.'
But still they hurtle back. 'What have we here? A
Gang of lolloping dinosaurs. I'll fire
My shotgun.' Bang. They gracelessly retire.

Then, with occasional humanoid intrusions,
He makes repairs and confidently sings
About an age of meliorist illusions,
Gas, electricity, and other things,
Science, an end to fideist confusions,
Socialists shawing upwards on webbed wings,
Mending old follies with a rational suture.
Apemen lurch on. She thinks this is the future.

On, on, into the real it. Notting Hill,
The girl consumed in a black bacchanalia.
'It ain't no sin,' black infant voices shrill,
'To roast them pigs with the pinko skin.' A failure
Of integration, says the Traveller. Kill
Or mutilate. I'll chew your balls, impale your
Prick. Recognition pricks, and he looks for
His house, replaced by a snuff porno store.

Two louts seize the machine, evaporate,
Then reappear, howling of horror, horror.
Police and the mobs now lock in mutual hate
(They saw a horror worse than this Gomorrah?).
Death dances off. The Traveller, isolate,
Wonders if he now dare fare forward for a
Glimpse of the final hell. Go back, you stranger as-
Tray. But Nietzsche said life must be dangerous.

Dangerous, dangerous. 'Were they right, I wonder,'
He sings. 'Stay as you are, refuse to move,
Brick yourself in, safe from the wind and thunder,
Stick yourself in a comfortable groove.
So, little dog, be safe and warm, lie under
A cretinous eiderdown. No, no, I'll prove
A man is not a dog. Dare the unknown,
Dismember Time and bite it to the bone.'

'A lot of nonsense.' Dorothy attacked
A small warm Gordon's in the theatre bar.
Most of the quack quack comments (quack) that quacked
Agreed. Tim said: 'I'm pretty sure there are
Remnants of Wells reserved to the last act,
Or so I heard. The sun a burnt-out star,
Dead earth, a pop song for its epitaph.
The end of man. Anything for a laugh.'

No Middle Ages now, with witches, warlocks,
Burnings and bishops. Pre-industrial man
(Smocked peasants who went aaargh and touched their fore-
                                                                            locks)
Metamorphosed to the Victorian
Proleship that's now become the race of Morlocks;
Genetic mutants, each a Caliban,
Cannibal really, masticate *en masse*
The effete Eloi, once the ruling class.

The girl the Traveller lost in the first portion
Emerges as the blonde anaemic Weena,
Spouting unspeech, abetting an abortion
Of literate lyrics. Eloi croon and keen a
Crowing, Morlocks grind out a distortion
Of hound-howls, growls, grunts, while the Time Machine, a
Witness of hell, lastly at least can cough
Civilised language as it whistles off.

And so the end of time, the sun near spent,
A slowing earth, degenerate monsters. He
Lets stirring words crash through the firmament:
'Victorian man survives, Victorian me.
We'll conquer yet.' Drums and trombones give vent
To triumph, and the Traveller's home for tea,
Hymning an unborn flower in his lapel.
Curtain. The audience took it fairly well.

'Not enough songs. Otherwise not too bad.'
They filled a corner table in Bernini's –
Tim, Brian, Dorothy, the Cockney lad
Who took the lead, the girl who shared the scene, his
Bed-sharing girl in fact, a girl who'd had
Fire, fornication, and an esculent finis,
A sinuous, delectable but dumb thing,
And also the librettist, Norbert Something.

A *trattoria*, not a *ristorante*,
Full of framed portraits, spotty and cooked brown,
Of Gino's ancestors, all of them ante-
Rather than anti-Fascist: manic frown,
Lethal waspwaist, oiled quiff. A schoolroom Dante
Was in the hands of Gino, just brought down.
'I think it's Canto XXVIII,' Tim said.
It was. Gino melodiously read:

'*Com'io vidi un così non si pertugia,*
Rotto dal mento infin dove si trulla.
Tra le gambe pendevan le minugia – '
'Clearly,' Tim said, 'anathema to the mullah.'
'*Che merda fa di quel che si trangugia –* '
Tim slapped with an imaginary ruler:
'You've missed a line. *La corata pareva*
E 'l triste sacco. Don't dilute the flavour.'

'For ladies, no,' said Gino's fat grave grin.
'This lady didn't cop a dicky bird,'
The girl said, forking antipasto in.
'This is the content, though not word for word,'
Tim said. 'His body's split from arse to chin,
Guts hang between his legs, A wretched turd-
Outchurning sad sack, food to fecal stuff – '
Dorothy said: 'We're eating. That's enough.'

'Shit really, *merda.* Listen. "He gazed at me
And ripped his chest wide open. Thus I saw
Mohammed mutilate himself, who said: 'Now see
The weeping Ali – ' " ('That's his son-in-law')
" 'Face ripped from chin to hairline.' " He and he,
Sowers of discord, get their ever raw
Wounds rendered rawer: each demonic sword
Rams home the eternal justice of the Lord.'

'Where did you learn the wopspeak?' 'He's a priest,'
Brian unexplained. 'Dante,' Tim then expanded,
'I honour as a saint – well, blessed at least.'
The girl ate her *vitello* single-handed,
Munching: 'Do priests fuck now?' This priest released
Some rank cigar smoke with: 'Well, to be candid,
Some priests may snatch a fumble in a hallway
But leave the whole hog to His Grace of Galway.'

'Your thing was nonsense' (Dorothy). 'Oh, really?'
Yawned Brian, with the tone of Maynard Keynes.
'We thought we'd fixed a frame around it. Clearly
You missed that. I, with Norbert, was at pains
To flout progressivism and not merely
Construct a construct that – well – entertains.'
'Them big words.' The two Cockneys chewed like cows.
She spilt veal sauce upon her Magyar blouse.

Brian spilt nothing on T-shirt or jeans;
Even his Mickey Mouse watch appeared polished.
He did not flaunt blue blood by any means,
But no demotic stance could have abolished
The aristocratic aura. Kings and queens
Might see their ancient hierarchies demolished,
But he had been bequeathed a certain quiddity
Hard to define but of a hard solidity.

'I saw this TV thing – a second law
Of thermo something.' A duet: 'Dynamics.'
A solo: 'Entropy.' The girl's dropped jaw
Went 'Jesus.' Brian went on: 'Smashed ceramics,
Spilt milk, bombed cities all add one bit more
To universal breakdown's jar of jam. Ex-
Cept in films you can't wind back the action.
Addition's never fashioned from subtraction.'

'That's it,' Tim cried. 'A film that no one's seen.
When Wells had done his *Things to Come* with Korda,
He swore they'd follow with *The Time Machine*.
But "Music first, then script – that's the right order,
Like *Things*." But the composer Bliss had been
Disgusted by the soundtrack. "Can't afford a
Re-recording," Korda said. "Scraped tin,"
Yelled Bliss. And that's where you-know-who came in.

'Meaning there was a score.' 'There *is* a score,'
Frowned Brian. 'I cleaned up its bloody mess.
Later, later.' Their talk had been a bore
To one at least, who chewed: 'Do all priests dress
Like you do?' 'You mean scruffy?' She searched for
A word. 'Incog.' Norbert said: 'Mufti.' 'Yes,
Meaning an expert in Koranic law.
Afta's the root. My twin could tell you more.'

'You're seeing Tom?' asked Brian. 'Yes, D.V.
Venice, tomorrow.' 'Venice? Lucky you.'
'Not at this season, darling. Will you see
If Tom can knock us out a verse or two
In hundredth-century London English? We
Need something better for these two to do
Than amorous gibberish. It was bad tonight.
We're always mending aircraft in mid-flight.

'A musical is planned and replanned, rereplanned and
Planing and chiselling are never done,'
Gloomed Brian. 'On the last night it's abandoned.'
He signed the *conto*. Norbert: 'I must run.
Ta for the scoff. See you.' He waved his hand and
Left. To Tim the girl said: 'Bye, have fun.
Tutti frutti.' The Traveller, waving: 'Cheers.'
She: 'Give my love to all them gonorrhoeas.'

'Well, now –' Brian unleathered two Coronas.
'We have to talk about Byrne's resurrection.'
He lightered Tim's cigar and then his own as
Pangloss whispered to Tim of the perfection
Of God's creation, still but dimly known, as
The giant weed slid snug into the section
Undigited. God knew what he was at:
The nose for spectacles, and that for that.

The weeds, of course, had first been circumcised.
The golden cutter all the way from Tiffany
Brian now span. 'A concert I've devised,
And not for Easter but Polyphony,
I mean Epiphany. I realised
The scope when all that stuff came. Speak now, if any
Doubt's in your mind about the project's merit, as
You and your twin are the true sole inheritors.'

'Stuff?' 'Yes, his scores, sent to me from Nairobi,
Some paintings also. If I'm not mistaken,'
(Fingering the gold ring stuck in his left lobe) 'he
Was doubly great. We have to bloody waken
The bloody world to what it ought to know. Be
Ready for some shocks, though. Francis Bacon,
Now larded, lauded, being dead, knew terror,
But Byrne knew terror's mother, and no error.

'As for the music – well before its time.
Ironic sentiment. Inverted commas
Inside inverted commas. The sublime
Turned into slime. Street crime. The hum of bombers,
The crash of cities. Love. Reason and rhyme
Upon the rack. The bloody heart torn from us,
Messages, codes. And all that's just from grazing
The scores. The sound is going to be hair-raising.

'You, Dorothy, have those pictures at your place,
Daubs, you once said, that you'd be sick to see.
Let's have them out.' Disgust suffused her face.
'Cobwebs and filth. I threw away the key.
My mothers told me they were bestial, base
And brutish.' He: 'However that may be,
The properties belong to Tom and Tim.
Tim's here. Tom's there. It rests with him and him.'

Tim said: 'I can deliver Tom's consent.
You are the artist, sort of. So no no
From us layfolk. Posthumous punishment
Or pardon, which?' 'I only wish to show
Neglected talent. I've prepaid the rent –
The Barbican, also the LPO.'
She: 'Palestine? Tea-towelled Arafat?'
'The Philharmonic. You'll have heard of that.'

He puffed. 'Polyphiloprogenitive.
He wasn't negative. Is that a crime?
Is it a crime to live? He bade us live.
We are three bicycles that ride on time,
Forged in his gonads. And his works will give
Salutary palpitations. Therefore I'm
Firing his guns while he rests on in peace.
Nihil nisi nihil de mortuis.

'Shoving the needle in a different groove'll
Confound my bloody critics,' Brian said.
'Approval, yes? You're nodding your approval?
You're nodding anyway. It's time for bed.
And Gino here requires the prompt removal
Of bodies moderately drenched and fed.
Ci dispiace, Gino.' Out they got. A
Wide yawn caesura'd Gino's *buona notte.*

71

A Neapolitan – not just his accent,
Also a *cena* worse than mediocre.
Lacrima Christi's fumes, all lava-black, sent
A shaft through Tim hot as a sizzling poker,
While the half-smoked Corona answered back (scent
Of foul Cuban *retretes*). All bespoke a
Sore need in Tim to renovate his system.
He handshook Brian; his half-sister kissed him.

She bruised her lips on his designer stubble. 'You
Had best send Tom's approval in a fax.' 'He
Won't disapprove.' Then Brian's BMW,
Silver agleam, blue surface over-waxy,
Rolled up. 'You want a lift?' 'No, we won't trouble you.'
Less than imperiously Tim hailed a taxi.
The chauffeur opened up, Brian was sped
Home to his catamites and triple bed.

'Recalled to life,' said Dorothy. She'd seen
That Dickens thing in 1989,
When, to mixed feelings, *la Terreur* had been
Unbottled like a long sequestered wine,
Reminding Europe what *l'Europe* could mean
If France's ideologues kept it in line.
'Recalled to life,' twice or thrice more she said,
Like Dickens, adding: 'Is he really dead?'

'As a doornail.' Tim cited the same writer.
'Definite from the Lagos legation.'
He read NO SMOKING, put away his lighter,
And said: 'Call Brian's thing the last purgation.
Let the old bastard take a final bite, a
Bold nip at ears and eyes, be a sensation,
And then, insensate, yield to the worms' hunger,
Deader than what you get at the ironmonger.'

She opened up and hurried in to check
That her indifferent video recorder
Had chronicled Brazil's arboreal wreck
And, here at home, domestic sin and sordor.
Timothy eased Brancusi from his neck
As she called up: 'Everything is in order,'
Like a returning housewife glad to learn
The puppy didn't shit or the roast burn.

He woke at three, nursing a half-subdued
Engorgement helped on by the tears of Christ.
Unchain the beast after long hebetude?
Odd heavy-breasted images enticed.
He thought he heard tiptoeing feet light-shoed,
Yukari's whisper. Flesh that was too long iced
Must melt, the Time Machine be oiled. Inept
Prospective rider. Jesus wept. He slept.

Yukari, bright at eight, brewed him strong tea,
Squeezed orange juice, cooked British sausages.
'*Choozume.*' Tim wondered why that should be,
Origin Spanish. All these mysteries.
'No, no, this sausage. Different thing.' And she
Among the old copper solidities
Showed herself a true daughter of the sun
With microwaves, sung signals of toast done.

'In Nagasaki you eat sausage?' 'Canned.
Our brotherhood was British and frustrated.'
Frustrated? A slight tremor of the hand.
Yukari's very British apron dated
From when the Union Jack had been a brand
Of hedonism jokingly related
To patriotism, the beginning of
Sexual intercourse, though hardly love.

Beneath she wore knickers and brassière
Of chocolate-coloured substance. He had read
That one could buy esculent underwear
And wondered was this it, but ate instead
His sausages, baptising the brown pair
With IQ sauce. He, crunching toast, then said:
'Were many there at Mr Woo's or Foo's?'
She also wore, he noted, high-heeled shoes.

'Good tip I get. Here she not pay too much.
More good she not. Not stay in all the night,
Watch *terebijon*. Here you not see such
Like Tokyo. More sexy.' Down the flight
Came Dorothy's fast feet. 'It I not touch.
She late for breakfast news. Not do it right,
She say, record wrong thing.' More sexy? Loud
Roared objurgations of a Muslim crowd.

Outraged believers in Islamabad
Demanded filthy Dante's execution
Outside the US Embassy. A sad
And academic voice poured a cold douche on
A hot *imam*. Iranian leaders had
As yet not issued a stern resolution
About the doing of the sinner in.
That would come with a later bulletin.

Dorothy entered in a dressing gown,
One of her mothers', doubtless, poured a cup
(The lacy nightdress too), said with a frown:
'How can you lap that horrid offal up
So early?' 'Priestly habit.' She sat down,
Tentatively taking in a scalding sup.
'Christ's body's insubstantial. Something ample
Must follow. John Polack sets an example.'

74

'Your staying here – will it be permanent?'
'Yes, if I permanently break the yoke.'
Mishearing (yolk) she retched. 'I'll pay you rent.'
She waved the rent away, with his rank smoke.
'Will there be women in your life?' The scent
Of dreams of armpits smote him as he spoke.
'I hadn't thought,' he lied. She weighed and gauged
And said: 'You're old.' He said: 'Try middle-aged.'

'He not.' Yukari seemed to ooze authority.
'Not fat. Some hair he got. And he got tooth.'
'Enough to bite your chocolate – Sorry, sorry.' Tea
Gulped washed down his embarrassment. Uncouth.
He'd never spoken thus to a sorority
Of virgin fillies, doling out God's truth.
Yukari pinched his flesh, as of a Christmas
Turkey. She had a sweet morning strabismus.

'I get that thing.' 'What thing?' 'To make hair black.'
She raced off with a flash of bold bare thighs.
'You need a suit,' said Dorothy. 'You lack
The look of one who's used to high-class lies.'
Shrewd, very shrewd. He said: 'I'm bringing back
Old clothes Tom doesn't need. We're size for size.
Even perhaps some clobber apt for tennis.
Tom said he'd bring a suitcaseful to Venice.'

'Is Tom in pain?' 'It's eased with Tetraphone
Or Trampoline or something. The cold steel
He naturally wishes to postpone.'
'God, where's God's justice? Don't you ever feel
It should be you? On TV twice they've shown
This Early Church thing. They said holy zeal
Made this man do it with a single snip, as
Easy as cutting nails with your nail-clippers.'

75

'Enervate Origen.' 'I didn't catch
His name.' Yukari dashed in to deploy
A brush and bottle on his thinning thatch.
He read the ideogram which said *kuroi*,
Or black. She blacked his eyebrows too to match.
Curious: an image of a Polish boy
As she removed his glasses. His libido
Seemed to await redemption on the Lido.

Dorothy too caught swiftly the similitude:
She knew at least Visconti's masterwork.
'This will not make you change your nature, will it? You'd
Better not turn into a sort of Dirk
Bogarde. Disgusting. And the silly billy chewed
Infected strawberries. Some folk go berserk
In Italy, especially old men.
It's AIDS now, but it was the Black Death then.'

Yukari womanhandled him to show
Tim Aschenbach, moustacheless, in the glass
That flanked the cooker. So, then. Time to go.
He kissed her porcelain cheek, patted her arse,
And gave her '*Kansha suru*', bowing low.
For Dorothy he made a priestly pass,
Gripping his grip. 'My love to Tom, remember.'
'God bless.' He strode out into spring December.

Green Park to Piccadilly. Bakerloo:
He rode to Oxford Circus, Regent's Park,
And last to Baker Street. A twinge or two,
Rheumatic. Glassless vision blurred the stark
Outlines of things. A gritty warm wind blew
Spent fastfood cartons. Foreign races, dark
And not so, milled possessively about.
The Anglo-Saxon breed was dying out.

Ten five. A little late. He had to hurry
To Dorset House and Brian's agent's office.
The ground-floor Crown of India breathed faint curry.
The porters, ebonite and milky-coffee-s-
Kinned, sent him up. He tasted a slight worry,
For Brian's agent was a Shoreditch toff, ess-
Ential barrow boy, East Endly fecular,
Totally absolutely crassly secular.

He was already slitting open mail,
Dressed as if to engage the Stock Exchange,
One of the money bugs poised to prevail,
Agential boasting in a four-walled range
Of naked posters whose wide spectrum – pale
To puce – would irretrievably estrange
The Calvinists. 'No problem. Go in there.
We wouldn't want to give the sods a scare.

'The pen-name's Southwell, right?' That pseudonym
Grew shady here. *'As I in hoary winter
Night* er *stood shivering –* ' Tim gaped at him
In disbelief. 'Er *in the snow –* ' A splinter
Of culture? 'Er *Surprised I was –* ' The dim
Glow of a soul? *'By sudden heat –* ' A hint, a
Wink of heaven? *'That made my heart to glow.*
That wouldn't make the top ten, would it?' 'No.'

'But always do your homework, sunshine. And
Always have coffee ready for the Yanks.'
He set it bubbling with a practised hand.
'You want some?' 'Makes my heart to thump. No, thanks.'
'Don't mention fucking money, understand?
These fuckers have no problems with the banks.
They own the fucking things. Calvin was Swiss.
We'll make a fucking killing out of this.

'They're 'ere.' They were – the Reverend Eli Sewall,
Sam Wadsworth. Tim asked the grim cleric whether
He was of the diarist Sewall's clan. He knew all
Of one brief entry: *Swallows, six, together*
Flying and chittering rapturously. 'You al-
Ready got 'em?' – Wadsworth. 'Crazy weather.'
'No, I cite Sewall. "Chittering" is superb.
Chitter – a good old Massachusetts verb.'

'No time for chitter, chatter. We admired
Your film of the Malacca colony
And how those lax Mohammedans acquired
A less lax Catholic Christianity.'
The Reverend beetled. 'But was it inspired
By your own – ?' 'Never, sir. My sympathy
Is all with faith expressed in rigorous laws,
Commitment to the Calvinistic cause.

'My life, you might say, has been dominated
By an innate Genevan point of view.
British permissiveness has nauseated
A soul essentially ascetic. True,
I've Jacob-wrestled with and execrated
Slimy seductive devils of the new
And won, I think. Now I can laugh at Rome
And Canterbury too. I'm safely home.'

'You've been in orders?' – Sewall, rather shrewd.
'My talent's propagandist, hardly pastoral.
I've brooded and pursued in solitude
A methodology to make our Master al-
Ive, a living force. However crude,
A film that screams of imminent disaster, al-
erting us to God's, or Calvin's, wrath,
Is solid meat. Sermons are tepid broth.'

78

'*My* broth was well digested in its day,'
Said grumpy Sewall, every inch the cleric. A
Savile Row suit showed Wadsworth to be lay.
(His cupric hair opposed his partner's ferric.) A
Card he now proffered said: 'CLNA:
The Calvinistic League of North America.'
'That's who we are,' he said. 'And now you know –
The offspring of the *Institutio*.

'John Calvin's life – twelve one-hour episodes.
That's what we want. Think you can undertake it?'
'I sure can,' answered Tim. The breezy modes
Of US speech came naturally. 'Make it
Convince, hit home, impress, cram it with loads
Of flesh and blood. For sweet religion's sake it
Has to have impact, right?' He added: 'Wham.
Ready to go?' Timothy: 'I sure am.'

'The Calvinistic epic must be told,
Resistance to its message overcome,'
Said Sewall, 'seen and heard, above all, *sold*,
Bringing in an incalculable sum – '
(Here the back-seated agent slyly rolled
Mercurial finger against horny thumb.)
' – To finance missions in the name of Calvin.'
He seemed to suck a succulent bivalve in,

Though ready to regurgitate it whole
When Tim said 'Art'. Wattles somewhat ashake,
'Art,' he pronounced, 'misleads the human soul.
Art.' (Bitter capsule bitten by mistake.)
'It devastates all spiritual control.
Pernicious doctrine – Art' (gulp) 'for art's sake.
It led your Oscar Wilde to condign hell.
We want no art. We want the thing done well.'

'OK, let no seductive art intrude,' ass-
Ented Timothy, adding 'He's not my
Oscar, by the way. There'll be no crude ass-
Ertions of the flesh.' 'We want this guy,
British of course, that I saw playing Judas.'
Agential interest but a sort of sigh
From Sewall. A sign-of-the-cross nostalgia?
The sort of wince that's ground out of neuralgia?

'A transatlantic voice would be inept,
I take it?' 'Calvin was a European,'
Said Sewall gravely. 'French.' Regret had crept
Into his tone. 'But soon we hope we'll see an
Epic account of how New England kept
The faith, a supreme televisual paean
To what became American theocracy,
Vox populi vox Dei, hence democracy.'

Timothy offered: 'The late Van Wyck Brooks
Regretted there's a truth you'll hardly find
Registered in the US history books
About the making of the US mind –
It's Janus-faced, with contradictory looks:
Two equally unsocial trends, a kind
Of transcendentalism, idealistic,
And the catchpenny –' *'What?'* – 'Opportunistic.'

The listening agent, hearing hints of cash,
Made a throatcutting gesture, frowning much.
'A European?' 'No, a sourish mash
Of Pilgrim Father and commercial Dutch.'
'Wholesome mercantilism libelled by a brash
Uncalvinistic sceptic.' 'Just a touch.'
'You've read quite widely.' 'Yes, even in odd
Corners of dusty libraries I seek God.'

80

'A question I must put – Michael Servetus –
What do I do about his martyrdom?'
'No martyrdom!' Sewall grew as irate as
If a crass hammerblow had smashed his thumb.
'Foul father of the Unitarian traitors,
He seethes in hell. Their hell is yet to come.
I shudder at that vicious analogue –
The Trinity as a three-headed dog.'

'I too, I too.' Sewall grew proprietorial:
Should they pay less for infranumerary fingers?
'Some accident?' 'Alas, the sad memorial
Of a quite unheroic act, a thing as
Common as dirt these days. No front-page story. Al-
Low me my reticence. The pathos lingers.
A little girl, a dog, the dog grew rough,
A Rottweiler. Its one head was enough.'

The contract? Contract. An agential nod.
'We pray.' Sewall flopped down with practised ease
Upon the broadloom, giving a sharp prod
To coffee-draining Wadsworth. Knelt. Tim's knees
Were calloused and habituated. 'God,'
Prayed Sewall, 'Look down kindly. If it please
You, let your servant tell the sacred story,
Nine fingers tapping your and Calvin's glory.'

He turned his black back on financial sordor,
Inviting Tim to lunch. Early and light.
A salad bar. Lettuce would be in order.
At two o'clock they had a Boston flight.
'Alas,' Tim said, 'or not. I too must board a
Plane, though Geneva-bound. Must get it right –
Predestination, banks and clocks, the sheer
Calvinity of the whole atmosphere.'

'Geneva.' Sewall swallowed somewhat sourly.
'The banks, true, are a Calvinist solidity.
Accurate public clocks remind you hourly
Of death approaching with its sly rapidity.
But sin and sex abound. There's lust's foul flower. Li-
Aisons, mistresses, *putains*' putridity.
The lewd proposal from the carmined mouth. Well,
Well, preserve your innocence, Mr Southwell.'

Innocent? He? The tube train to Heathrow
Threw up the debris of a tattered *Sun*.
His body did not lie, he gloomed to know,
Responding to its tits. What had he done
Mentally, morally? Glowed at the glow
Of thirty thousand dollars. He'd begun
The well-greased progress of the hypocrite.
Why, this is hell, nor am I out of it.

South Kensington, Earls Court, then Hammersmith,
Soon Acton Town, South Ealing, Boston Manor,
All stations of a shaky ligneous myth,
And *in hoc signo vinces* a torn banner?
Osterley, Hatton Cross. He got up with
His grip well gripped. His shaky limbs began a
Terminal search. Earth travel here hath ending.
He limped to his ascent, his soul descending.

Udara Indonesia first to Munich,
Then Alitalia for the other leg.
A beauty, half-Malay, in a tight tunic
Sold him raw gin, then served him a cold egg
On colder rice. He frowned away the runic
Of Oriental news sheets, had to beg
A dozing black's discarded *Telegraph*.
The news was good for a sardonic laugh.

82

But 'NOTICE: The failed artist Michael Byrne
Invites the fruits of his insemination,
Legitimate or not, to come and learn
His final will and testament. Location:
Claridges, London. Tourist air return
Fares reimbursed. Drinks and a cold collation.
At 8 p.m. this coming Christmas Eve.'
This was a thing that Tim could not believe.

But it was also in the day's *giornali*,
Seen on the Venice flight. Also *Die Zeit*.
Dead as a doornail? No, no Jacob Marley.
Le Monde. *El Pais*. Still alive, in spite
Of ninety-odd years' sinning. Fit to parley
With truculent descendants on the night
When shepherds glimpsed an untoward stellation
And Scrooge was smacked to his regeneration.

Tom too had seen it. Tom awaited him
At Venice airport. Rain smacked the lagoon.
The empathy called twillies smacked at Tim,
Who felt Tom's pain. It modulated soon
Into gemellar warmth, warming the grim
Venetian night with no Venetian moon.
In Brian's agent's twang, let's tike a pause 'ere
While the twins dare the choppy water's nausea.

For me, I face a fresh prosodic duty.
Rhyme for a time must be quadruple-barrelled
As well as treble. The occluded beauty
Of winter Venice, bilious-sea-apparelled,
Calls me to try on Byron's other suit. He
Used the nine-fingered stanza in *Childe Harold*,
Borrowing it from Spenser's *Faerie Queene*.
I'll rest before I ride that time machine.

THREE

'How is it?' Tim enquired as they both got
Into the *motoscafo* rocking rocking.
'Oh, androblastomas and God knows what.
The elevation of the plasma – shocking.
There's seminomas, teratomas blocking
The seminiferous ducts. The Leyding cell
Or the Sertoli cell or something.' Mocking,
He grimly grinned. And Tim said: 'I can tell
It hurts like bloody hell.' 'It hurts like bloody hell.

'Still, they'll soon have it off, with me reduced
To the fat squeaking eunuch of Stamboul
Or somewhere. How can no-balled me get used
To being seedless as a bloody mule
Or blasted bullock? The heaven-hailing tool
Diminished to a lowly waterspout,
The drying up of our genetic pool
Stagemanaged by that polycarpic lout
Who's doubtless left bastard breeders enough about.'

Tim would say nothing of the *vita nuova*
Envisaged for himself. Best to keep mum.
With gloom referred he let his eyes look over
The grey lagoonscape, very winter-glum,
Lights on the Grand Canal and lights on some
Brisk oriental shipping's horny fuss.
'We're staying with – Giudecca, here we come –
A woman writer, quite notorious.
Sex is her line. Ironical for both of us.'

'How?' A long island, shops and *trattorie*,
Casette undetached. They crashed its side.
A carious baroque church. The landing quay, a
Reserve for *vaporetti*, was denied
To their spark-puffing Charon. Thomas cried
Over the gale: 'I once gave her a hand
In Strasbourg as her francophonic guide
At a book-signing. She was grateful and
Said "Any time".' They climbed to dry or wettish land.

'She lives here?' 'There's some Yank organisation
That owns the place and lets it out to writers.
She's working on a novel, its location
Unserene Serenissima. Quite bright as
Pop-writers go. Nice of her to invite us.
Delighted when I told her you're a priest.
There's an unfrocked one in her book. You might as
Well tell her how God chains the sexual beast
Or vice versa. Buys a night's repose at least.'

'The Congress doesn't run to a hotel?'
'*Run from* was the procedure I employed.
When you've delivered better get the hell
Out. The dear delegates – needful to avoid
The swine when they're off duty. Overjoyed
They'll not be with your thesis. There'll be raps you'll
Not relish. Christ, the French will be annoyed.
Latin – it yearns to turn to French. Perhaps you'll
Be knifed. This bloody awful pain.' He took a capsule.

Timothy knew himself to be among
The world's last Latinists. But, all the same,
The resurrection of the Roman tongue
As Europe's lingua franca, with the name
Of Novolatin, was his aim. 'A game,'
Tom said, 'beyond the EEC's mentality.'
'Still, I propose it, and that's why I came.
Also the fee has its own mild reality.'
'Fare and food only. Priests should be above venality.'

Their hostess was Rayne Waters, Tim was told.
He knew the name, had even seen her picture
(Blonde, hungry, about forty-five years old).
A parish girl had said: 'See how she's pricked your
Progenitive balloons and also kicked your
Male chauvinism' ('*Not* mine') 'in the balls.'
A pert young miss. 'Your sacerdotal strictures
Are pissy slogans daubed on shithouse walls.
Up all your costive arses, starting with St Paul's.'

That girl had been much moved by Mistress Waters,
Whose novels answered Freud's frustrated whine
About what women wanted. All Eve's daughters
Now knew what women wanted – to decline
Sex as pure thrust. Sex they must redefine
As clitoral ecstasy, best with a vibrator,
Neck of a bottle of expensive wine,
Even a male as slavish excitator,
Coolly and fully used, coldly discarded later.

The lady, trousered, tall, came to the door
When Tom had knocked her knocker. She said: 'Hi.'
'A thing,' Tim teased, 'I didn't know before –
You're an Armenian.' 'Me Armenian? Why?'
'*Hai* is Armenian for Armenian.' 'I
Had to invite two eggheads for my sins.
Come in,' she said, 'and get your asses dry.
Jesus, but you're identical as pins.
Right, that's the epitaph for special brands of twins.'

'Epithet,' murmured Tim, but 'Epitaph,'
Tom nodded twice, 'for twins of a different sort.
Right, right.' She pealed a sympathetic laugh,
Well knowing what impended in his thought,
Or rather not impended, while Tim caught
In the old furnishings a dusty whiff
Of Unamerica. Clanking, she brought
America right in: martinis, stiff,
Probes for the teeth and for the brain a buoyant biff.

'We can defer our homage to Bellini'
(That mixture of Spumante and crushed peach)
'Until we eat our meatballs and linguini.
Well, well.' She lounged and looked from each to each.
'Were those nine fingers fixed so as to teach
Folk how to tell one brother from the other?'
She gave a tiny self-excusing screech
(An indiscretion droll eyes tried to smother.)
'Nature did this,' Tim said, 'our dear considerate mother.'

'When?' she asked Tom. 'We have to finish first
This nonsense that I had to organise
So that some Eurocash could be disbursed.'
'Why not to me?' growled Tim. 'An exercise
In nothing, then a nothing I disguise
As homage to the European mind.'
'You've had this Eurocrap up to your eyes,'
She said, 'Real Euroculture's what you find
In Eurodisneyland. Better if you resigned.'

'Homage?' Tim frowned. 'Next Wednesday the *Musée*
In Strasbourg, with my help, is to parade,
With all the medial bullshit of the day,
A kind of ideational cavalcade,
Great Eurothinkers, visually displayed –
Dante, Descartes, Pascal, Rousseau, Kant, Nietzsche,
Others. The academics have put paid
To my quite mild entreaty that they feature
Bill Shakes. They shook their beards. Hardly a Euroteacher.'

'This Muslim rage at anti-Muslim Dante,
Starting in Bradford – don't say you've not heard.
It's spreading.' 'Yorkshire news is pretty scanty
In Strasbourg. No, I haven't heard a word.
Jesus,' he yelled. The sleeping crab had stirred.
'I'll gulp my pills and get to bed.' 'Eat first.'
'Funny, the stab's moved upstairs. A referred
Pain, like a bloody boil that wants to burst.
O Jesus Christ,' he prayed. 'O Jesus Christ,' he cursed.

And so he knocked himself out for the night,
And Tim and Mistress Waters supped alone.
'So you're a priest.' Tim munched and said: 'That's right.'
Afar, Tom snored after a final groan.
'The ball-less twins.' She used a bantering tone.
'We're different, for my celibacy's just
A thing that I elected on my own.
Part of the priestly package that I must
Regard as a technique for overcoming lust.'

'Lust? Can a priest feel lust?' 'That's the whole point.
Lust racks and rends on every corporal level,
Burrows through bone and jumps in every joint,
A slavering incarnation of the devil.'
Tim was enjoying this. 'Lust can dishevel
The well-coiffed locks of faith.' Her eyes were wide.
'A good priest groans at the dysphonic revel,
Then grins. He's supersensually satisfied,
Until the time comes for the next satanicide.

'Mind if I smoke?' 'I do. Smoking's a sin.'
'Sin's focus has been changed.' Tim rudely flicked
His lighter, lighted, drew the sweet smoke in.
'Thou shalt not smoke,' he mocked, and then he nicked
The burnt end off. 'That's insolent.' She kicked
Him under the table. 'And thou shalt instead
Cosset the ecology, and interdict
All interdictions on raw sex,' he said.
'That was delicious. Now I'd better go to bed.'

The bedroom that she opened up for him
Was chill, austere, its odour monkish-cellish.
The ceiling though had flaking cherubim,
A noseless Venus. These failed to embellish
The narrow bed with any sensual relish.
He lay in threadbare sheets, untouched by fear
Of what might come. (Tom's snore, next door, was hellish.)
He knew she would pursue research in here.
Tim had confessed some writers in his long career.

He'd even, on a long-dead eve of Christmas,
Confessed the dubious Catholic Graham Greene.
He recognised him through his rhotacismus.
The sins were quite conventionally unclean,
Though glamourised by an exotic scene.
Tim hurled inordinate penance through the dark.
Evelyn Waugh's transgressions though had been
Mere scruples, Tim was saddened to remark.
It was too late to hear the sins of Muriel Spark.

He kept the light on. When she padded in,
La Waters, not la Spark, he grinned and nodded.
Her strawy hair was loose, she diet-thin
But, on the whole, quite curvilinear-bodied,
High-bosomed and firm-buttocked. Flaccid-rodded,
He lay beneath her. There was hardly room
For lateral lying. Fingers sharply prodded;
Her skin diffused a faint (*Rive Gauche*) perfume.
'Hardly a compliment.' 'A compliment to whom?'

'To you – a substance that I hardly know,
Or to generic woman? I'm for use
Remote from amatory – isn't that so?
Something to pump up your creative juice.
Arousal of the nerves. Stale clichés – loose
Tresses and looser lips. Should I be flattered?
Your heroine, I take it, must seduce
A priest and laugh to see his semen spattered.
Heaven versus woman, heaven's legions scattered.

'Love is the answer, love – you know the term?
The body sacramental to the soul.
No automatic spurt of neutral sperm.
My nerves are well excited, on the whole.
The context's masturbatory, your role
A stereoscopic centrefold. And mine?
A stereotypical cleric. If your goal
Is pinning me on pages, I decline.'
'All I could want,' she lied. 'OK, you're doing fine.'

'You're pinned already, *father*. Highly laudable,
Your attitude.' She jerked her long legs out,
The wirebrush pubic skirr just about audible.
She stood there, blazing naked, and her pout
Belied what her few crisp words were about.
'Besides,' he said, 'my brain's suffused with Latin.
Tomorrow's session.' 'Yeah,' she said, 'no doubt.
And what is "lust" in Latin?' Getting that in,
She got out angrily, but first she let a cat in.

The cat, Venetian, gravid, tortoiseshell,
As clouds with rain, swollen, ready to shed
Her kitten-load, uttered an urgent yell,
Disputing his possession of the bed.
Tim gave her room, she leapt. The Church still said
That sex meant progeny. This beast, concurring,
While Tim, tired, joined the temporary dead,
Parturiated in the dark, conferring
New life on Venice, waking Tim with deafening purring.

The blindlings pressed and sucked and Tim arose,
Found the disordered kitchen and there tapped
Its slim resources. Milk spilled on bare toes.
Six, seven, he counted, while the mother lapped.
He watched benignly, blessing, sitting wrapped
In his old dressing gown. Thus, to be freed
For sex meant being genitively trapped.
The mother leapt, her brood resumed its feed.
No freedom, taught that damned and dour Genevan creed.

At sun-up Tim woke Tom. Tom's brain was furred
But pain greatly diminished. Tim selected
A suit of decent grey. Their hostess stirred,
But only in her sleep. 'She's disaffected.
Europe, except as décor, is rejected,'
Tom said. His pain was grumbling. Tim was deft
At boiling eggs and coffee. They inspected
Venetian winter morning, sun-bereft,
Collected bags and left a thank-you note, then left.

'The last day, God be thanked,' Tom said. 'Your flight's
At three. At half-past five I hit the road.
I've no throat for the fishbones of tonight's
Dinner at Mestre.' Winter Venice showed
Small glamour. Here a belching steamer towed
A garbage barge. And there their talking shop,
San Giorgio, Euro-rented, dully glowed
In baroque honey from its mastoid top
To its canal-girt base: one *vaporetto* stop.

Across the Grand Canal imposed St Mark's
With desolate pigeons. Venice, Tim was thinking,
A gift to man from prudent politarchs
Who, sick of Attila, Italia's shrinking
From landlocked ruffians, ordained the sinking
Of piles to bear a city, while the Hun,
Boatless and huddled in his mareskin, stinking
Of mareflesh, squinted at its rising sun,
Wondering at a wonder. No Hun writ there could run.

Once did she hold the glorious East in. What
Had fleaed the lion's rump and pared his claws?
Pollution flowed from Mestre. She was not
The queen she had been. Ruskin had to pause
When writing *Fors Clavigera* because
Sickened by vapour from the *vaporetto*.
Decay came early. What were the seven laws,
Time's ruin? Shylock loosed from his *borghetto*
The plague. All else was for Canale Canaletto.

In the palazzo (Marble? Travertine?)
The Eurodelegates, sent here to measure
Limits of Euroculture, which was seen
By Frenchmen as a pure Cartesian treasure,
Saw Tom and Tim with no apparent pleasure.
Twinhood. A British trick. Some catch in it.
Tom took the chair. Tim, at his urbane leisure,
Tried wooing them with self-abasing wit,
Most stonily received. Tom winced. His twinges bit.

Our Roman heritage (Not ours – the Huns'),
Everything renderable (Megabytes?
Jets? Hamburgers?) The French discharged their guns
With 'French is Latin'. 'English claims no right
To be more than the dialect of flight,'
Tim said. 'I say this as an anglophone.
Mater Aeterna nostra – Latin.' 'Quite,'
A fellow-priest said. 'Kick the pope,' a lone
Red Ulsterman proclaimed. Tom gave a ghastly groan.

Tom tumbled from the chairman's chair he sat in,
Dead out. The session was dissolved. Tim bent,
Concerned. *'Eheu'*, he said in Novolatin.
He palped Tom's belly. Tom at once gave vent
To echo-rousing screams. Tim swiftly went
To a Titian beauty *in vestibulo*.
'Subito – get an *ambulanza* sent.
Un'emergenza. Il telefono.'
A Frenchman pushed him. 'You will know the *numero*.'

The ambulance was rather slow to come.
It came at last, not ambulant but biting
Foul water. Tom lay, breathing still but dumb.
A coffee klatsch found his near-corpse exciting.
Two orderlies in white, politely fighting
Through with a stretcher, joltingly then bore
Tom to the landing stage, first though inviting
Tim to embark. A loud ironic roar
Of *'Vale, fratres'* rang from Euroswine on shore.

Poor Tom saw nothing of the Grand Canal,
Palazzi, scafi, Peggy Guggenheim,
Caffè, alberghi, Harry's Bar et al.
They chugged past the Rialto, fighting time,
And reached at length the *ospedale.* 'I'm
Done for,' Tom gasped, as the few crewmen got
Grips on him for the lurching shoreward climb,
'Amen,' a gust of sempiternal rot
Gushed from the depths. 'Oh no,' Tim countergasped, 'you're
                                                       not.'

Tim waited long among the whirring skirts
Of nursing nuns, with baggage at his feet.
Padre he called himself (it never hurts
To pull one's rank). He soured the air with sweet
Pulls at a rank cheroot, then stood to greet
White gravity. *'Dottore, che cos'è?'*
'Appendicite, padre.' Two discrete
Agonies, simultaneously at play.
Could one knife cut the two appendages away?

'*Posso vederlo?*' '*Certo.*' Tim was led
To where pyjama'd Tom lay part-sedated
Under a cross and in a narrow bed.
'Listen,' he breathed. 'It grieves me that you're fated
To do my job in Strasbourg.' Unelated,
Tim nodded. 'Ring Claudine. I have at home a
Young girl in hiding. Who'll explain.' Tim waited.
'The keys are in my bag.' He sank to coma
Then surfaced. 'My car's parked on the Piazzetta Roma.'

Tim blessed his brother. A preoperative
Trolley was trundling. Tom had ample cash,
Lire and francs in jacket pocket. Give
Name, phone, address. A nun with faint moustache,
Almoner, wrote. A girl in hiding? Rash,
He always had been. Puzzled, Tim now let a
Sospiro out. He saw a *scafo* splash
In at his summons. Boarded. *La Piazzetta.*
Better to take the road by day. Considerably better.

He landed, paid, then sought Tom's grey Mercedes,
Saying a sour goodbye to the Adriatic.
Across the way the Serbs were playing Hades
With ethnic cleansing. Only a fanatic
Could dream of Euro-unity. Erratic
That dream of Latin as a unifier.
I come to bring not peace but. Poets, vatic,
Knew all about the ever-widening gyre.
Tim found the car. It had a flabby offside tyre.

He opened, entered, switched on the ignition,
Eased out and scraped a rather dirty Fiat.
A left-hand drive. The left-hand door partition
Held maps. Mestre. Verona. He could be at
Milan by nightfall. Nothing much to see at
Milan. Ticino next. What must he do
At Strasbourg? First of all, insert the key at
Numéro neuf, rue Halévy. But who
Was this damned girl? Claudine, of course, he knew.

Claudine, Tom's colleague, was a tall and willowy
Alsacienne he'd met with Tom in Rome,
A classic blonde, superbly bosomed, pillowy,
Her long locks unsubmissive to the comb,
Divorcing at that time a sort of gnome
Of Zürich. Why did goddesses select
Models of ugliness to build a home?
Foils to their beauty? Tim could half-detect
Unpriestly urgings, though modified by respect.

Civilisation rayed out of Claudine,
Sweet Venus black-gowned as a polymath.
Not like that – Tim felt terribly unclean:
At Strasbourg he would have to take a bath.
He wondered was it really true: Hell hath
No fury like a woman sc— His hide
Crimped paperishly. Keep out of her path.
He and a Eurotruck failed to collide.
Old habit drove him to the wrong, or British, side.

Now concentrate. Check gas, oil, air and water as
You get geared to the Continental mode
(Napoleon and his tramping blueclad slaughterers
Monopolised the left half of the road).
The sky by turns hailed, drizzled, grinned and snowed,
Celestial dandruff really. By Piacenza
Mist fingered and the speeding foglamps glowed,
And all through Lombardy the fog grew denser.
Let him drive on. Meet him three frontiers hence, a
Reunion with Ariosto too. My dried-up pen, sir,
Madam, gladly dispenses with that brief spell of Spenser.

FOUR

So, after Agip service, fog, rain, snow,
Much-broken naps curled up on the rear seat,
Tim reached the Rhine, like Siegfried, though with no
Horn-blasts, only the monosonic bleat
Of Tom's befouled Mercedes. Where to go?
Foredawn. The syntax of the one-way street
Abusable through lack of traffic flow.
In searching for the place that Tom called home,
He met the Gothic *cathédrale* or *Dom*.

Should I correct that stanza? As you see,
It has an extra line and rhymes too much.
Curious, rather, wouldn't you agree?
– The way mild Spenser holds one in his clutch.
I quit his rhyme-scheme with a certain glee
But find it hard to disengage his touch,
Though I'm no longer drawn to his hexameters.
Rechain me, Ariosto's verse parameters.

Strasbourg, the Eurolawbox, much contested
Town of two cultures, Gallic and Teutonic.
The Germans had consistently been bested,
Though *Baekeoffe* and *Kougelhopf* were chronic
Items of the cuisine, where also nested
Choucroute garnie. Tim nodded at a sonic
Confusion from the coffee-serving wench,
Who, saying *Danke*, said it in *echt* French.

But *donc* she pointed out rue Halévy.
He parked and peered, had trouble with the lock.
Someone within was quicker than the key
And opened up. It would have been a shock
To see what he was now compelled to see
Had he not (nerves, as now, right as a rock)
Had that Venetian visit, though more crude
Or lewd: an adult female in the nude.

'Oh Tom, thank Christ you're here.' And she embraced him,
Debagging him as he put down his bag.
The light was dim and dawnish. As she faced him
He saw she was no man-exploiting hag
But young, bewildered. Pity then encased him
As she decased him of his inmost rag.
'Oh Tom, I've shivered all the fucking night,
And when I've dropped off waked with fucking fright.'

This was no time for stating his identity
Any more than when hearing a confession.
She dragged him to the bedroom, a male entity
She thought she knew, and he had the impression
It was sheer warmth she wanted. As he lent it, he
Felt in the stimulation of the flesh an
Untoward sense of holiness hold sway,
Like Flaubert's Julien l'Hospitalier.

But this girl was no leper, merely bruised
And shocked, and her right hand was bandage-bound,
Young, British (why?), and bodily abused,
Although her sexual appetite seemed sound.
She sighed, he warmed her, but as yet refused
Erotic contact. Her left fingers found
His scrotum, and she cried, as well she might,
'Oh Jesus Christ, they've put the bugger right.'

So 'Listen,' he said kindly. 'Merely listen.
I'm Tim, not Tom. Tom's being operated
On, now, in Venice. Please consider this an
Innocent swap. We're one. We emanated
From the same egg. One thing he has I miss – an
Annular digit – feel. It's compensated
By what poor Tom has forfeited – the status
Of owner of a full-fledged apparatus.'

She counted calmly. 'Tell me – who are you?'
'That means we've fifteen fingers altogether.
I'm Angela De'ath.' 'How do you do?'
Each introduced to each, he wondered whether
Their total nakedness was somewhat too
Intime for shaking hands beneath the feather-
Stuffed duvet. Still, they knew now who they were.
Tom sought a brief biography from her.

'I'm one of those enrolled in fucking CHAOS,
One of the mercenaries who save the sum
Of things for pay for anyone who'll pay us.
From Beirut, Ulster, Italy, I've come
Rhinewards. The swine are tough. They say *obey us*.
CHAOS – an acronym – Consortium
For Hastening the Annihilation of
Organised Soc – ' 'All in the name of love.

'I know the bloody business. So you maim
Yourself with an ill-handled hand grenade
Meant for some innocent, in the bloody name
Of bloody love. Some loveless bastard paid
To kill poor bastards. Supersessive shame
Or pain or fear or shock or something made
You see the evil. What's your origin?
Where are you from? How did this shit begin?'

She howled and clung to him. 'They ran away,
The swine. Tom found me bleeding in the dark,
Got me to hospital, came every day.
Tom's good. He'll get me home to Belsize Park
When I get better, book my flight and pay.'
'So no more love?' Tim's crabbed acerb remark
Made her howl worse. 'It's,' as her eyeballs flooded,
'Those bloody books on anarchy I studied.

'Love me, for God's sake, give me proper love.'
Well, here it was. Compassion mixed with rage,
A soupçon of contempt, all bade him shove
Priestly misgivings and the shame of age
Into the dark. Then a bedraggled dove,
No paraclete, flew from its unclean cage
And let its liquid siftings drip on him,
Clean Timothy aghast at filthy Tim.

Where did one draw the line? Pity will serve:
It often tastes like love. And briny kisses,
Pressed breasts, stroked thighs, probed anus, twitching nerve
Of frantic glans, cardiac frenzy – this is
Venerean heat a cold brain can observe –
A bestial barrage of blatant blisses,
The satyr mad to saturate the nymph
With exudations of ecstatic lymph.

They came, with morning, saw each other clearly –
On her bruised lips and unwashed hair, in him
A duplicate of Tom, or very nearly.
Chaos – no longer a mere acronym
But a too apt description of what really
Was female fetor – cup with bloody rim,
Canned slop half-eaten, hairballs and smoked butts
Confirmed that girls were fornicating sluts.

108

This naked bridges-burnt-behind-him man
Surveyed Tom's kitchen, gagging at the mess.
But then his thoughts more charitably ran
To pitying the slut's one-handedness.
Rhine water rattled in the one clean pan.
He called out 'Coffee?' She called back a yes.
At least there was some bread, a slice at most, a
Raw rusk that would grow ruskier in the toaster.

He donned his dressing gown. The telephone
Burred Frenchly. Foul enough Tom's bookish den
But masculinely so. With a faint groan
He watched a planet swim into his ken,
Raying responsibilities. The tone
Of Claudine's voice was querulous. Again
He summed up what the circumstances were.
She summoned a commendable *froideur*.

The exposition of great European
Contributors to European thought
Was ready, and tomorrow there would be an
Official opening. Tim as Tom now ought
To schlepp his ass (astonished, Tim could see an
American vulgarian had taught
Her showbizspeak) pronto to the *Musée*
In the Place Kléber. 'See you there. *Oqué?*'

But 'Food,' Angela pleaded. 'Give me food,
But give me love first, then a cigarette.'
Though this command opposed his present mood,
Tim, for his manhood's sake, was forced to get
Into his former posture and renewed
The warm tonalities of their duet.
He gave her coffee and a small cigar
And realised how friable men are.

He dressed and sought the nearest supermarket,
Sensing that Tom's Mercedes was familiar
To two blond louts who frowned and watched him park it.
He shrugged, then shivered, for the air was chilly, a
Rawish wind blew, Germanically stark. It
Was warm enough within. Taped muzak, sillier
Than was appropriate to the French mentality,
Twanged transatlantic Christmassy banality.

He piled his purchases in a wire basket –
Canned food, some grammes of *beurre*, two steaks to grill,
Beefeater gin, *baguettes* – the sort of task it
Had been his dour housekeeper's to fulfil.
New Beaujolais sulked in a plastic flask – it
Seemed evident the European will
Had yielded to some gross anonymous
Being, omnipotent, ubiquitous.

He paid and left, half-conscious as he drove
That he was being followed by a kind of
Ancient Lambretta, coughing as it wove
Between the petulant liverish cars behind. Of
Course, it was pure illusion. As Tim clove
The traffic, he was strangely put in mind of
One he had once confessed, a man who'd built
A world of helmeted emissaries of guilt.

So he got back and found her out of bed,
Thank God, in filthy T-shirt and torn jeans.
'Here's *déjeuner*, hardly *petit*,' he said,
Grilling the steaks and heating Boston beans.
He cut for her. She blubbered as she fed:
'A one-pawed hag still in her bloody teens.'
'How old exactly?' Tim asked as he sliced.
'Just gone sixteen.' (O Jesus bloody Christ.)

And bloody Tom. Yes, blood. Tim realised
He hadn't phoned. He phoned. Tom had been cut,
Appendix also testicle excised.
C'erano complicazioni, but
He'd live. Plenty of bed-rest was advised.
Full-fed and purring smoke, the green-eyed slut
Wished love as a dessert. Tim, somewhat sickly,
Drained gin and said it had to be done quickly.

The new museum, a converted warehouse,
Off Place Kléber, near the Librairie Fnac,
Was a grey brooding squarish, not quite square, house.
Tim frowned then shrugged. Its blunt and brutal lack
Of elegance was neither here nor there. HOUSE
OF EUROCULTURE blared, white upon black,
In French, of course. A structure hard to love.
Tim entered with his left hand in a glove.

Elegance was within – a massive hall
With nacreous lights and statues of the great,
Plastic, deplorable, but ten feet tall,
Forged by some hireling of the Eurostate
Who'd worked in films. Robed Dante led them all,
Beaked by the entrance, there to indicate
A sign: '*Speranza*' – hope – '*voi che entrate.*'
Tom cunningly had cut out the *lasciate*.

You dialled to hear Tom, prerecorded, say
'*Cogito ergo sum*' or 'God is dead',
And there were books and pictures on display,
Brisk commentaries on what these men had said,
And barks about their pertinence to today.
'We know' – green light that shook – 'more than the dead,
But it's the dead we know' – like greengage jelly. At
Least Tom had sneaked in something by Tom Eliot.

Claudine swished up, lean legs, flame hair, green eyes,
Unready to rebuke Tim's being late
(He gave no reason). Tim's fraternal guise
Was God's own blessing. 'Enemies await
Tom's absence', or, to transatlanticise,
'Too many top guys kicking ass. It's great
You're here. I guess they'll all be too damn dumb
To spot the difference, stoopid as they come.'

'Where did you learn to speak like that?' he asked.
'Rayne Waters said my English was too formal.'
(O Jesus Christ.) Tim gulped and quietly basked
In a blonde beauty that was supranormal.
Lust, for the time, was thoroughly decasked,
Nay drained, thus granting space to nourish warm al-
Ert desire to know, not to possess.
'Let's have a drink,' he said, and she said yes.

A drink was Pernod in a back *bureau*.
Tom's situation was, it seemed, precarious.
His British irony was growing so
Ironical that all the multifarious
Top functionaries wanted him to go,
Finding his epigrams less than hilarious.
Some grousers at the bureaucratic pinnacle
Thought that his attitudes were over-cynical.

And, an occasion for the grossest humour,
An imputation of his null virility
Had swollen here to far more than a rumour,
A total intellectual debility
Associated with a scrotal tumour.
All this, she sneered, was crass male imbecility,
The kind of diabolic grace that falls
On men whose brains are wholly in their balls.

112

That was the gist. Her exposition, Gallic,
Cartesian, was more rational and refined.
'When Tom returns,' Tim said, 'his lack of phallic
Endowment may well elevate his mind.
There'll be no outer change, even vocalic,
No elevation there, Tom reassigned,
Since his *vie sexuelle* is negative,
To the great tribe of those who think to live.'

'Can you assume his role – a month at least?'
'I have my own responsibilities.'
'You mean your function as a parish priest?'
'Well, no, no more. My late apostasy's
Ready to hatch, and the whole worldly feast
Is spread before me, meagre though it is.
Fresh steaming dishes bid me lift the lid,
Assuming too what Tom has forfeited.'

They looked each other in the eyes. Her blush
Dawned and then set. 'You two have known each other
How long?' A pause. 'I never wished to rush
Into a close relationship. Your brother
Was soaked in *Tristan* and proposed a lush
Liebestod for himself before the smother
Of the *élan vital* came in a fateful minute.
I told him no. I saw no future in it.'

'Where is your future?' 'There's no doubt it could
Have been with him, but I'm no Eloïse
To match his Abélard. I see no good
In popping passion into the deep freeze.'
'Two angels holding hands in bed. That would,'
Tim nodded, 'be a concept hard to seize
For anyone who's not been raised upon
Shelley's perverse *Epipsychidion*.'

'Tonight what are you doing?' asked Claudine.
'You need to eat. Why not come home with me?'
'I must work out a speech as well as clean
A dwelling much neglected. Still, *merci.*
Demain peut-être?', wondering if she'd been
Apprised of that young succuba. No, she
Had not, it seemed. She asked no question now.
'*Demain, d'accord.*' They parted. '*Ciao.*' '*Ciao.*' '*Ciao.*'

He pierced the Strasbourg dusk and was surprised
To find that Tom's street door was open wide.
Someone had come – so much was advertised.
He parked with haste. With haste he ran inside.
She'd gone. A flash inside his brain advised
Now of a nexus – louts, pursuit. He cried
Aloud on the stupidity of youth, paced
Up and then down. He caught a whiff of toothpaste.

A message on the bathroom shaving glass –
THEYVE TAK – and then the flat tube's inanition.
Peppermint on the air. Alas, alas
For youth, for her. Some new disruptive mission.
Abduction. Pain. For God's sake let it pass.
Curing the postlapsarian condition
Was someone else's duty to fulfil,
And the damned girl was gifted with free will.

Clean up, clear up, erase, try to restore
Scholarly order, meaning tolerated
Disorder. Let the ancient Hoover's roar
Rampage, and let black plastic bags inflated
With rubbish rubbish sulk outside the door.
He mopped the kitchen and then dissipated
With *Fleurs des Forêts* an old stench of fish (an
Odour devised by some devout technician).

114

So then a supper of canned *bisque*, torn bread,
Gin and a Schimmelpenninck, while he wrote
A note or so. And then he went to bed.
He had not changed the sheets. A whiff of goat,
Female arousal, sperm-spill, blood-gouts, shed
A pagan benison. And so to float
Off to a noon of rank Sicilian charm, pits
And flesh of peaches, fauns scratching their armpits.

Or Irish oxters, Oxtail University,
Course in French letters with the great god Pan
Presiding, dribbling, mouthing. Then, oh curse it, he
Assumed the lineaments of a burnished man.
Seeds spilt like pennies from a great burst purse. City
Darkness and alley whispers, a split can
Of nameless effluent, the great black crack
Back of a sack of a slack zodiac.

Tim, late awake, had breakfast and a shave.
He rang up Dorothy, who'd just recorded
The morning's tale of infamy, from grave
Through gritty and grotesque to frankly sordid.
Tim gravely took it in and then he gave
His own sharp narrative. And, one word more, did
She know of the conclave that was advertised?
Yes, Brian rang. Brian was not surprised.

Next Tim, with some small difficulty, got
His curate, Father Benlowe, on the phone.
He had a problem. Oh? Precisely what?
A Pakistani girl, who'd not made known
Her wishes to her elders – she durst not –
Had come to see him, lateish and alone,
And shown a strong desire to be instructed
About the faith, eventually inducted.

'*Liberum arbitrium*,' Tim sighing said.
'Not even Muslim nonsense can deprive
The questing soul of that. Go right ahead.
But one who is Islamically alive
May not prefer to join the Christian dead.
Between the two of you you may contrive
To bring about a literal martyrdom,
But she can choose – *liberum arbitrium.*'

Michael Servetus, martyr, chose to swim
Into his brain. He stared at Tom's black blank
Computer screen, and it stared back at him.
Work beckoned, though the whole conception stank.
He freely willed to propagandise grim
Determinism. Money in the bank.
Free will perhaps was the destructive siren. He
Knew Calvinists would not perceive the irony.

But first things first. This opening first of all.
He chose a sober suit and tie and dressed.
His left hand bore a wool-stuffed fingerstall –
A whitlow, hangnail, something. For the rest,
Tim was pure Tom, though ready to appal
(That Venice failure still oppressed, depressed)
The non-Latinophones (in Francophonian
Allophones though) with something Ciceronian.

Driving the car, he mouthed his Latin loud.
He was on time. Claudine's bright loveliness
Irradiated a large subfusc crowd.
Here was the mayor. There, sour under duress,
The Eurodelegates. Tim bobbed and bowed
And, with Claudine, gold in a golden dress,
Elbowed and thrust, as through a football scrimmage,
To a rostrum under rostral Dante's image.

'Urbis praefecte honorabilis'
(Epithet used just once by Cicero),
'Legati, nuntii' (was that a hiss?),
'Civites, vos salvere jubeo.'
He got no further in his speech than this.
The bomb was deafening, a gleam, a glow,
Screams, shouts, collisions, runnings, eyes dilated,
Horrified howls. Dante disintegrated.

Tim grabbed Claudine sheer clear of the hit head;
A fingerless hand struck his, pure paint and plastic.
The cameras flailed. *'Les Musulmans,'* Tim said.
Some things cohered. Claudine's faint gasps and spastic
Shudders grew worse, while Dante's ruins shed
Odour of something apt, infernal. Drastic
Inquiries called for. Tim remembered now
Algerian doormen. That was wrong somehow.

Probably all this would be blamed on Tom.
Perfide Albion. Lawrence d'Arabie.
Tom-Tim should have nosed out that bloody bomb.
The Dante head frowned hard at him and he
Kicked it. It turned to filthy ash, wherefrom
Comminatory smoke rose. Tight-held she
Knew new distress. The mayor was loud and voluble.
Descartes shook, and the crowd grew highly soluble.

Descartes was merely shaky. Islam held
Nothing against him, knowing nothing of him.
'Cette exposition est ouverte,' Tim yelled
And bore Claudine away. The lights above him –
Nous connaissons les morts – spilled down and spelled
A quite dire message. Crowds began to shove him
And Claudine out, still tremulous, tremulous she,
And he a little with the ignition key.

Her deafness, unabated, worried most.
He drove her to Tom's dwelling, set her down,
Fed her some cognac. Then, a mixed-up host,
He changed the bedsheets, saw her golden gown
Was gritty, ashy; she, aghast, a ghost,
Wore pallid plaster as a comic crown.
A bath, a bed, or both, something to wear?
Tim shrank into a *bonhomme à tout faire*.

Later, in bathrobe, glowing, hair near dry,
She was no longer deaf. 'A childhood scare.
Italian Alps. *Caduta Massi*. I
Was six years old. A rock fell. A mere hair
Divided me from it. Such terrors lie
Awaiting wakening. It was like that there.
I'll sleep a little.' 'Do so. I'll prepare
Some broth.' She tottered bedwards, he elsewhere.

He mixed some gin and Pernod to reprove his
Shivering still. The TV news showed all.
Special effects, though, in disaster movies
Would have made more of it. So. What we call
Real life, in shifting to a fictive groove, is
Seen as inferior fiction. 'What's the fall
Of Dante,' Tim groused to his gin and Pernod,
'To a multimillion Hollywood *Inferno*?'

But then the news said that the Rhine police
Had grabbed three terrorists, two self-confessed
Tools of disruption, garnished with a piece
Of cinefootage. Just as Tim had guessed,
Angela featured, howling without cease
Though without sound: innocent, pushed, forced, pressed.
Her name, De'ath, meaning *La Mort*, was seen
As guilt enough, so said the *speakerine*.

Switch off, doze, wake, give the *bouton* a push, de-
Siring news of bigger worlds without.
The sex-life of ex-President George Bush, de-
Linquencies no one cared a bit about.
A failed West End assault on Salman Rushdie.
Islam again. A loud Koranic shout
From Teheran, an imperious demand
That Dante's works be mondially banned.

Tim felt uneasy. He'd as good as doffed
The Christian armour meet for holy war.
The secular hardware was over-soft.
Should tolerance meet intolerance? Once we bore
Paynim-defying banners high aloft.
The Christian West was rotten to the core,
A culture facing in its deliquescence
The rigour of a million stars and crescents.

She stirred, she yawned. The cupboard was near-bare.
Some onion soup? He looked in on Claudine.
She was awake and in her underwear.
'Better?' he gulped. 'Better.' He said he'd seen
The news. She nodded, gave him a green stare.
'One bed,' she said. 'Two people'. Gulp. 'You mean – ?'
He coughed, and in his pocket had to root am-
Ong used Kleenex to entrap the sputum.

He coughed and coughed and what he coughed was crimson.
Had Dante, pulverised, assailed a lung?
Phlegm deep encrimsoned. In his lower limbs an
Unwonted trembling started, so he clung
To the night table. The sheer sight of Tim's un-
Stanchable flow froze Claudine's eyes and tongue.
And then he stopped, but held on to his fright.
There'd be no casual dalliance tonight.

119

Claudine, quite clearly, did not care for sickness.
'Give me my dress, lend me a raincoat. I'll
Call for a taxi.' Tim surveyed the thickness
Of a haematic blob with a sour smile.
She dressed with an exemplary quickness.
'I'll drive you home.' But still he let her dial
The number with a panicky velocity.
'I hit a vein. Senescent varicosity.'

She left, like someone fleeing from *la peste*,
Abandoning poor Tim to soup and smoke.
He twirled a Schimmelpenninck. It was best
To let the bronchii rest and not provoke
Another crimson fit. He grew oppressed
By a conceit, a sort of holy joke:
To match the sinful seed that he had spent
Christ's blood streamed in the inner firmament.

The hound of heaven snuffled at his back.
He pissed white wine then gazed on his reflection.
Inveterate grey had swamped Yukari's black.
His eyes were glazed, his body a collection
Of bones grown brittle and of skin grown slack.
He hawked, spat in the bowl. A close inspection
Showed that Christ's blood or his had sidled off,
Permitting him a candid smoker's cough.

Rejuvenation? Never. Not a hope.
The wooing of Claudine by candleshine
While Strasbourg snow like fluffy shaving soap
Lay on the Tudor-looking roofs. Red wine
And smoking *Baekeoffe*. No grab, no grope,
Avoidance of a Casanovan line.
His need and hers. He watched *perhaps* collapse.
His teeth, he saw, had unattractive gaps.

He wondered: should he cry himself to sleep?
Thought better of it, downed some gin, soon snored,
Leaving it to the Strasbourg sky to weep,
Rose early, shopped, drove back. He had on board
Enough provisions, so he thought, to keep
A winter trapper. Reverently he poured
A sacramental malt, reverently sipped,
Then sat to process half a yard of script.

Start in the middle. Could Servetus be
The bloody villain Sewall had alleged?
Tim thought of Michael, Miguel, and could see
The poor boy in warm water, parent-pledged
To papal choir castration (of course, he
Had no say in the matter). The blunt-edged
Shears snipped potential manhood. Sexicide.
He'd sing soprano till the day he died.

But Miguel joined the medical fraternity,
And killed and cured throughout the whole Hispanic
Terrain, heaped gold, although he had to earn it. He
Was calm when plague made every province panic.
The rational approach – he had to learn it. He
Combined the syllogistic and organic,
And while to most the blood was merely bloody,
He made its logic his profoundest study.

Long before Harvey, Dr M. Servetus
Saw that the blood sustained an ordered motion.
Like earth itself, it had to circulate. As
Stream blossomed into river, river ocean,
And then through rainclouds back to streamy status,
So it. That cycle earned his full devotion.
Rejecting blood as a red static pillar, he
Pursued its course – artery, vein, capillary.

Of course, he played the earnest pedagogue,
Expanding though, for, to his own surprise,
A theological near-analogue
Forced him, alas, to sneer and stigmatise
The Trinity as a three-headed dog,
Meaning the orthodox concept – unwise –
Replacing it – three persons quite distinct
But, so to speak, haematically linked.

This to the old devout must seem strong meat.
The ultimate in heaven was not stasis
But motion. God rendered himself complete
Through filiality, incarnate basis
Of a kinetic stuff, the paraclete
The network where eternal change takes place. Is
Not this, thought Tim, although it warmed his heart, a
Vision most apt for a prospective martyr?

Servetus published his *De Trinitate*.
Both Rome and Wittenburg emitted thunder;
Zwinglians, Hussites tore the work apart. He
Tried to contend the text expressed a wonder:
Essential three in one. God's subtle art. He
Showed his true oneness manifested under
Mere outward show: call that the Holy Trinity,
Himself the blood, the cyclical divinity.

So Tim interpreted the doctrine. Though
He could not well remember what he'd read,
He well recalled how Miguel had to go
From land to land to land to beg his bread
And save his body from the burning, so
Finally trod where it was death to tread,
Seeking the hagiocracy where faith
Was logic, not a mythopathic wraith.

He landed in Geneva. To his inn
A state official bearing a white rod
Came right away, announcing with a grin
That the Genevan state, body of God,
Arrested him. Here secular crime and sin
Were one. The official used his rod to prod
The victim: he must go at once to state
Incarceration and a lengthy wait.

The gaol was filthy, and the leering warders
Derided his soprano squeak. They saw
His ball-less groin and roared, obeying orders
To check that peccative, or papist, flaw.
Then came a long procession of recorders
Recording what incensed Genevan law
Or theocratic doctrine. From the horse's
Mouth, or whinnying mare's, nightlong discourses.

Servetus met his judges. Honest John,
Or crafty Calvin, kept out of the way,
Although the judgment was his own. Upon
The teachings of that dwarf whose blood was whey,
Semen pure water, a phenomenon
Whose only beauty, so they tell us, lay
In an exemplary prose style, was based
The doled-out doom the shivering Spaniard faced.

The public burning was a fine diversion
To citizens deprived of basic joys.
Lausanne arranged a holiday excursion.
Black-suited bankers turned to boisterous boys
Remembering pre-Calvinist immersion
Into a brantub full of toys. The noise
Of 'Heretics to hell' was sweetly festive.
The wood was damp, though, and the crowd grew restive.

The flames leapt late. Servetus reeked of crackling
After his stuck-pig squeals. John Calvin shammed
Delicacy through absence, frowning, tackling
A riddle: why this damned one felt undamned,
Screaming to God, his skin scorched devil-black (Ling-
Ering, yes, shrieked fury) while red torment crammed
Each orifice, stink of an outraged God.
Yet it was God he called on. Very odd.

There was a Calvin problem, was there not?
God made his mind up, right from the beginning,
That some were damned, some saved, and strictly what
You did with life, saintly by choice or sinning,
Mattered to God not one benighted jot.
You prosper? That probably means you're winning.
You're losing, lost – the sudden voices shout it.
You're lost, and nothing can be done about it.

Conviction of damnation, so they tell,
Afflicted Calvin later. The good Lord's
Guerdon for faithful service? Fiery hell.
Well, no – no punishments and no rewards.
Servetus rose and his accuser fell?
That's all too possible, and it accords
With logic, justice being man's creation:
Its symbol is a public conflagration.

It would not do, the damned thing would not do.
And *homo fuge* sang from blood released
On one of Tom's white shirt cuffs. So it's you,
Truepenny. Then the sanguine spasm ceased.
Veins brittle in the throat – that might be true,
But something whispered of the encroaching beast.
Why should his twin be stricken and he not?
The dart was blind: it fired at any spot.

A doctor. Who? Well, possibly Denise's?
That gush of red, though, had been alienating.
He'd wait for Tom's return and help to ease his
Way into eunuchdom. Life was all waiting,
N'est-ce pas? Nicht wahr? But still it didn't please his
Habit of priestly pressure (fulminating:
'Give up that sin that eats you to the quick!')
Delay, and you confirmed that you were sick.

This was a case where languages looked in.
A foreign tongue bestowed an A-effect:
Somebody else had the disease, or sin –
Lust or leukaemia. In this respect
The surgery and confessional were akin.
When Christ spoke to the lost and the elect,
He'd have to, Tim supposed, be polyglot.
One's mother tongue spoke true, the others not.

And so he'd wait until he'd winged his way
Back to the warm vernacular, GPs
With common colds and common phonemes, grey
Worn suits and cardigans, and Melanese
Receptionists, and no damned fees to pay.
He was entitled to a large disease:
He'd made his dogged weekly contribution
To the decaying liberal institution.

And now he thought he'd better telephone
To Brian's agent. After 'Can I 'elp
Yew?' and a rasping nailfile, he made known
His summary rejection. A foul yelp
Of Cockney execration in a tone
Apt for a brawl ensued. The unwiped whelp,
The moneyloving lout, could not conceive a
Conscience. So Tim down-slammed the damned receiver.

He cooked, drank, smoked a little, roamed the city
In snow or slush or rain. The *tussis* racked him
Hardly at all. A lone week. Neither pity
Nor friendship gave Claudine cause to contact him.
He spent long hours in the cathedral, pretty
Well reconciled to going back to black. Tim
Saw the priest's duties now as purely formal,
A trade a trade, the situation normal.

And yet – the fantasy applied to Thomas
Rather than Timothy – if only God
Would grant a sign – no need for stops and commas –
Some hieroglyph, graffito, half-baked clod
Of cuneiform-marked clay, an ill-aimed bomb, a s-
Usurrus, fart, intrusion of the odd
Into the even mainstream of the day,
A prodigy. God didn't work that way.

He trudged back to Tom's place. The telephone
Was trilling to itself. He lifted it.
Tom's voice, assertive, male (the eunuch tone
Did not ensue when shears or scissors bit
Post-pubertally). 'Coming home. Alone?
No, no, accompanied. Feeling not too fit.
Weak rather. Hm. Don't think I like that cough.
Back Tuesday night. Then you can bugger off.'

Kind. Brotherly. Tim did not like it either.
He spat a rust-gout in his handkerchief.
Was he a little thinner? Oh well, by the
End of the week the dubious relief
Of solid knowledge. Then perhaps to die the
Death. An endless silence after a brief
Earth-sojourn. All the putative joys untasted.
Circular speculation. A life wasted.

The bed must now be Tom's. Tim's place of rest
Could be the armchair or the filthy floor.
Then off off (bugger). Fly. Change ticket. Best
Find out the worst in Manchester. Restore
Faith in the craft, leave unfaith unconfessed.
Stand up for Dante's faith, if nothing more.
Accept with glee the bells Holst tolls in 'Saturn',
Glad in a sense life can disclose a pattern.

'Hi,' jeered Rayne Waters. 'Ah. Armenian still.'
He might have guessed that she might be his brother's
Compagnon ∂e voyage. More weak than ill,
Tom tottered bedwards. She displayed no mother's
Solicitude nor any nursing skill,
No *tenerezza*. Men were just The Others.
She dumped the ball-less Tom, then went away:
She'd other fish to fry or ploys to play.

Tim sat down by his brother. 'The girl's gone.
She went, was taken, played a minor part
In blowing up your Dante. She was on
The TV news. I saw her howl her heart
Out. Poor girl, poor child.' Tom turned upon
The muftied priest with 'Christ, you'd better start
Getting your pontiff to get furious.
This can't go on.' Tim said: 'It's up to us.'

Tom paused awhile, and then said: 'What's the view
Of Holy Bloody Mother Church about
Sapphic activities?' 'What's that to you?'
'Nothing directly. I must live without
Physical love, but what these lesbians do
Has some residual interest, no doubt.
Rayne Waters kindly offers, *sans pu∂eur*,
The washed-out pleasures of the mere *voyeur*.'

127

'With whom?' 'Why, can't you guess? Claudine, no less.'
Tim's heart might well have dropped at that disclosure.
Only his face fell. 'What a bloody mess,'
Tom groaned. 'You're clearly shocked. That only shows your
Innocence.' 'It's what women don't confess,'
Tim said. 'The theological exposure
Of non-productive sex cannot include
What women do in bed, however lewd.

'The only sexual sin is waste of seed,
And women clearly have no seed to spend.
Therefore the lesbian embrace is freed
From total censure. But the sexual end
Is several miles off Nature's simple need
– Viz. procreation. Hence we can't defend
Sapphism. It sits tentatively in
The book of law. Call it a venial sin.'

'Call it a damned perversion,' execrated
Tom. 'Life denial, voluntarily chosen.
It's only now that, detesticulated,
With my paternal promptings permafrozen,
I see, like poor Macbeth, an elongated
Procession, files and flanks and ranks and rows, an
Image of progeny now unfulfillable,
Time negative, breathless, down to the last syllable.'

'An animal fulfilment.' 'All we are.'
Tom sipped some Scotch. 'I leave you at first light.'
Tim downed unwanted gin, smoked a cigar,
Coughed, doused it, said: 'I think you'll be all right.
The larder's stocked, there's petrol in the car.'
And then: 'We can expect a lively night.
Christ and the Antichrist. I'll see you then.
Let's sleep now. Angels guard you, me. Amen.'

Tim, hurling back to London, left a coin
Of scarlet tribute in the toilet bowl.
He tubed to Green Park. Twinges in the groin
Bound him to Tom, but sordor in the soul
Was all his own. He shrugged and went to join
A brief confession queue at Farm Street, stole
Out of his past the trick of sincere penance,
Then in a pub toasted himself with Tennant's.

Yukari was alone. 'So. You come back.'
'Where's Dorothy?' 'Doloti she not here.
Leave you a letter.' 'Give me.' *I must attack*
This ghastly disbelief in hell, my dear
Timothy. Though I don't expect to pack
These village halls, just one retentive ear
Justifies slamming home the word believe.
I'll be back home just before Christmas Eve.'

And then they looked each other in the eyes
And Tim, in a slow rhythm, shook his head.
Temptation? Certainly. Therefore unwise
Even to snooze a half-hour on that bed.
'I go. I come again.' Formal goodbyes,
And then the tube to Euston. Coughed up red
Did not recur until the train reached Crewe.
In Manchester it was a flag. It flew.

Dr Mackenzie had Tim's chest x-rayed,
Then sent his inner portrait to the Royal
Infirmary, an appointment being made
With the great Dr Gogol, who was loyal
To cancer, his first love. He'd plied his trade
In Europe and on transatlantic soil.
His origin was Minsk or Pinsk or Moscow. Pe-
Rusing Tim's chart he called for a bronchoscopy.

129

Tim, somnolent, was raped via his nose
By tubes that told the truth about each lung.
The truth was far from welcome: in repose
After the process he was briskly stung
Awake by Gogol's waiting to disclose,
In a Slav version of Tim's native tongue,
A stern prognosis crassly negative:
Inoperable; say six months to live.

Tim now became a *Hermes psychopompos*,
Leaving the living to his loving curate
Who, as a guide to life, was still in rompers.
The sick and dying Tim must now assure, at
Any rate, that he too could encompass
Similar fears, despairs, also endure at
Much their own level what death had in store,
God being the great blackness, nothing more.

As for the Pakistani girl, the would-be
Convert, Tim found no hardship in dissuasion.
'I say these words, my child, for your own good. Be
What you have been and don't grant an occasion
For filicide, sororicide. It should be
Enough to live. The ultimate invasion
Of nothingness, by sword or scimitar,
Says, too late, *Lay off faith*. Stay as you are.'

Quantification. Quantification. Tim
Coughed blood. The whole world is our hospital,
Endowed by the ruined millionaire. The grim
Contractive nature of the interval
Did not exorbitantly trouble him.
We meet the real – axiomatical –
Sooner not later. It would be a rather
Strange Christmas gift, recovery of a father.

Tim told Tom nothing, but Tom sent a scrawl:
'Some nastiness, quite unanticipated
Since unanticipatable, for all
Nature must go against it. Terminated
At month's end job. Scandal, or what they call
A scandal. Once the great cantant castrated
Had sexual glamour. Difficult to conceive.
Sheer nonsense, really. See you Christmas Eve.'

FIVE

Christmas Eve morning, cold in the old style,
With even snow, a homage to Charles Dickens,
And Tim and his half-sister held their bile
Back, back: can art be art if it so sickens?
Their private preview, nearly half a mile
Of gallery, wrung them, like the necks of chickens.
This exhibition – what could one learn from it?
The diarrhoeal link of paint and vomit?

There was one theme, just one – corporeal outrage.
No skill in texture, no 'fag on at flesh'.
No teacher with a salutary clout, rage
At technical incompetence, no mesh
Of rules had tripped him, instilled wholesome doubt. Rage
Raged from the canvases, all strangely fresh,
And strangely gleeful, as if human pain
Were necessary bread. It was insane.

'It's hell,' cried Dorothy, as she surveyed
A sexual posture and three screaming faces.
'No, rather it's what leads to hell.' Tim made
A sickened gesture at some foul embraces
That, surely, sheer anatomy forbade,
Forbade. 'Bad, bad,' Tim groaned. 'There must be traces
Of him in us. God, are we really free
Or sick from birth with sap from the parent tree?'

They slithered to a pub he knew in Pimli-
Co. They could not eat. 'There's a rehearsal
This afternoon.' Tim downed his brandy grimly.
'He curses through the eye and now the curse'll
Come through the ear.' She sipped her sherry primly.
'It won't be Bach or Beethoven or Purcell,'
Tim said. 'There won't be any Christmas jollity.
But Brian said look in and taste the quality.'

He went alone. Brian, stern on the dais,
Rebuked a rather swollen LPO
(Eight horns, extra percussion). 'What you play is
Inferior to Beethoven, we know.
But, trumpets, your (bar twelve) sardonic bray is
Unwanted commentary. You all can show
Contempt a little later, over beer.
It's bad musicianship, you bastards, here.'

Strangely enough, the brief *Swiss Overture*
(Why that, for God's sake?) was a counterpart
To Tim's own feelings. Clockwork rhythms, pure
Calvin chorales on alpenhorns. Not art
(Civic commission?). Towards the end the dour
Texture slowed down to mock a thumping heart.
Whose? Then it broke. Was that Servetus yelling?
Music is only sound. There was no telling.

The bass trombone concerto – soloist
G. Gregson – seemed to speak rather than sing.
A strong dot-dash component braved a mist
Of mock Wagnerianism. Was the thing
Venturing on a message? The humorist,
Sardonic, very dry, in Byrne, let ring,
On four tuned cymbals and an anvil ding,
Inverted and reversed, 'God Save the King'.

Add a mixed chorus and percussion players
With instruments Tim had not seen before.
These slushed through darkest Africa. Foul layers
Of dissonance obscured a primal core
Of all too primal squalor. Conrad. Flay us,
Go on, tear off our hides. The heart of. More
Dissonance. More. Then – Mistah Kurtz he dead.
'A *Zigarettenpause*,' Brian said.

And so it went. Today's rehearsal ended
With music for an unfilmed *Time Machine*,
A suite that, mostly tonal, condescended
To populism. The Victorian scene
Was not derided, and the music tended
To teatime tenderness when earth had been
Denuded, slowed, reduced to tuba groans
With microtonal burps on five trombones.

The son had taken nothing from the father.
'Look at this score,' said Brian in the bar.
Tim peered at it. A symphony, or rather
A dysphony. 'You can see where you are –
Flutes top, bass bottom. See that midway lather
Of horns and trumpets. See? He's gone too far.
Too far. Take in that devastating chord – it has
Twenty-four different notes. God help our auditors.'

'Where is he? Where's he come from?' 'Came last night
With big black escort. Some quite vague location
Upon the Kalahari border. Quite
The tribal patriarch, due for immolation,
Entitled, though, to ask for death to smite
On his own birth-soil. No real new sensation
For Claridges. Our damned Hibernian jester meant
Nothing, I think, by a last will and testament.

'They speak a language there called !Ku or !Kung.'
(He scrawled the names in beer). 'Palatal stop,
That exclamation point. This Bushman tongue
Has just a hundred consonants – the top
Linguistic mondial phonemic rung.
Talk about riches in a rag-bone shop.
That's the twins' legacy. The other stuff
Is mine. Genetical amends. Enough.'

So, Christmas Eve – ah, bitter chill, etcetera.
The Mayfair trio kept the appointed date,
Tim dog-collared. Tom sent another letter, a-
Ssuring them that he'd be there, though late.
The darkling room where all the gathering met, a ro-
Coco misfit, not full, had many a plate
From which the reek of meat, coffined in bread,
Proclaimed that eating meant eating the dead.

The jugs of drink looked urinous, and smelt so.
Some oil lamps stank of human hair and soot.
The first arrivals, Brian said, had felt so
Crawsickened that they'd left. 'Mischief's afoot,'
Gagged Dorothy. 'Let the assembly melt so
That just the authentic residue stays put,'
Said Brian. 'All these brownskins here won't do,
Except the odd photographer or two.'

Now tetraphonic speakers spoke, or crackled.
'Christmas is jingling towards us. Santa
Claws at the reins. His reindeer, firmly shackled,
Snarl at each other, set then to a canter
Over the snow to Bethlehem,' they cackled.
'Maria wonders (birth-pangs start instanter)
What her place is within the scheme of things.
Music. She has her carol. Hark. She sings.'

138

In this spinning room,
Reduced to a common noun,
Swallowed by the giant belly of Eve,
The pentecostal sperm came hissing down.
Lullay lullay.

I was no one,
For I was anyone,
The grace and music easy to receive,
The patient engine of a stranger son.
Lullay lullay lullay.

His laughter was
Fermenting in the cell.
The worm, the fish was chuckling to achieve
The rose of the disguise he wears so well.
Lullay haha lullay.

And though by dispensation
Of the dove
My flesh is pardoned of its flesh, they leave
The rankling of a wrong and useless love.
Lullay.

Four blacks, vast, nearer seven feet than six,
Trampled the floor with corresponding weight,
Feet shod and capable of lethal kicks,
Cheaply smart-suited, the smooth-shaven pate
Of each agleam amid the candlesticks.
The hotel lights switched off, a sort of state
Of primitivity ensured a scare
Among the twenty-odd who waited there.

The fourfold voice resumed. 'That Yuletide carol
Was penned to lift your hearts and make you feel good.
Better to tap a celebratory barrel
And groan dyspeptically after your gross meal? Good.
I've figuratively donned the bard's apparel
To give five restive sonnets to John Gielgud,
Who'll read them now. They sum up all our annals
In five disjunctive but connective panels.'

I

Sick of the sycophantic singing, sick
Of every afternoon's compulsory games,
Sick of the little cliques of county names,
He bade the timebomb in his brain go tick
And tock. As binary arithmetic
Resentment spent its spleen. Divided aims
Meant only 2. But, quivering in flames,
He read: 'That flower is not for you to pick.'

Therefore he picked it. All things thawed to action,
Sound, colour. A shrill electric bell
Summoned the guard. He gathered up his faction,
Paused on the brink, thought, and created hell.
Light shimmered in miraculous refraction
As, like a bloody thunderbolt, he fell.

II

Bells clanged white Sunday in, a dressing-gowned day.
The childless couple basked in the central heat.
The comics came on time. The enormous meat
Sang in the oven. On thick carpets lay
Thin panther kittens, locked in clawless play.
Their loving flesh was O so firm, their feet
Uncalloused. Wine they drank was new and sweet.
Recorders, unaccompanied, crooned away.

Coiled on the rooftree, bored, inspired, their snake
Crowed in black Monday. A collar kissed the throat,
Clothes braced the body. A benignant ache
Lit up a tooth. The papers had a note:
His death may mean an empire is at stake.
Sunday and this were equally remote.

III

A dream, yes, but for everyone the same.
The thought that wove it never dropped a stitch.
The absolute was everybody's pitch,
For, when a note was struck, we knew its name.
That dark aborted any wish to tame
Waters that day might prove to be a ditch
But then were endless growling ocean, rich
In fish and heroes – till the dredgers came.

Wachet auf! A fretful dunghill cock
Flinted the noisy beacons through the shires.
A martin's nest clogged the cathedral clock,
But it was morning: birds could not be liars.
A key cleft rusty age in lock and lock.
Men shivered by a hundred kitchen fires.

IV

They lit the sun and then their day began.
What prodigies that eye of light revealed,
What dusty parchment statutes they repealed,
Pulling up blinds and lifting every ban!
The galaxies revolving to their plan,
They made the conch, the coin, the cortex yield
Their keys, and, in a garden, once a field,
They hoisted up the statue of a man.

Of man, rather: to most it seemed a mirror;
They strained their necks with gazing in the air,
Proud of those stony eyes unglazed by terror.
Though marble is not glass, why should they care?
Eat now, and vomit later, the sweet error:
Someone was bound to find his portrait there.

V

Augustus on a guinea sat in state,
The sun no proper study, though each shaft
Of filtered light a column. Classic craft
Abhorred the arc or arch. To circulate
Blood or ideas meant pipes, and pipes were straight.
As loaves were gifts from Ceres when she laughed,
Thyrsis was Jack. Caruso on a raft
Sought Johnjack's rational island, loath to wait

Till sun, neglected, took revenge, so that
The columns nodded, melted, and were seen
As Gothic arches where a goddess sat.
It seemed then that a rational machine
Granted to all men by the technocrat
Was patented by Dr Guillotine.

The voice said. 'Good. Better to understand,
Goodbody, Light and Dunkel will hand on
Fair copies. And my will is there. My land
Is rich in omnium: fresh research upon
Its fissile properties is ecstatic and
All it requires is cash – they have the data.
Squabble about it at your leisure, later.'

'Plagiarism, bloody plagiarism,' Tim groaned.
'What that word mean?' Yukari asked. 'A poet
Confessed to me in Tangier. He atoned
For a protracted adolescence. So it
Got to the wrong hands, did it? It was loaned
Me for an hour or so. Ah, let it go. It
Summons up something. Now a fresh sonority
Calls. The thugs leave, they recognise authority.'

It was a kind of distant bird-scream. Then
The ancient Byrne was borne in on a litter,
In papal white, light burden for four men,
Old, unbelievably, unfleshly, fitter
For gnomic scrawls from an Egyptian pen
Than life. He bird-eyed with a toothless titter
At the assembly. Then his bird-voice cried
That the door had been locked from the outside.

Hardly a voice, though, from that shrunken wreck.
Ninety? A hundred? Rather a dry reed
Eroded, forced out of a ruined neck.
'I'm he,' it crarked. 'You wretches have no need
To prove identity. Here at my call or beck
All that you seek to demonstrate indeed
Is greed or curiosity. My features
Gleam in a few. The rest are nameless creatures.

'There's a musician son who called me back
To hear by ear what I hear in my head,
Encoded messages. Evil or slack,
Intelligence officials' ears were dead
To brassy information from the black
Nazi interior. Let that discord shed
Generalised light upon a vicious era
And once banned scrawls render the vision clearer.

'You, Brian – Brian is the name? Please go.
You have to work on art's behalf. The rest
Must stay.' He bird-called. Open. Out. One, though,
Shadowily entered. Byrne obscenely pressed
His wrinkles close to Dorothy's. 'I know
You, I think, daughter. I was a paid guest
Of your three mothers. Yes.' He closer peered.
'Are you a witch? Hm, a moustache, a beard.'

Dorothy spat. He howled. Two of his mob,
Making adjustment, seized her. Tim thrust out
A missing-finger hand, then forced a gob
Of pulmonary blood. A porridgy gout
Rusted on Byrne's white cerement. A sob
Of startlement seized all the four. One lout
Screamed as he saw Tim now in repetition,
For it was Tom who had just gained admission.

Unceremoniously upon the floor,
Though littered still, Byrne raised his suppliant claws
To twin sons' hands. The panting groaning four
Howled for an exit, hammered without pause
Upon the adamantine bolted door.
Byrne lay upon a table. 'Ravening maws
Of anthropophagoi grind gutsy lusts.
Appropriate I lie here with the crusts.

146

'We die, my sons, my daughters. Though my race is
Not widely noted for its efficacity
In the promotion of the greater graces,
In fixing sudden death throes its capacity
Is known, I think. The IRA now faces
A Christmas of quite murderous audacity,
They promise bombs and guns and other gear,
Gifts of a Muslim leader, starting here.

'I've lived a life spurting with brave bravura
Into the *muliebris naturalis*,
Indifferent, *naturalis* as *Natura*.
It's done. You're the part product. Is that Karl, is
That Carlotta? Is that Aqua Pura?
Something. Names go. And rhymes and rhythms. Ah, Lys-
Ander, is it? Hero? Emanations
Of long completed casual copulations.'

(See how the form fades. This is Tomlinson,
Your poetaster, dying not in Berkeley
Square but in a room in Islington.
I cough blood too, thin, thick or lightly, darkly.
Byrne is the killer. See his dim eyes run
On faces that he thinks he knows, as starkly
They range themselves. I have not long to go
But I'll outlast that Swiney Tod, I know.

Names, eh? Oh, there's Crovalis and Novalis,
Pontius, Patroclus, Singapurapura,
Piggery, Pokery, Talis, also Qualis,
And Candelabra, Kish, and Candalura,
Paralysis, Polaris, and Poralis,
De Minimis et Maximis Non Cura
Est est est. Let the bastard snort and snivel,
Audibly fade out, aye, visibly shrivel.)

'You might as well go with me. You have done
Nothing to change the world.' 'You evil fool,'
Tom growled, seasonably drunk. 'Here is a son
Who's cracked a wearisome genetic rule.
Feel, fool.' He thrust his full-clothed crotch upon
The father. 'No,' the father yelled, 'No, you'll
Not do that to me.' Tom did what he did
– Martelling on a fancied coffin lid.

'An ithyphallic thrust is not a key,'
Tom said, and pumped his mild voice to a shout,
With perfect phonemes in a cantrip. He
Knew the damned inventory inside out.
TE YESU LL'Ā HA TAE KATA HA TSISI
TSIU HA KABE SITA . . . Had perhaps that tout
Of Brian's, called an agent, stood him lunch? 'I kn-
Ow one thing. Always do your homework, sunshine.'

The homework worked. The door flung open. Four
Black louts first out, a booted octopus
Or pod. The others followed. From the door
They all looked back on Byrne, whose tremulous fuss
At being left alone roused little more
Remorse than Hitler and his succubus
Dying. A rather well rewarded part
For Guinness, though life pays too much for art.

So there they were outside. Tom said: 'You ladies
Go home. I'll follow. Tim and I must quaff
A Christmas Eve potation.' Brisk wind made his
Nose start to glow, Yukari dance. 'He's off
To do his Midnight Mass. So I'm afraid his
Quaffing is out, I'd quite forgotten.' Cough
Not quaff. Tim gave some blood to Davies Street,
A red host that the holy air could eat.

148

'Well, that's the situation,' Tom explained.
'Fullsize erections, greater than before.
Where does the semen come from? I've obtained
No special message from the prostate. More
Spiritual, surely. Paradise regained.
But Mistress Waters conjured hell. She tore
My bloody bedsheets when I leapt between
The two of them. It quite amused Claudine.'

Crisp bombs erupted in the West, in bookshops
That doubtless sold Dante's *Commedia*,
Provision stores, humble Italian cookshops
That purveyed Dante olive oil (top grade); here
Also a pasta (reaped by that nose-hook?). Shops
Did not concern the IRA. The arcadia
Of posh hotels crashed. In the tube booking hall
Tom asked Tim: 'Have you heard these lines at all?

'I have raised and poised a fiddle,
Which, will you lend it ears,
Will utter music's model –
The music of the spheres.

'By God, I think not Purcell
Nor Arne could match my airs.
Perfect beyond rehearsal
My music of the spheres.

'Not that its virtue's vastness,
The terror of drift of stars.
For subtlety and softness
My music of the spheres.

'The spheres that feed its working,
Their melody swells and soars
In thinking of your marking
My music of the spheres.

'This musing and this fear's
Work of your maiden years.
Why shut longer your ears?
See how the live earth flowers.
The land speaks my intent.
Bear me accompaniment.'

Spring then was needed – the green chirping token
Of sacrifice. Those baby limbs would grow
Into a Hillman's, scourged, finally broken.
Let the logician and the Godman show
The foolishness, but let the word be spoken.
Tim embraced Tom, embarking for Heathrow.
Smiling, Christmas-elated, somewhat sad too,
Blessing the filthy world. Somebody had to.

Ash Wednesday 1993